P9-CBM-426

HALO

ESCALATION

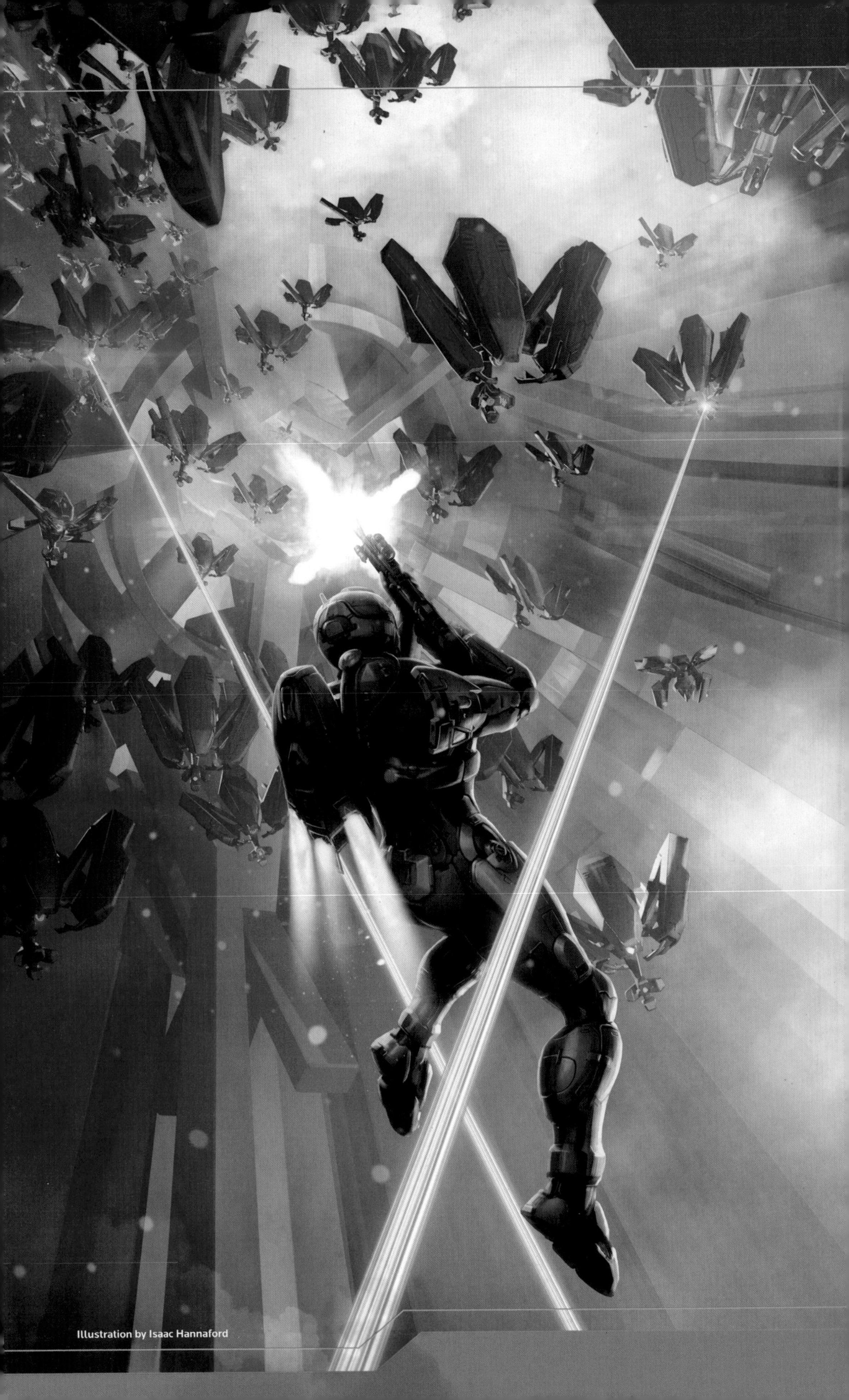

Illustration by Isaac Hannaford

ESCALATION
VOLUME 4

SCRIPTS
DUFFY BOUDREAU

PENCILS
IAN RICHARDSON
NETHO DIAZ
DOUGLAS FRANCHIN

INKS
DENIS FREITAS
CARLOS EDUARDO
JUAN CASTRO
ROB LEAN
DOUGLAS FRANCHIN

COLORS
MICHAEL ATIYEH

LETTERING
MICHAEL HEISLER

COVER ART
JEAN-SÉBASTIEN
ROSSBACH

DARK HORSE BOOKS

PUBLISHER
MIKE RICHARDSON

EDITOR
AARON WALKER

ASSISTANT EDITORS
EVERETT PATTERSON
ROXY POLK
RACHEL ROBERTS

COLLECTION DESIGNER
SANDY TANAKA

DIGITAL ART TECHNICIANS
RYAN JORGENSEN
CHRISTIANNE GOUDREAU

HALO: ESCALATION Volume 4

This volume collects issues #19–#24 of the Dark Horse comic book series *Halo: Escalation*.

Special thanks to Christine Finch, Nicholas Gallagher, Kevin Grace, Tyler Jeffers, Scott Jobe, Carlos Naranjo, Tiffany O'Brien, Frank O'Connor, Jeremy Patenaude, Kenneth Peters, Brian Reed, Sparth, and Kiki Wolfkill at Microsoft.

Published by
Dark Horse Books
A division of Dark Horse Comics, Inc.
10956 SE Main Street
Milwaukie, OR 97222

DarkHorse.com
HaloWaypoint.com

First edition: March 2016
ISBN 978-1-61655-881-9

1 3 5 7 9 10 8 6 4 2
Printed in China

Illustration by Jean-Sébastien Rossbach

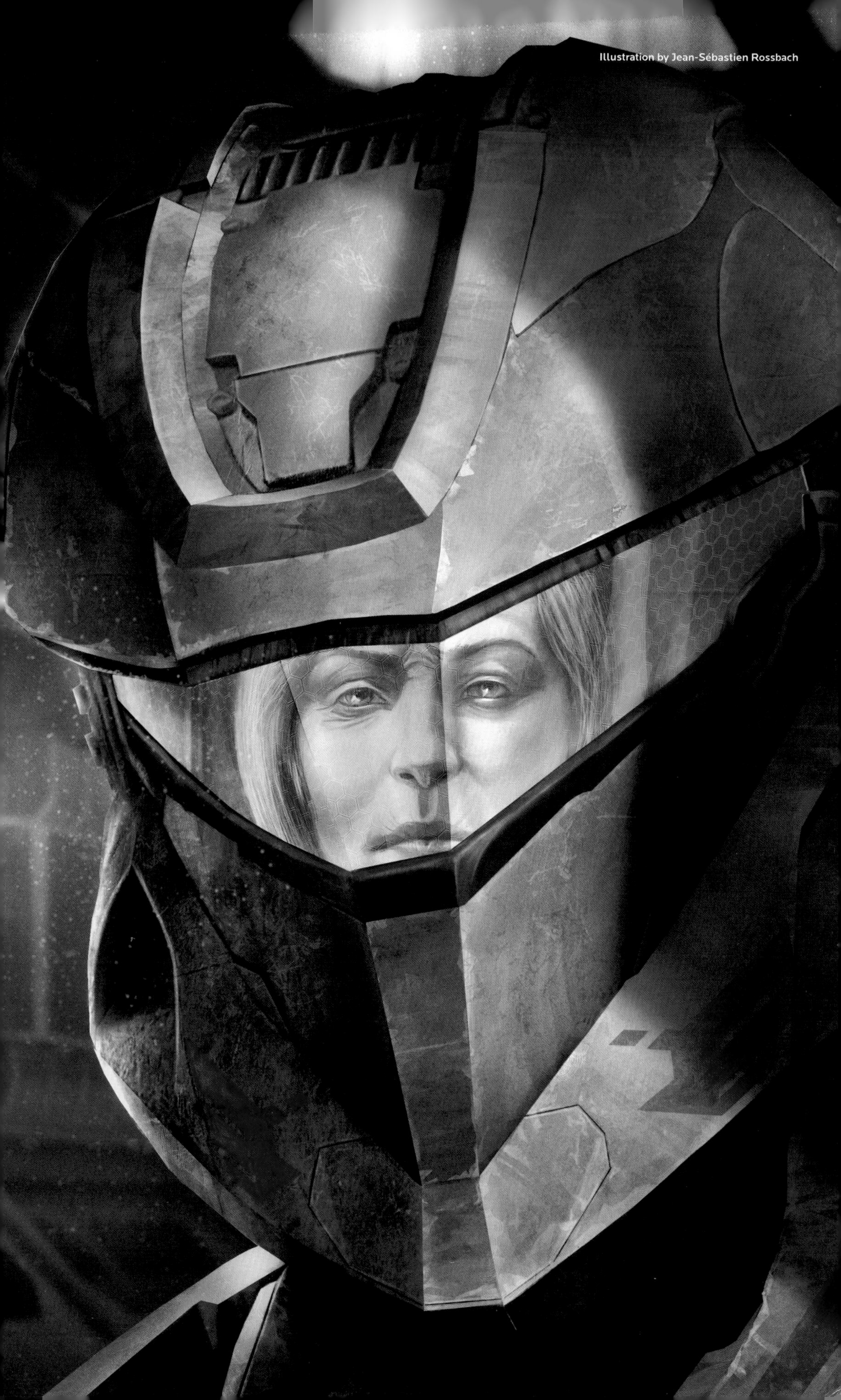

THE YEAR 2558: After battles on various worlds, both halves of the Janus Key are back in the hands of the fugitive Dr. Catherine Halsey and Covenant Commander Jul 'Mdama. With the key in their possession, this alliance of the UNSC's most wanted has the power to unlock the Forerunner facility known as the Absolute Record. Jul and Halsey now race to locate this hidden site before the UNSC tracks them down . . .

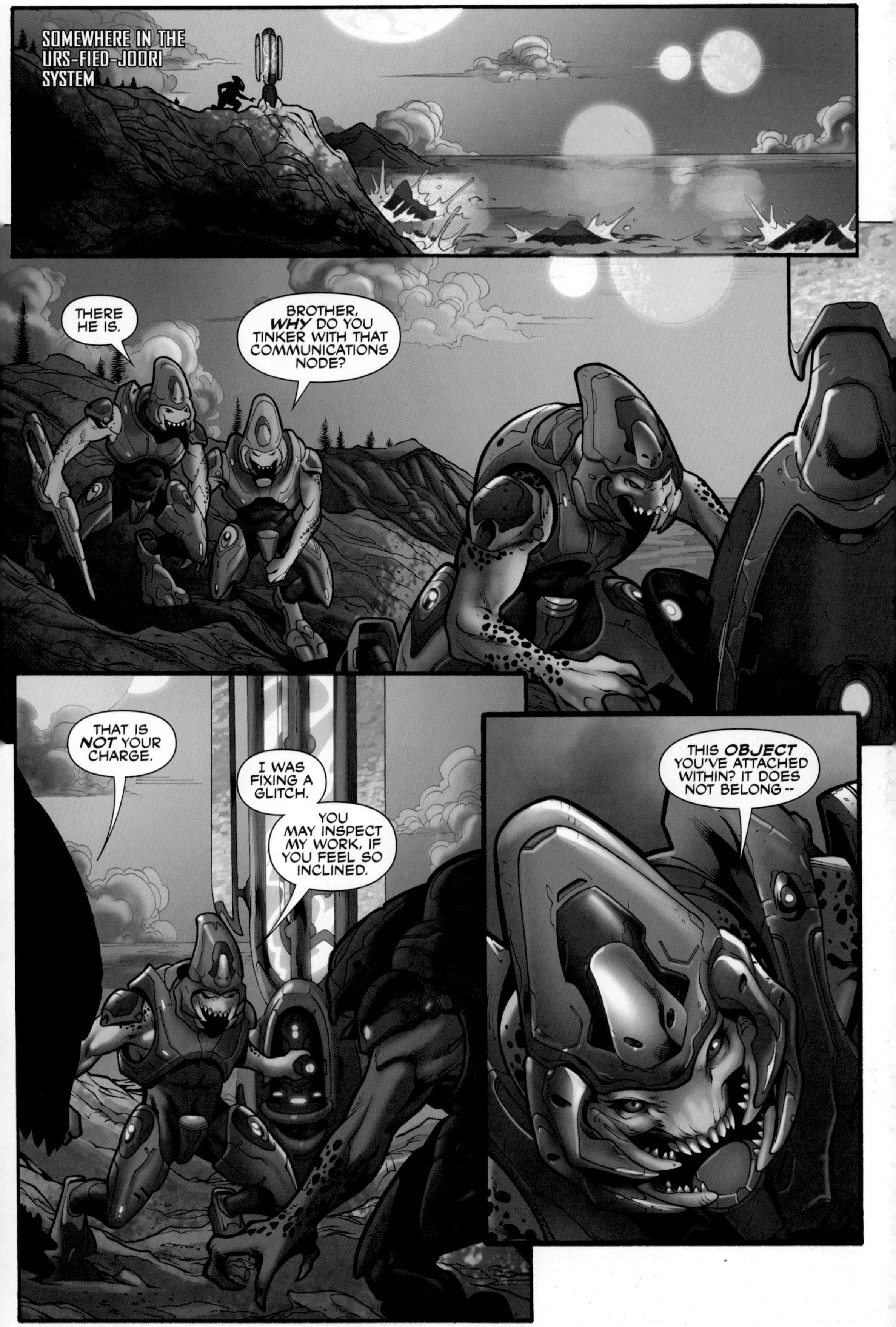
SOMEWHERE IN THE URS-FIED-JOORI SYSTEM
THERE HE IS.
BROTHER, *WHY* DO YOU TINKER WITH THAT COMMUNICATIONS NODE?
THAT IS *NOT* YOUR CHARGE.
I WAS FIXING A GLITCH.
YOU MAY INSPECT MY WORK, IF YOU FEEL SO INCLINED.
THIS *OBJECT* YOU'VE ATTACHED WITHIN? IT DOES NOT BELONG --

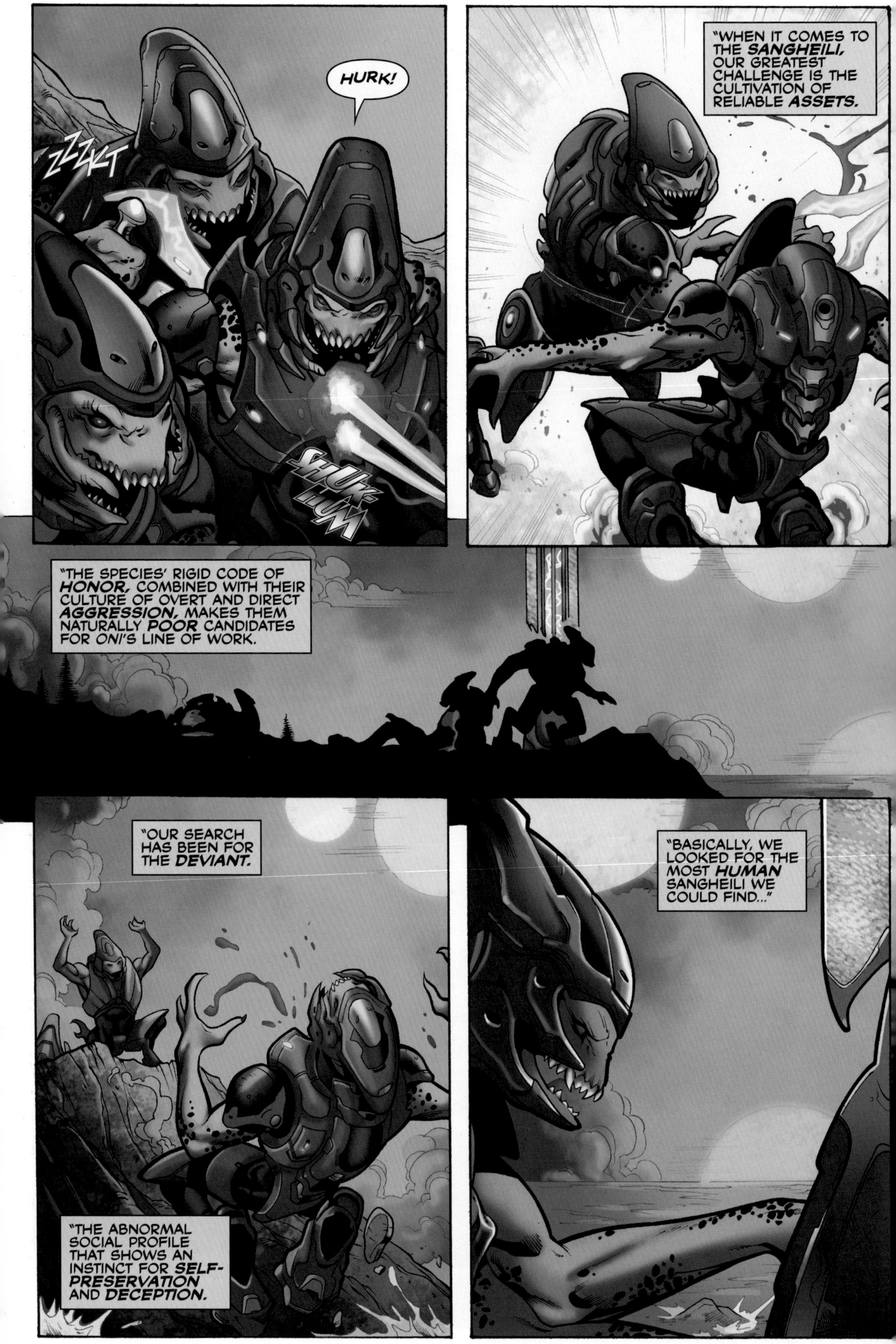
HURK!
ZZZKT
SHUK-THUM
"WHEN IT COMES TO THE *SANGHEILI,* OUR GREATEST CHALLENGE IS THE CULTIVATION OF RELIABLE *ASSETS.*
"THE SPECIES' RIGID CODE OF *HONOR,* COMBINED WITH THEIR CULTURE OF OVERT AND DIRECT *AGGRESSION,* MAKES THEM NATURALLY *POOR* CANDIDATES FOR *ONI*'S LINE OF WORK.
"OUR SEARCH HAS BEEN FOR THE *DEVIANT.*
"THE ABNORMAL SOCIAL PROFILE THAT SHOWS AN INSTINCT FOR *SELF-PRESERVATION* AND *DECEPTION.*
"BASICALLY, WE LOOKED FOR THE MOST *HUMAN* SANGHEILI WE COULD FIND..."

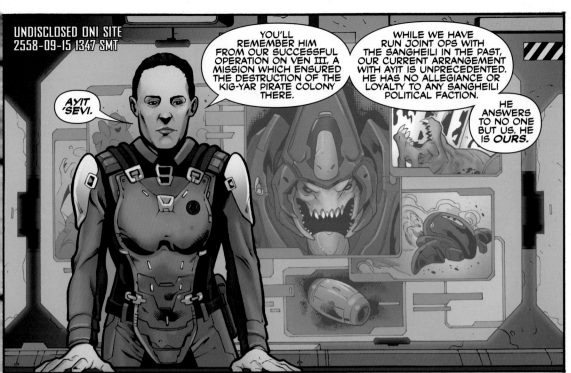

UNDISCLOSED ONI SITE
2558-09-15 1347 SMT
AYIT 'SEVI.
YOU'LL REMEMBER HIM FROM OUR SUCCESSFUL OPERATION ON VEN III, A MISSION WHICH ENSURED THE DESTRUCTION OF THE KIG-YAR PIRATE COLONY THERE.
WHILE WE HAVE RUN JOINT OPS WITH THE SANGHEILI IN THE PAST, OUR CURRENT ARRANGEMENT WITH AYIT IS UNPRECEDENTED. HE HAS NO ALLEGIANCE OR LOYALTY TO ANY SANGHEILI POLITICAL FACTION.
HE ANSWERS TO NO ONE BUT US. HE IS OURS.
AND HE'S CURRENTLY EMBEDDED WITHIN JUL 'MDAMA'S COVENANT, WHERE HE'S BEEN PROVIDING A STREAM OF VALUABLE INTEL.
'SEVI IS THE SOURCE OF THIS LATEST REPORT ON HALSEY AND HER CURRENT OBSESSION...
...A FORERUNNER SITE KNOWN AS THE ABSOLUTE RECORD.
AFTER MONTHS SCOURING THE GALAXY, HALSEY HAS APPARENTLY DISCOVERED WHERE THE SITE IS HIDDEN AND 'MDAMA IS READYING HIS FLEET.
UPON THEIR ARRIVAL, HALSEY WILL USE A SPECIAL ARTIFACT -- ONE SHE RECENTLY STOLE FROM INFINITY'S SPARTANS -- TO UNLOCK THE RECORD.
"SHE'LL THEN HAVE INSTANT ACCESS TO REAL-TIME LOCATIONAL DATA FOR EVERY PIECE OF FORERUNNER TECH IN THE GALAXY...

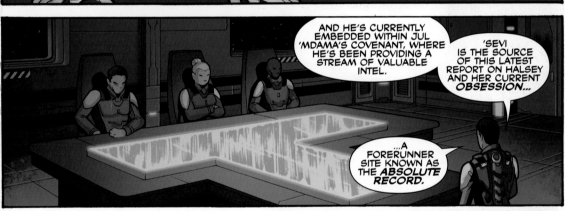

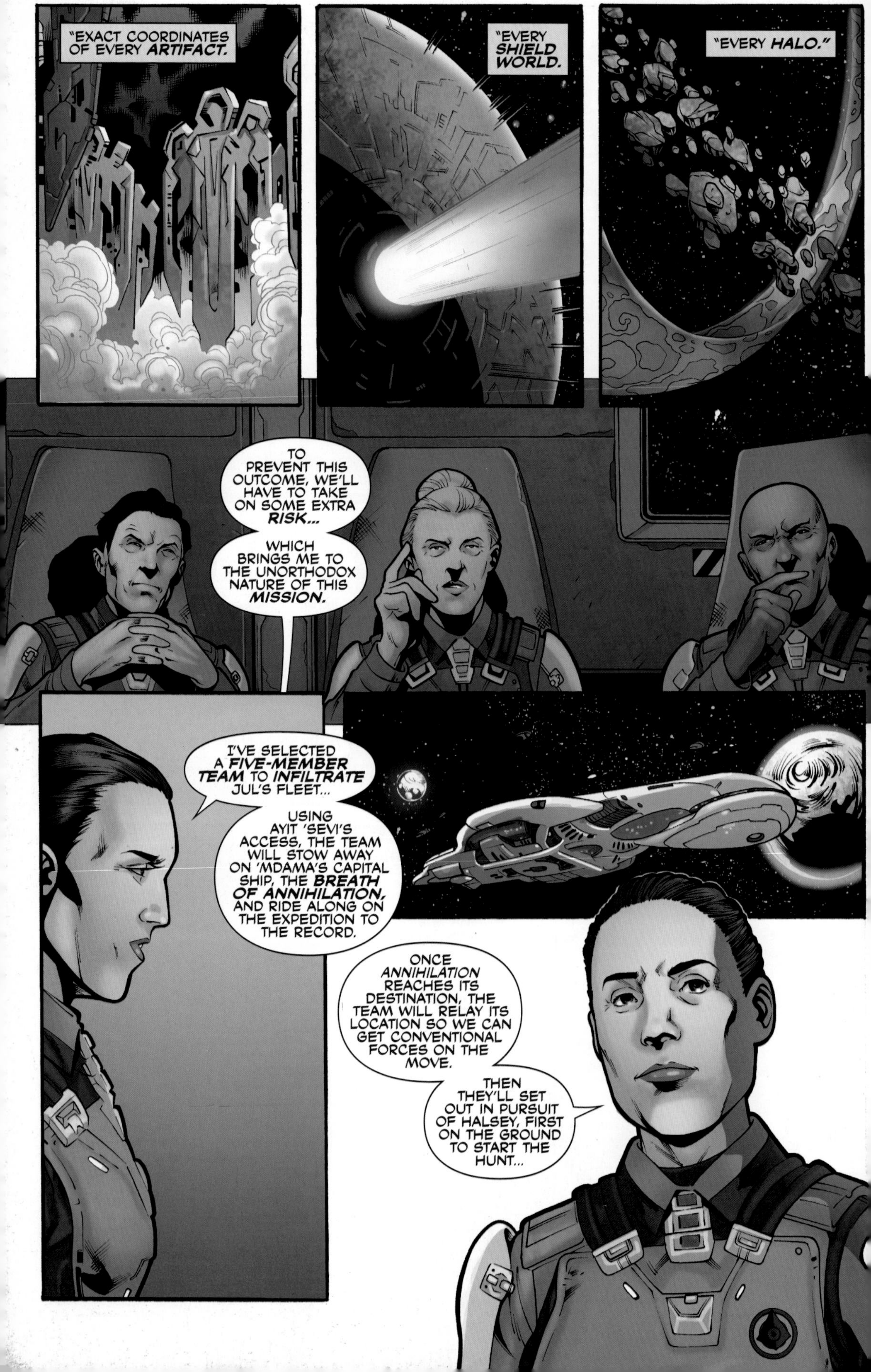
"EXACT COORDINATES OF EVERY ARTIFACT.
"EVERY SHIELD WORLD.
"EVERY HALO."
TO PREVENT THIS OUTCOME, WE'LL HAVE TO TAKE ON SOME EXTRA RISK...
WHICH BRINGS ME TO THE UNORTHODOX NATURE OF THIS MISSION.
I'VE SELECTED A FIVE-MEMBER TEAM TO INFILTRATE JUL'S FLEET...
USING AYIT 'SEVI'S ACCESS, THE TEAM WILL STOW AWAY ON 'MDAMA'S CAPITAL SHIP, THE BREATH OF ANNIHILATION, AND RIDE ALONG ON THE EXPEDITION TO THE RECORD.
ONCE ANNIHILATION REACHES ITS DESTINATION, THE TEAM WILL RELAY ITS LOCATION SO WE CAN GET CONVENTIONAL FORCES ON THE MOVE.
THEN THEY'LL SET OUT IN PURSUIT OF HALSEY, FIRST ON THE GROUND TO START THE HUNT...

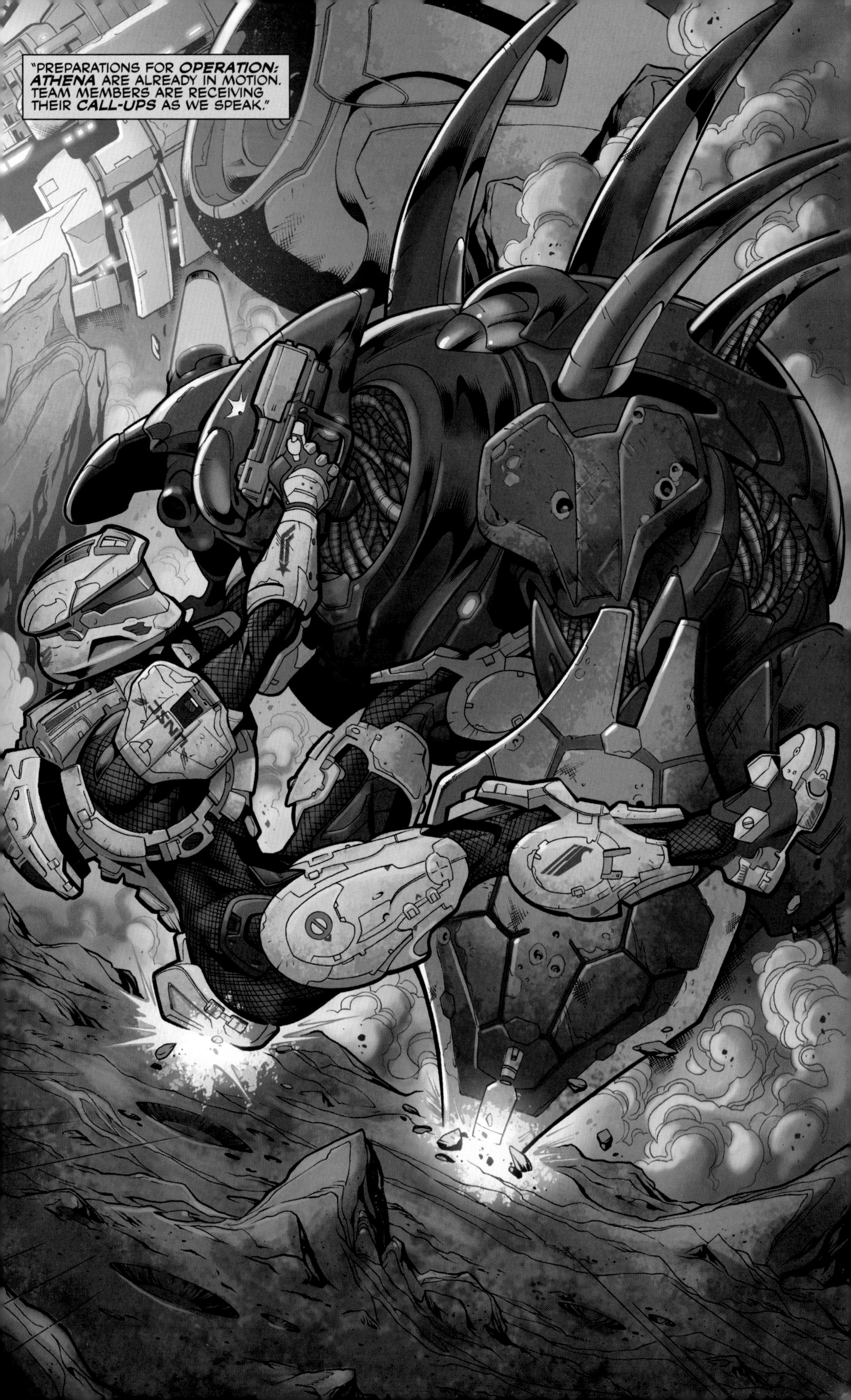
"PREPARATIONS FOR OPERATION: ATHENA ARE ALREADY IN MOTION. TEAM MEMBERS ARE RECEIVING THEIR CALL-UPS AS WE SPEAK."
UNSC

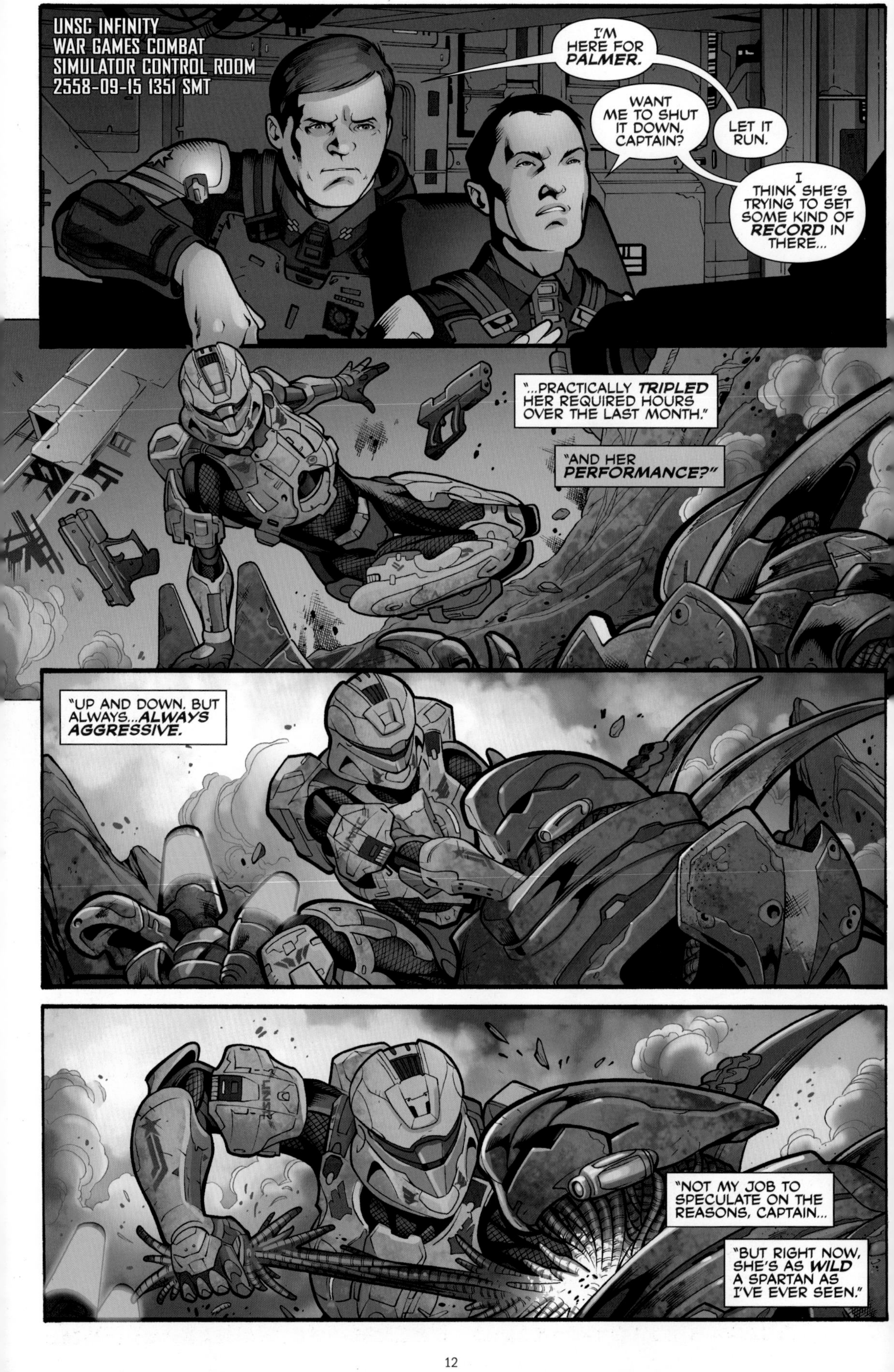

UNSC INFINITY
WAR GAMES COMBAT
SIMULATOR CONTROL ROOM
2558-09-15 1351 SMT
I'M HERE FOR PALMER.
WANT ME TO SHUT IT DOWN, CAPTAIN?
LET IT RUN.
I THINK SHE'S TRYING TO SET SOME KIND OF RECORD IN THERE...
"...PRACTICALLY TRIPLED HER REQUIRED HOURS OVER THE LAST MONTH."
"AND HER PERFORMANCE?"
"UP AND DOWN. BUT ALWAYS...ALWAYS AGGRESSIVE.
"NOT MY JOB TO SPECULATE ON THE REASONS, CAPTAIN...
"BUT RIGHT NOW, SHE'S AS WILD A SPARTAN AS I'VE EVER SEEN."

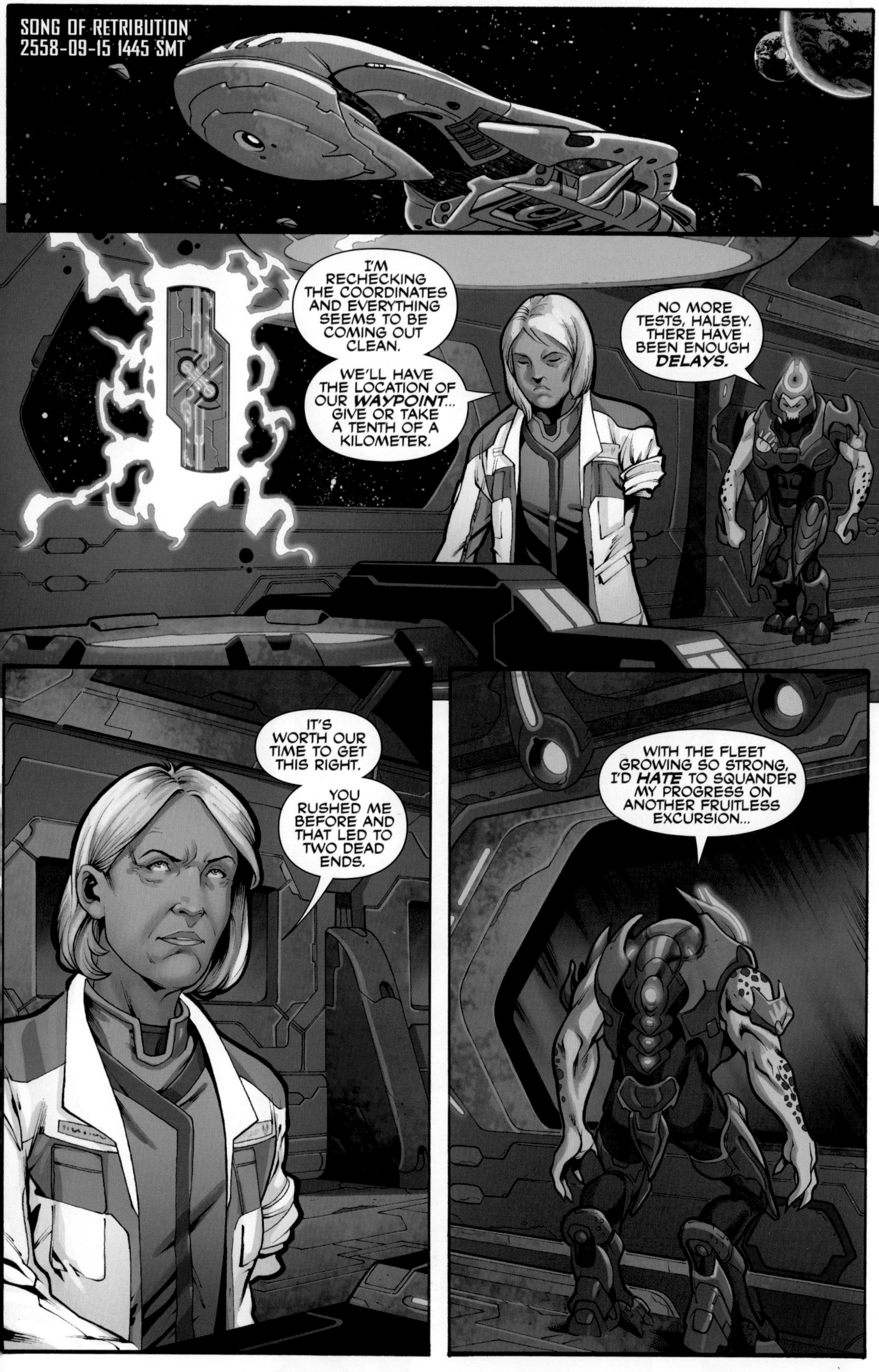
SONG OF RETRIBUTION
2558-09-15 1445 SMT
I'M RECHECKING THE COORDINATES AND EVERYTHING SEEMS TO BE COMING OUT CLEAN.
WE'LL HAVE THE LOCATION OF OUR WAYPOINT... GIVE OR TAKE A TENTH OF A KILOMETER.
NO MORE TESTS, HALSEY. THERE HAVE BEEN ENOUGH DELAYS.
IT'S WORTH OUR TIME TO GET THIS RIGHT.
YOU RUSHED ME BEFORE AND THAT LED TO TWO DEAD ENDS.
WITH THE FLEET GROWING SO STRONG, I'D HATE TO SQUANDER MY PROGRESS ON ANOTHER FRUITLESS EXCURSION...

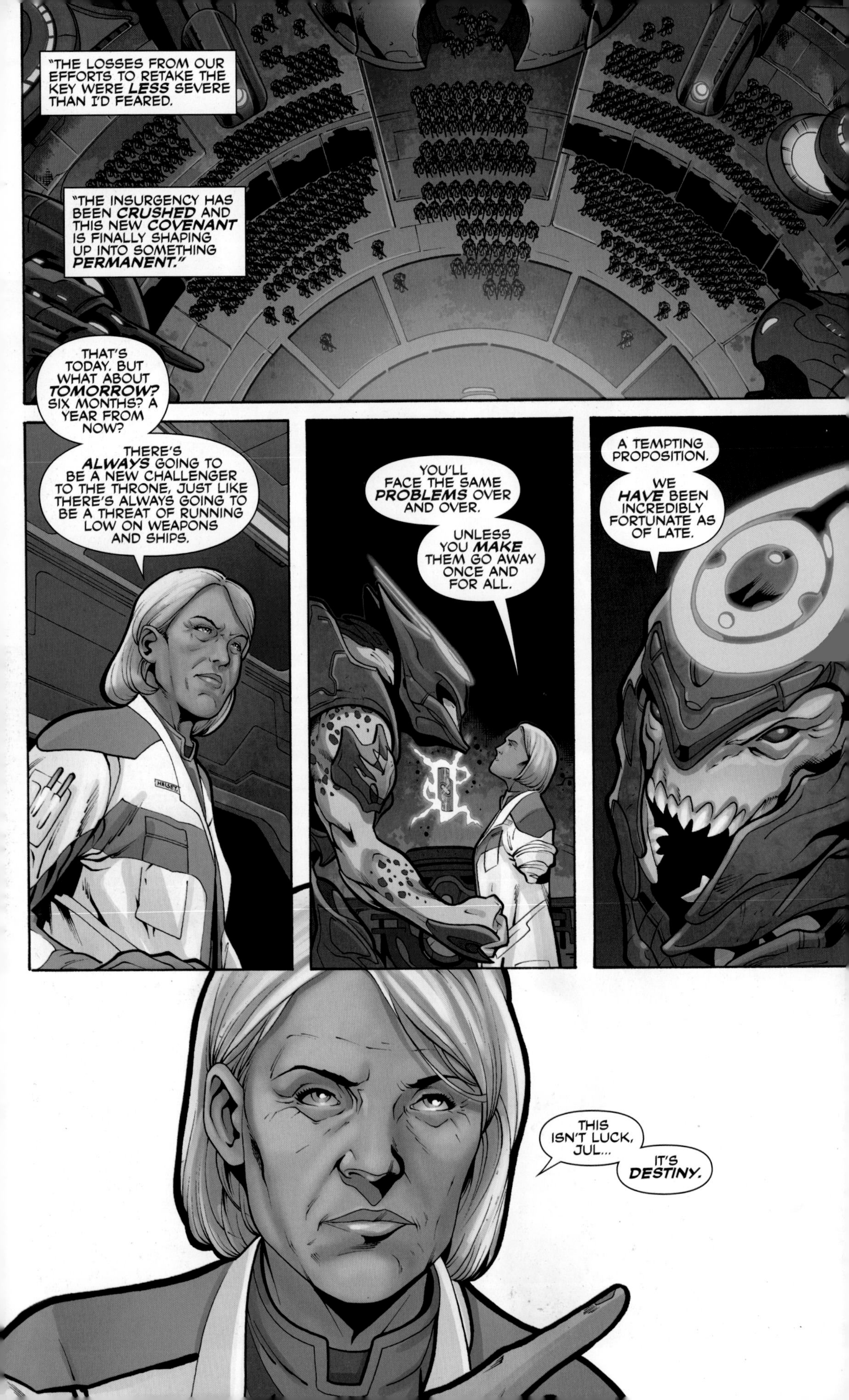
"THE LOSSES FROM OUR EFFORTS TO RETAKE THE KEY WERE LESS SEVERE THAN I'D FEARED.
"THE INSURGENCY HAS BEEN CRUSHED AND THIS NEW COVENANT IS FINALLY SHAPING UP INTO SOMETHING PERMANENT."
THAT'S TODAY. BUT WHAT ABOUT TOMORROW? SIX MONTHS? A YEAR FROM NOW?
THERE'S ALWAYS GOING TO BE A NEW CHALLENGER TO THE THRONE, JUST LIKE THERE'S ALWAYS GOING TO BE A THREAT OF RUNNING LOW ON WEAPONS AND SHIPS.
HALSEY
YOU'LL FACE THE SAME PROBLEMS OVER AND OVER.
UNLESS YOU MAKE THEM GO AWAY ONCE AND FOR ALL.
A TEMPTING PROPOSITION.
WE HAVE BEEN INCREDIBLY FORTUNATE AS OF LATE.
THIS ISN'T LUCK, JUL...
IT'S DESTINY.

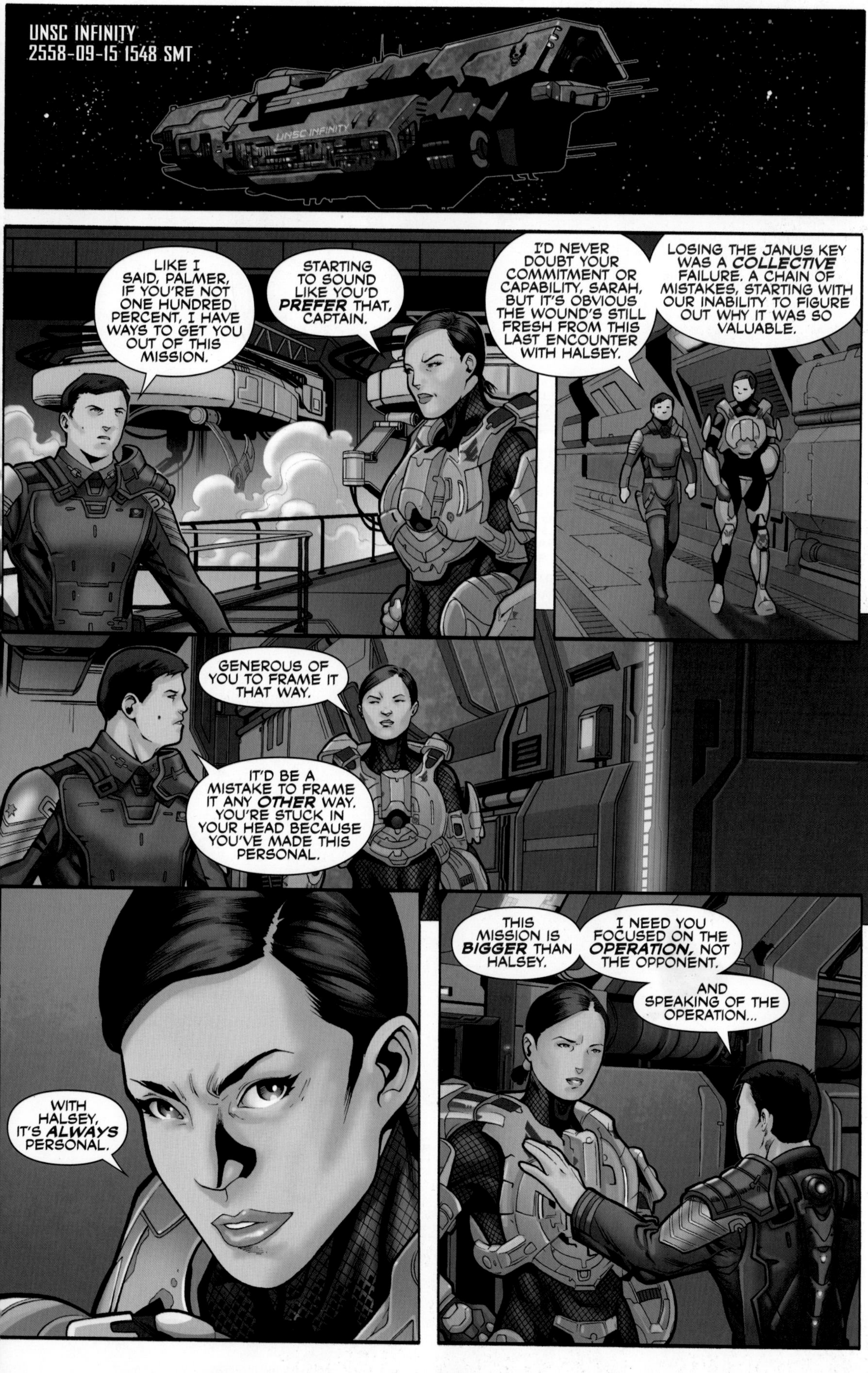
UNSC INFINITY
2558-09-15 1548 SMT
UNSC INFINITY
LIKE I SAID, PALMER, IF YOU'RE NOT ONE HUNDRED PERCENT, I HAVE WAYS TO GET YOU OUT OF THIS MISSION.
STARTING TO SOUND LIKE YOU'D PREFER THAT, CAPTAIN.
I'D NEVER DOUBT YOUR COMMITMENT OR CAPABILITY, SARAH, BUT IT'S OBVIOUS THE WOUND'S STILL FRESH FROM THIS LAST ENCOUNTER WITH HALSEY.
LOSING THE JANUS KEY WAS A COLLECTIVE FAILURE. A CHAIN OF MISTAKES, STARTING WITH OUR INABILITY TO FIGURE OUT WHY IT WAS SO VALUABLE.
GENEROUS OF YOU TO FRAME IT THAT WAY.
IT'D BE A MISTAKE TO FRAME IT ANY OTHER WAY. YOU'RE STUCK IN YOUR HEAD BECAUSE YOU'VE MADE THIS PERSONAL.
WITH HALSEY, IT'S ALWAYS PERSONAL.
THIS MISSION IS BIGGER THAN HALSEY.
I NEED YOU FOCUSED ON THE OPERATION, NOT THE OPPONENT.
AND SPEAKING OF THE OPERATION...

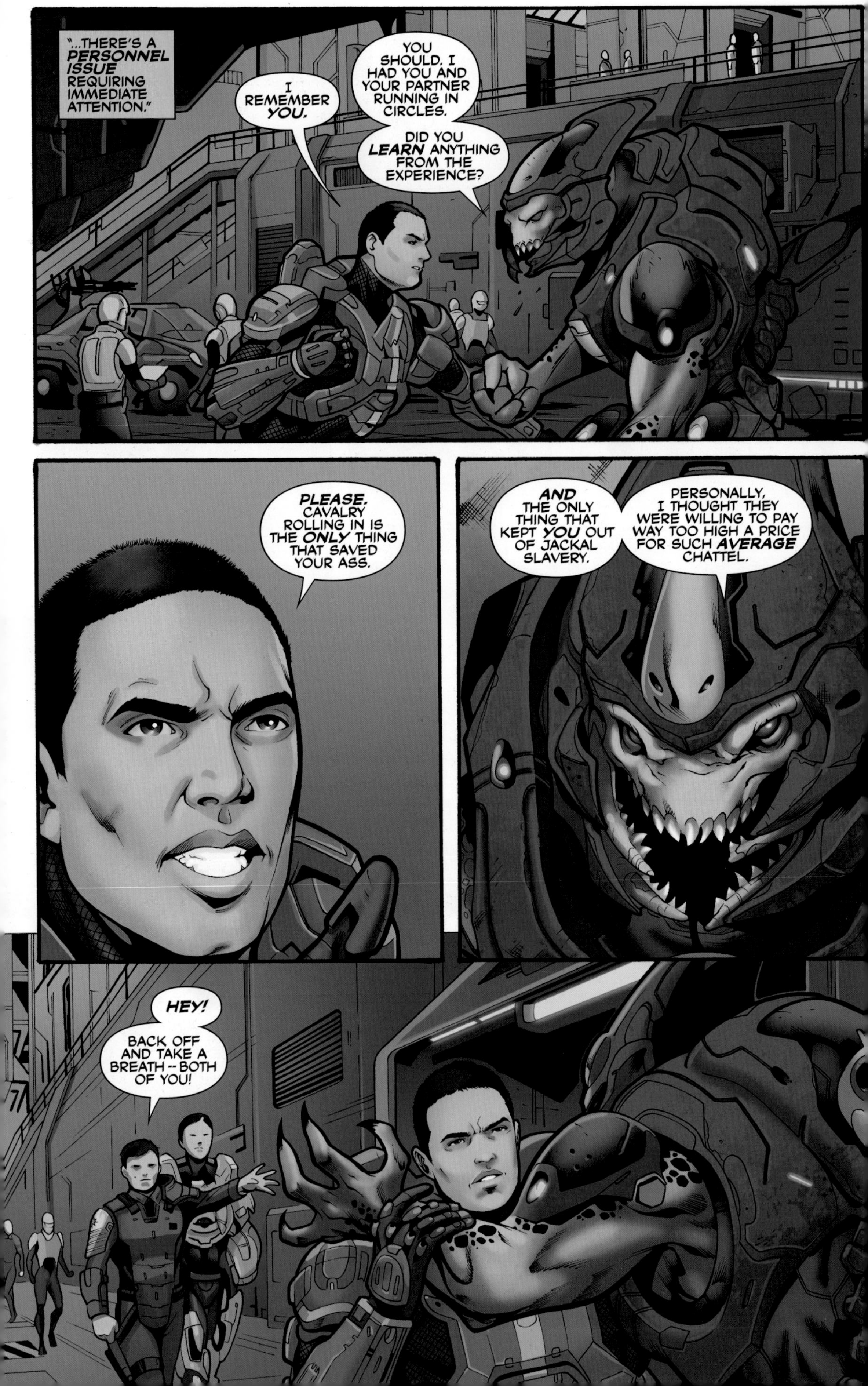
"...THERE'S A PERSONNEL ISSUE REQUIRING IMMEDIATE ATTENTION."
I REMEMBER YOU.
YOU SHOULD. I HAD YOU AND YOUR PARTNER RUNNING IN CIRCLES.
DID YOU LEARN ANYTHING FROM THE EXPERIENCE?
PLEASE. CAVALRY ROLLING IN IS THE ONLY THING THAT SAVED YOUR ASS.
AND THE ONLY THING THAT KEPT YOU OUT OF JACKAL SLAVERY.
PERSONALLY, I THOUGHT THEY WERE WILLING TO PAY WAY TOO HIGH A PRICE FOR SUCH AVERAGE CHATTEL.
HEY!
BACK OFF AND TAKE A BREATH -- BOTH OF YOU!

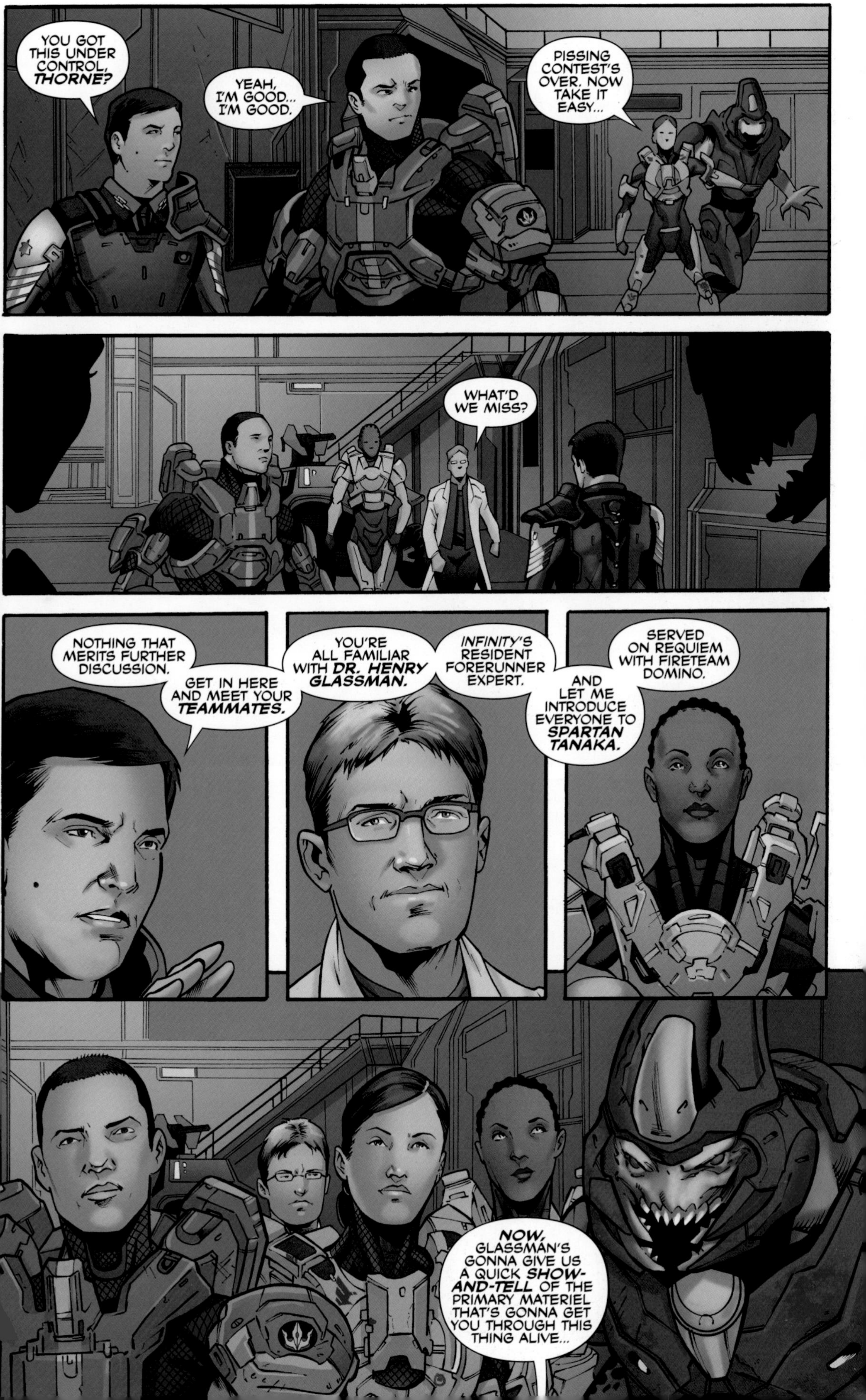

YOU GOT THIS UNDER CONTROL, *THORNE?*
YEAH, I'M GOOD... I'M GOOD.
PISSING CONTEST'S OVER. NOW TAKE IT EASY...
WHAT'D WE MISS?
NOTHING THAT MERITS FURTHER DISCUSSION.
GET IN HERE AND MEET YOUR *TEAMMATES.*
YOU'RE ALL FAMILIAR WITH *DR. HENRY GLASSMAN.*
INFINITY'S RESIDENT FORERUNNER EXPERT.
AND LET ME INTRODUCE EVERYONE TO *SPARTAN TANAKA.*
SERVED ON REQUIEM WITH FIRETEAM DOMINO.
NOW, GLASSMAN'S GONNA GIVE US A QUICK *SHOW-AND-TELL* OF THE PRIMARY MATERIEL THAT'S GONNA GET YOU THROUGH THIS THING ALIVE...

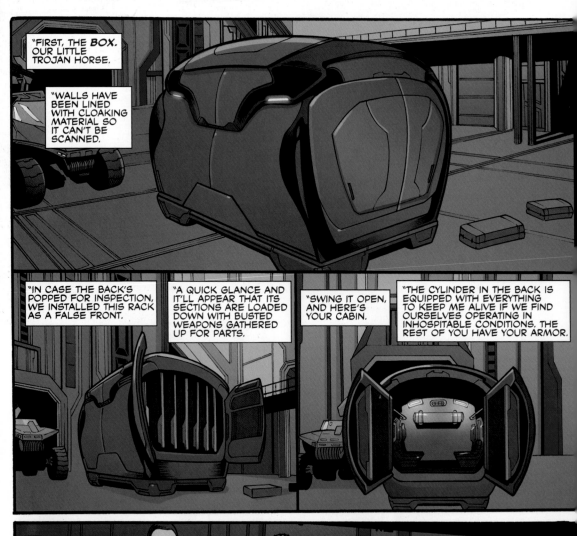

"FIRST, THE *BOX.* OUR LITTLE TROJAN HORSE.

"WALLS HAVE BEEN LINED WITH CLOAKING MATERIAL SO IT CAN'T BE SCANNED.

"IN CASE THE BACK'S POPPED FOR INSPECTION, WE INSTALLED THIS RACK AS A FALSE FRONT.

"A QUICK GLANCE AND IT'LL APPEAR THAT ITS SECTIONS ARE LOADED DOWN WITH BUSTED WEAPONS GATHERED UP FOR PARTS.

"SWING IT OPEN, AND HERE'S YOUR CABIN.

"THE CYLINDER IN THE BACK IS EQUIPPED WITH EVERYTHING TO KEEP ME ALIVE IF WE FIND OURSELVES OPERATING IN INHOSPITABLE CONDITIONS. THE REST OF YOU HAVE YOUR ARMOR.

WE'LL LOAD THE BOX INTO THE TROOP BAY OF AYIT'S PHANTOM.

ONCE COVENANT FORCES HAVE REACHED THE RECORD'S LOCATION, AYIT WILL SEPARATE FROM THE FLEET AND FIND A PLACE TO INSERT YOU ON THE GROUND.

BY THAT TIME, HELP *WILL* BE ON THE WAY -- COURTESY OF THIS *NEXT* GADGET...

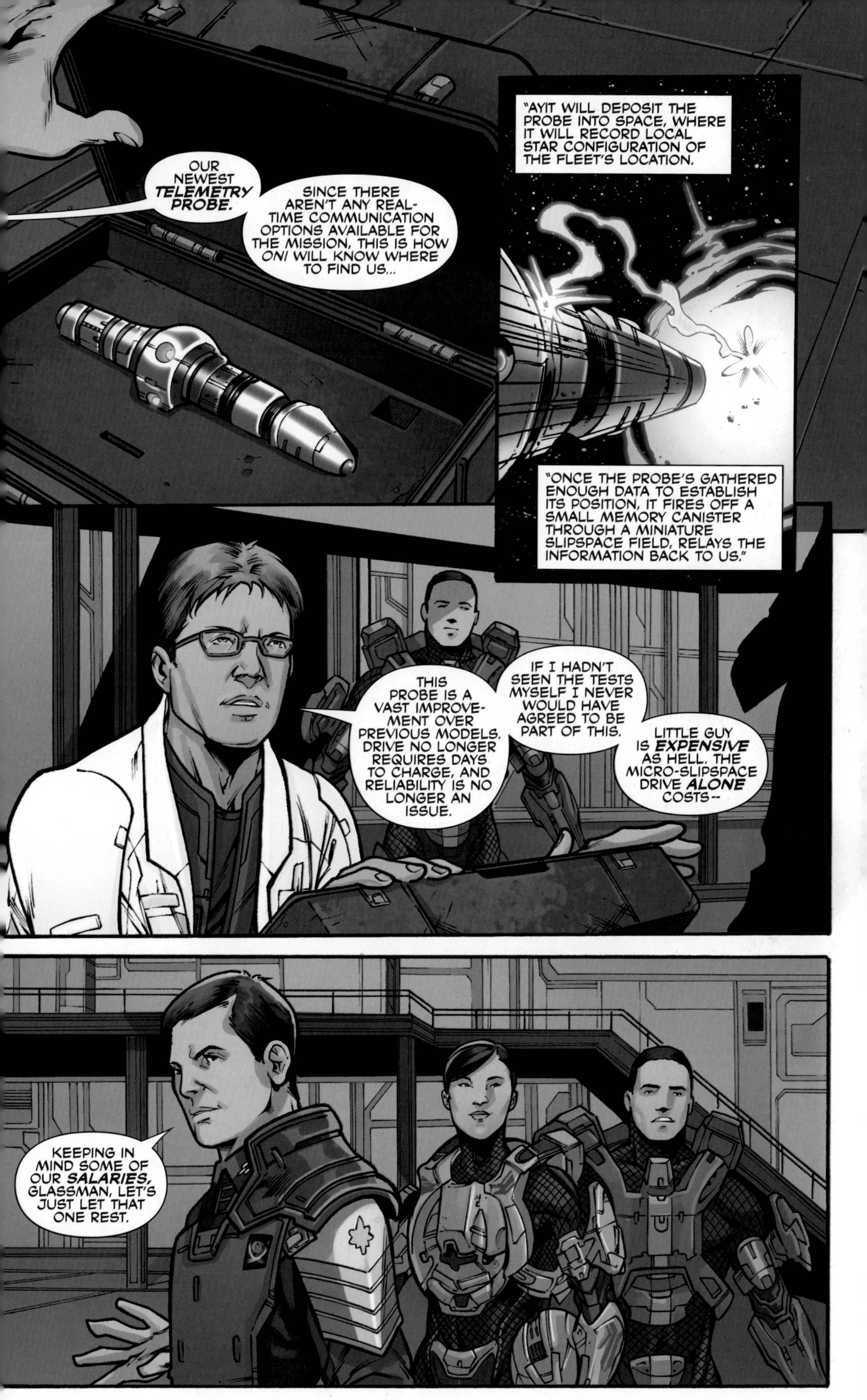

OUR NEWEST *TELEMETRY PROBE.*
SINCE THERE AREN'T ANY REAL-TIME COMMUNICATION OPTIONS AVAILABLE FOR THE MISSION, THIS IS HOW *ONI* WILL KNOW WHERE TO FIND US...
"AYIT WILL DEPOSIT THE PROBE INTO SPACE, WHERE IT WILL RECORD LOCAL STAR CONFIGURATION OF THE FLEET'S LOCATION.
"ONCE THE PROBE'S GATHERED ENOUGH DATA TO ESTABLISH ITS POSITION, IT FIRES OFF A SMALL MEMORY CANISTER THROUGH A MINIATURE SLIPSPACE FIELD, RELAYS THE INFORMATION BACK TO US."
THIS PROBE IS A VAST IMPROVEMENT OVER PREVIOUS MODELS. DRIVE NO LONGER REQUIRES DAYS TO CHARGE, AND RELIABILITY IS NO LONGER AN ISSUE.
IF I HADN'T SEEN THE TESTS MYSELF I NEVER WOULD HAVE AGREED TO BE PART OF THIS.
LITTLE GUY IS *EXPENSIVE* AS HELL. THE MICRO-SLIPSPACE DRIVE *ALONE* COSTS--
KEEPING IN MIND SOME OF OUR *SALARIES,* GLASSMAN, LET'S JUST LET THAT ONE REST.

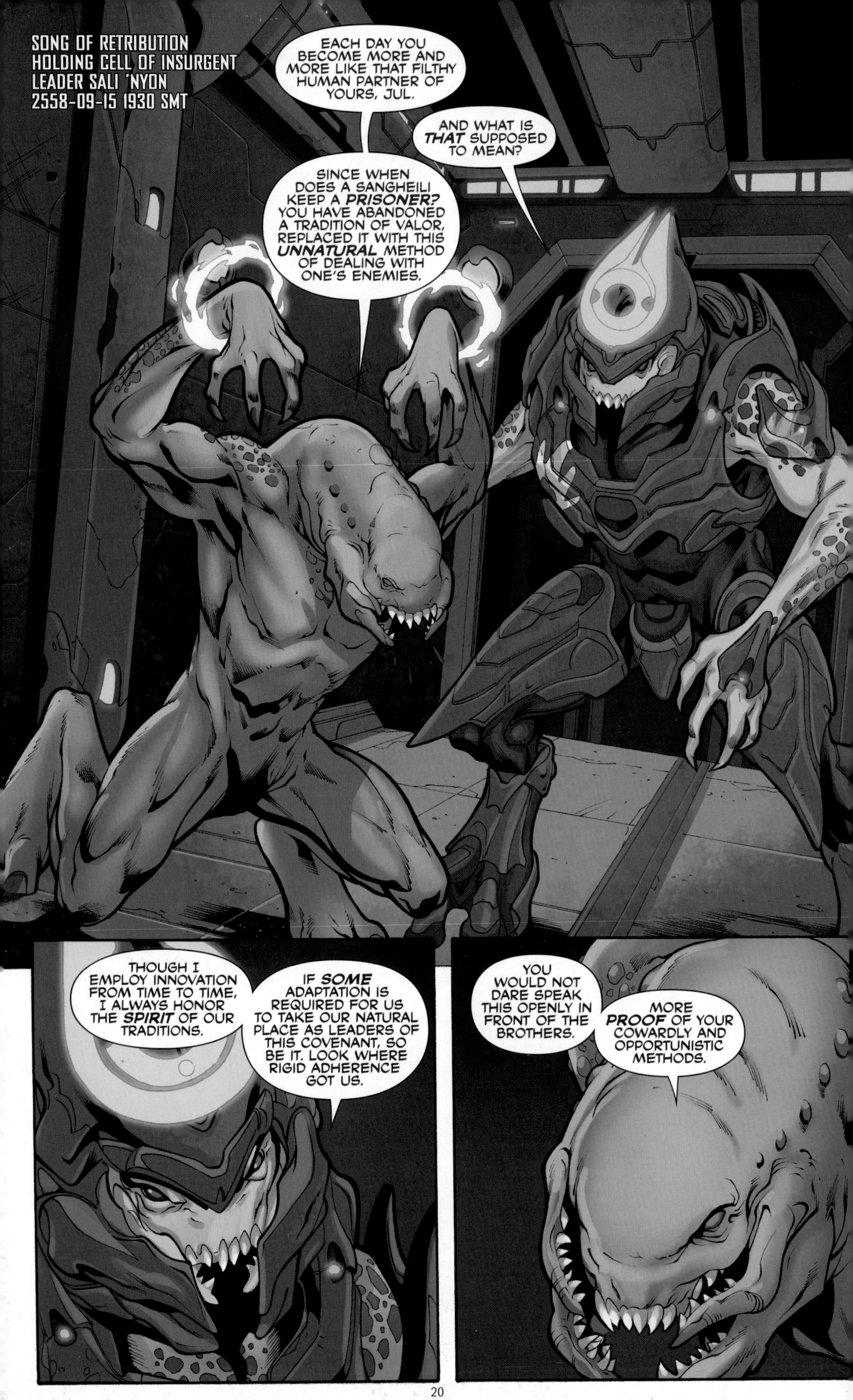

SONG OF RETRIBUTION
HOLDING CELL OF INSURGENT LEADER SALI 'NYON
2558-09-15 1930 SMT
EACH DAY YOU BECOME MORE AND MORE LIKE THAT FILTHY HUMAN PARTNER OF YOURS, JUL.
AND WHAT IS *THAT* SUPPOSED TO MEAN?
SINCE WHEN DOES A SANGHEILI KEEP A *PRISONER?* YOU HAVE ABANDONED A TRADITION OF VALOR, REPLACED IT WITH THIS *UNNATURAL* METHOD OF DEALING WITH ONE'S ENEMIES.
THOUGH I EMPLOY INNOVATION FROM TIME TO TIME, I ALWAYS HONOR THE *SPIRIT* OF OUR TRADITIONS.
IF *SOME* ADAPTATION IS REQUIRED FOR US TO TAKE OUR NATURAL PLACE AS LEADERS OF THIS COVENANT, SO BE IT. LOOK WHERE RIGID ADHERENCE GOT US.
YOU WOULD NOT DARE SPEAK THIS OPENLY IN FRONT OF THE BROTHERS.
MORE *PROOF* OF YOUR COWARDLY AND OPPORTUNISTIC METHODS.

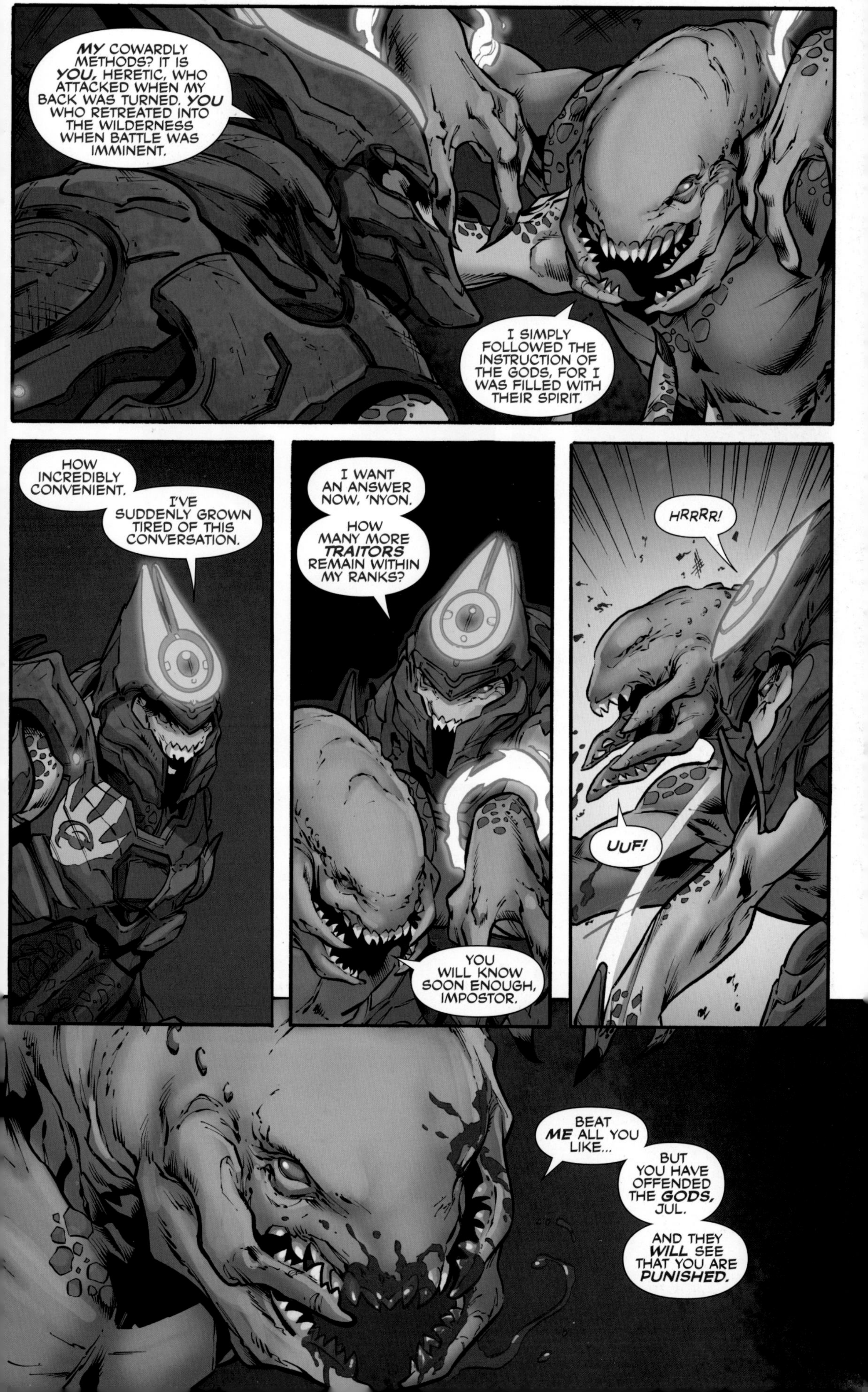
MY COWARDLY METHODS? IT IS YOU, HERETIC, WHO ATTACKED WHEN MY BACK WAS TURNED. YOU WHO RETREATED INTO THE WILDERNESS WHEN BATTLE WAS IMMINENT.
I SIMPLY FOLLOWED THE INSTRUCTION OF THE GODS, FOR I WAS FILLED WITH THEIR SPIRIT.
HOW INCREDIBLY CONVENIENT.
I'VE SUDDENLY GROWN TIRED OF THIS CONVERSATION.
I WANT AN ANSWER NOW, 'NYON.
HOW MANY MORE TRAITORS REMAIN WITHIN MY RANKS?
YOU WILL KNOW SOON ENOUGH, IMPOSTOR.
HRRRR!
UUF!
BEAT ME ALL YOU LIKE...
BUT YOU HAVE OFFENDED THE GODS, JUL.
AND THEY WILL SEE THAT YOU ARE PUNISHED.

URS-FIED-JOORI SYSTEM
2558-09-17 0810 SMT

I'M ABOUT TO MAKE CONTACT WITH ANNIHILATION...

ALL FURTHER COMMS WILL COME IN OVER THE CODED CHANNEL.

HERE WE GO...

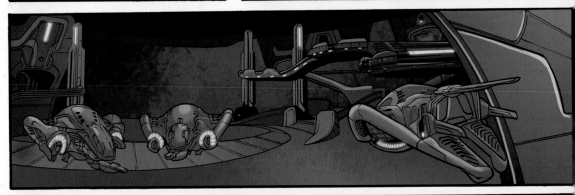

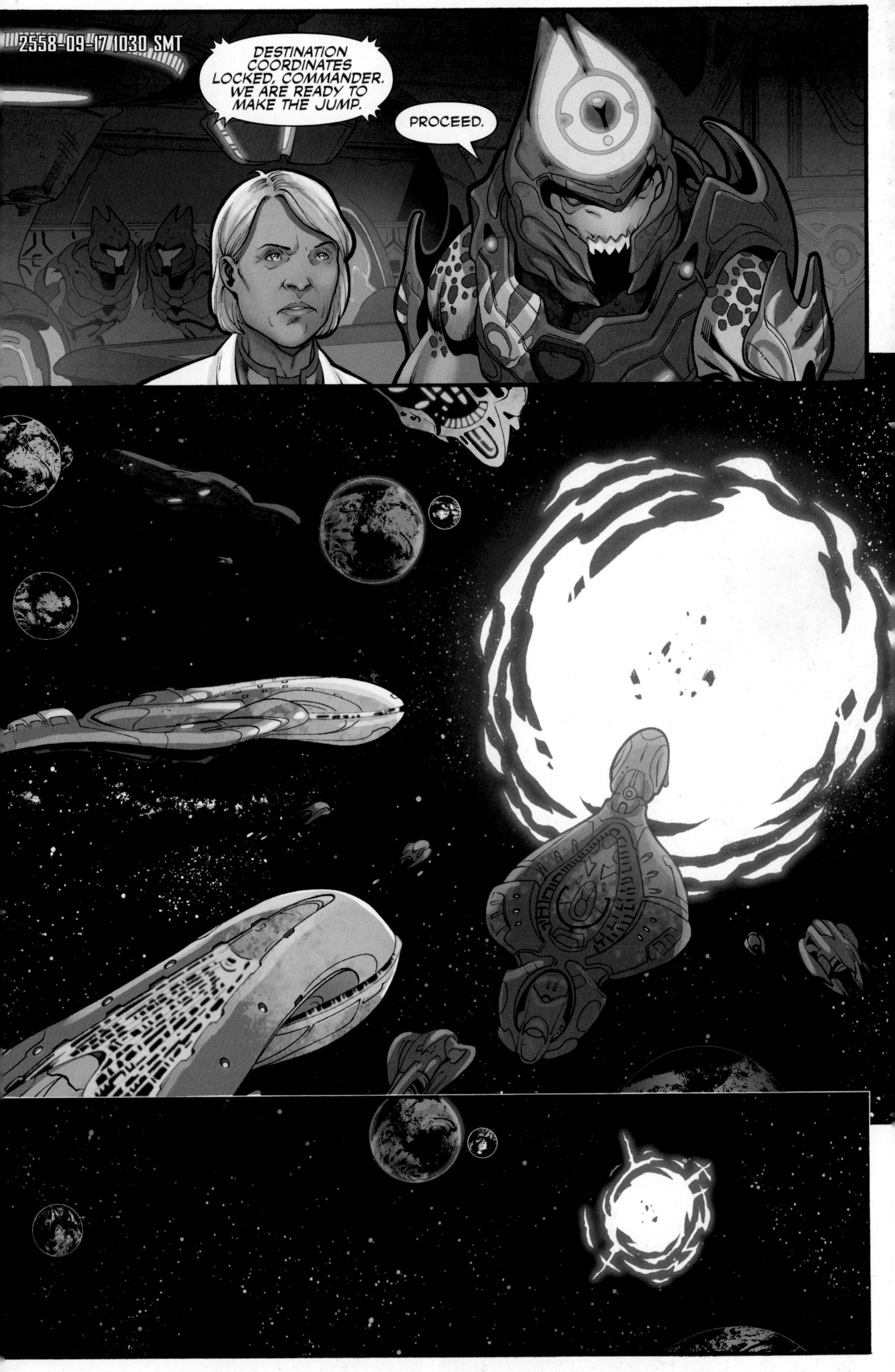
2558-09-17 1030 SMT
DESTINATION COORDINATES LOCKED, COMMANDER. WE ARE READY TO MAKE THE JUMP.
PROCEED.

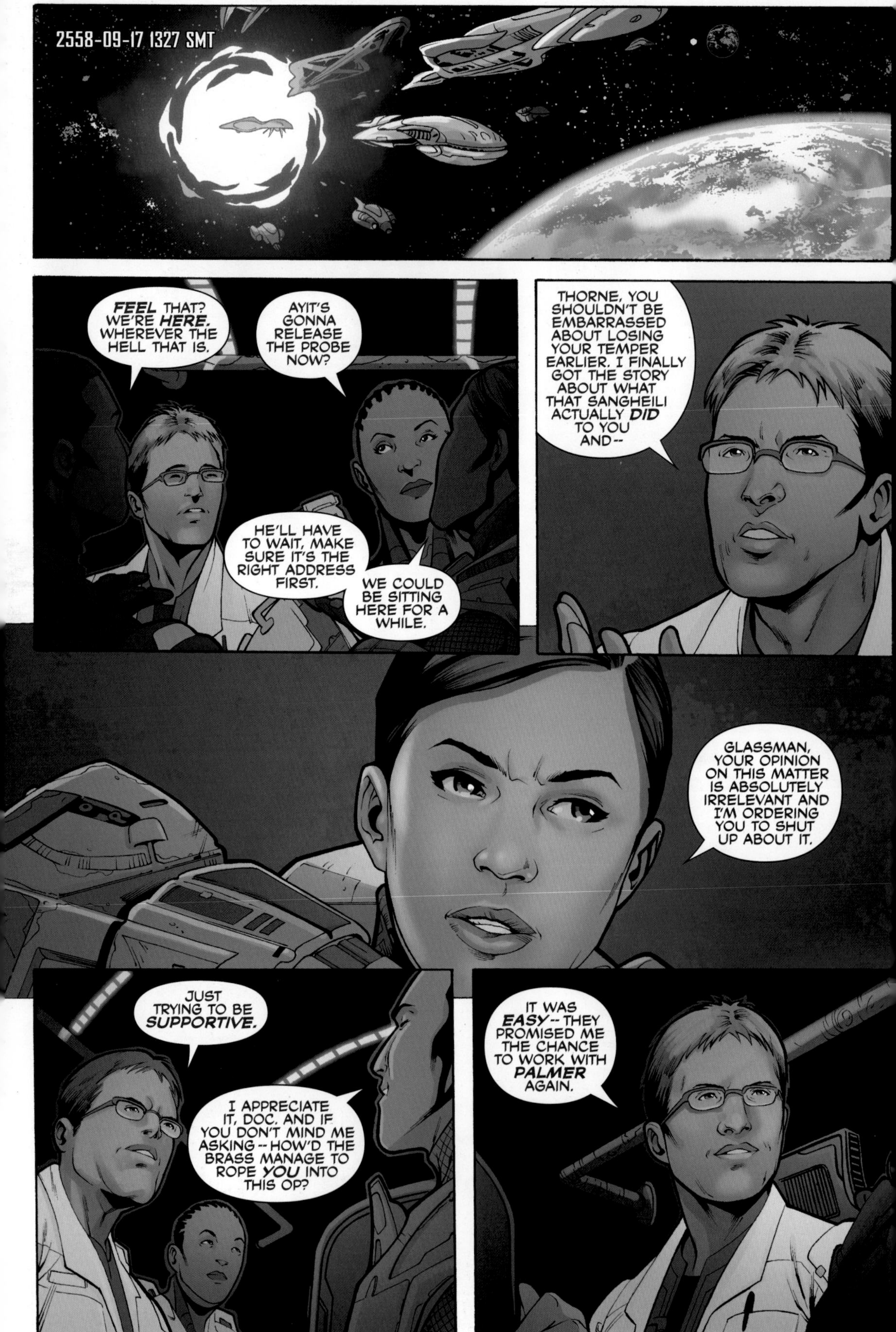
2558-09-17 1327 SMT
FEEL THAT? WE'RE HERE. WHEREVER THE HELL THAT IS.
AYIT'S GONNA RELEASE THE PROBE NOW?
HE'LL HAVE TO WAIT, MAKE SURE IT'S THE RIGHT ADDRESS FIRST.
WE COULD BE SITTING HERE FOR A WHILE.
THORNE, YOU SHOULDN'T BE EMBARRASSED ABOUT LOSING YOUR TEMPER EARLIER. I FINALLY GOT THE STORY ABOUT WHAT THAT SANGHEILI ACTUALLY DID TO YOU AND--
GLASSMAN, YOUR OPINION ON THIS MATTER IS ABSOLUTELY IRRELEVANT AND I'M ORDERING YOU TO SHUT UP ABOUT IT.
JUST TRYING TO BE SUPPORTIVE.
I APPRECIATE IT, DOC. AND IF YOU DON'T MIND ME ASKING--HOW'D THE BRASS MANAGE TO ROPE YOU INTO THIS OP?
IT WAS EASY--THEY PROMISED ME THE CHANCE TO WORK WITH PALMER AGAIN.

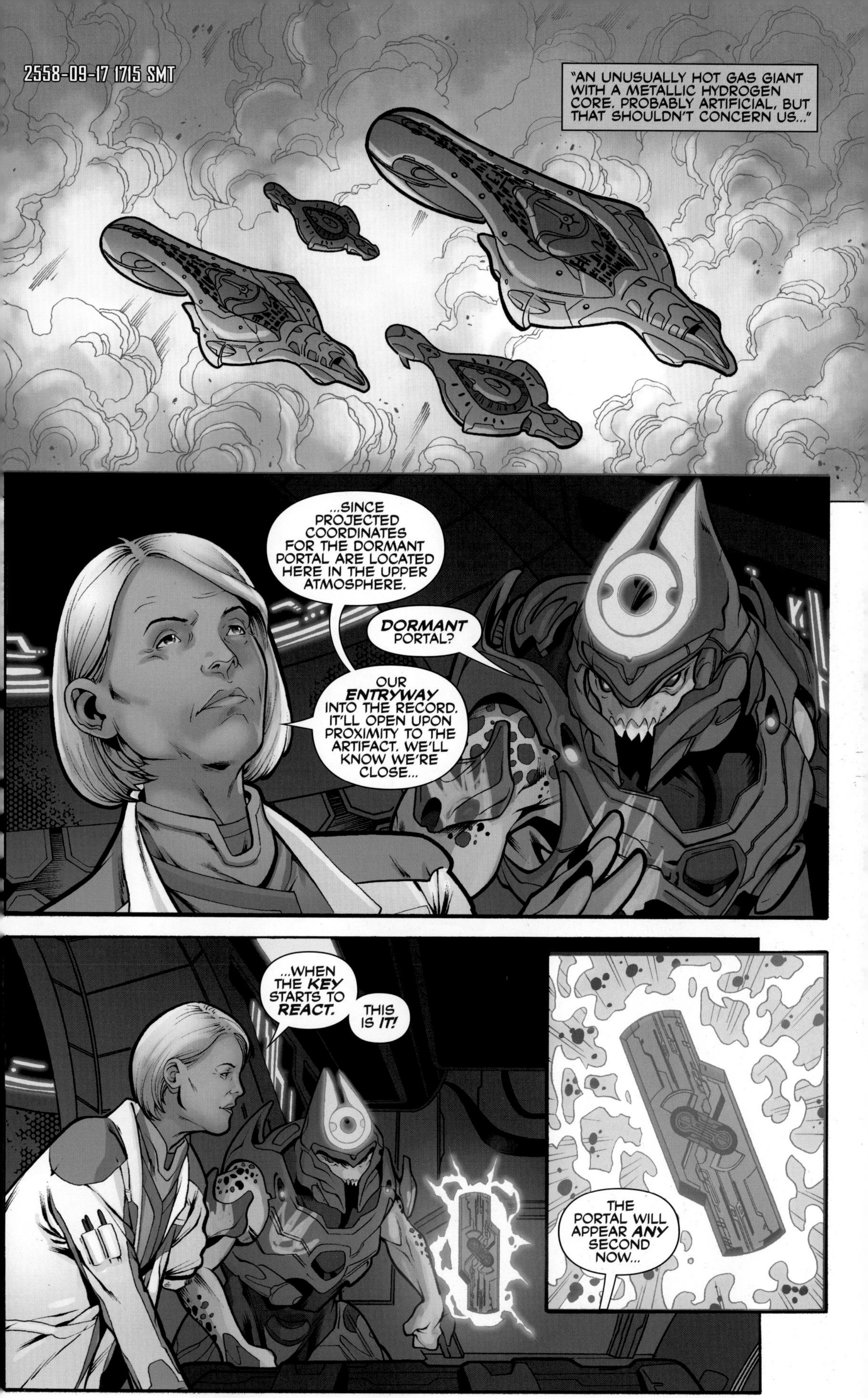
2558-09-17 1715 SMT
"AN UNUSUALLY HOT GAS GIANT WITH A METALLIC HYDROGEN CORE. PROBABLY ARTIFICIAL, BUT THAT SHOULDN'T CONCERN US..."
...SINCE PROJECTED COORDINATES FOR THE DORMANT PORTAL ARE LOCATED HERE IN THE UPPER ATMOSPHERE.
DORMANT PORTAL?
OUR *ENTRYWAY* INTO THE RECORD. IT'LL OPEN UPON PROXIMITY TO THE ARTIFACT. WE'LL KNOW WE'RE CLOSE...
...WHEN THE *KEY* STARTS TO *REACT.*
THIS IS *IT!*
THE PORTAL WILL APPEAR *ANY* SECOND NOW...

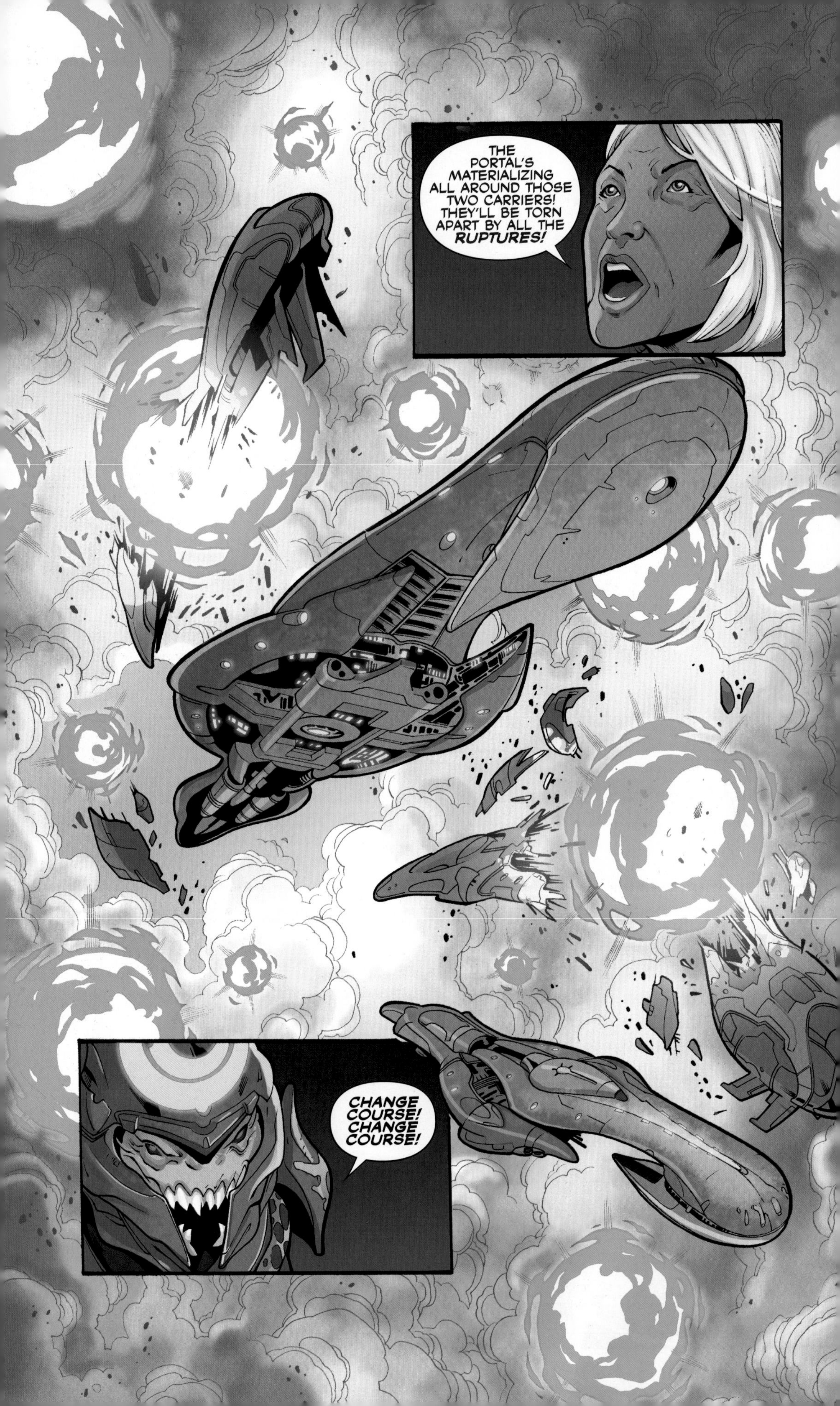
THE PORTAL'S MATERIALIZING ALL AROUND THOSE TWO CARRIERS! THEY'LL BE TORN APART BY ALL THE *RUPTURES!*
CHANGE COURSE! CHANGE COURSE!

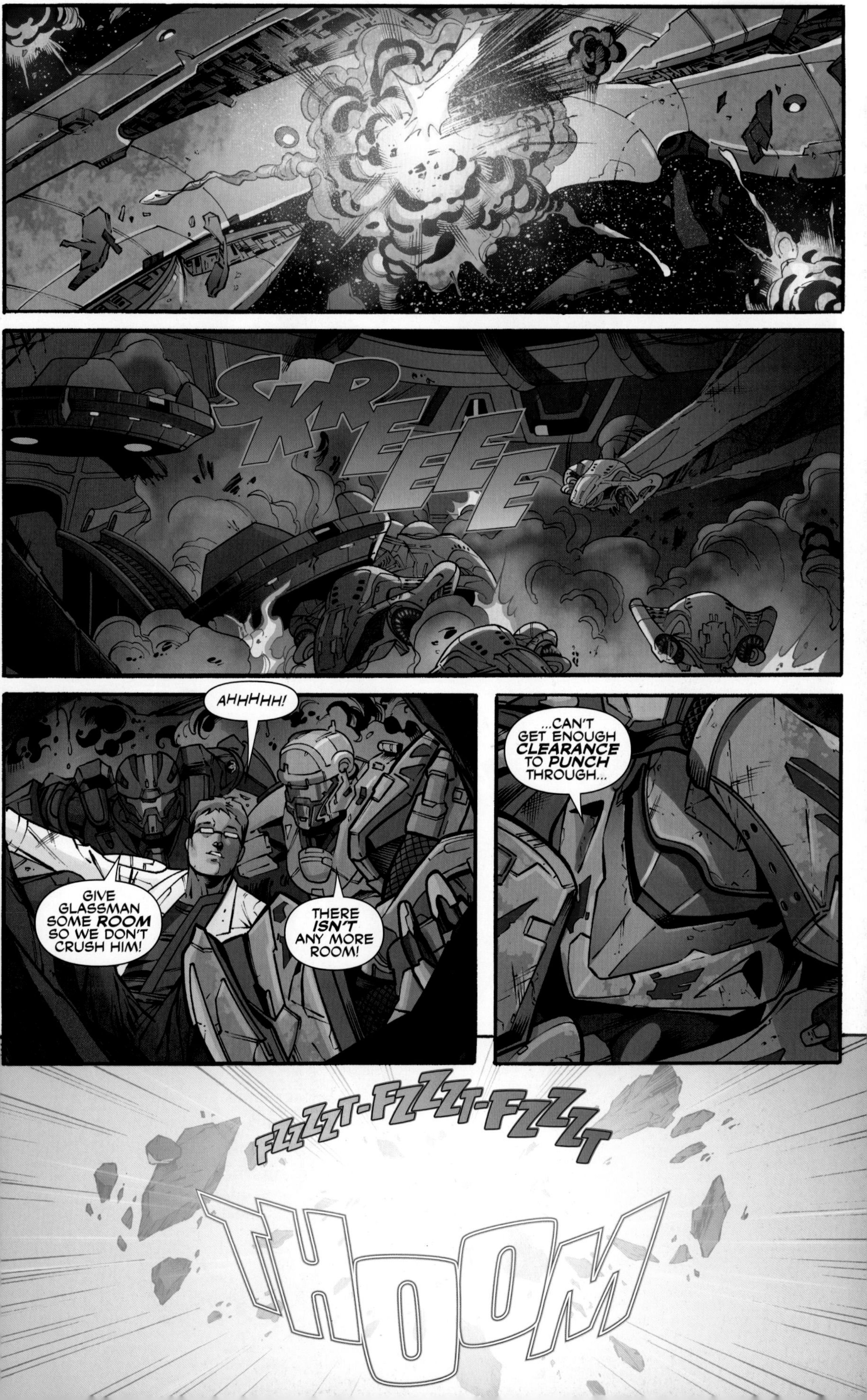
SKREEEEE
AHHHHHH!
GIVE GLASSMAN SOME ROOM SO WE DON'T CRUSH HIM!
THERE ISN'T ANY MORE ROOM!
...CAN'T GET ENOUGH CLEARANCE TO PUNCH THROUGH...
FZZZZT-FZZZT-FZZZZT
THOOM

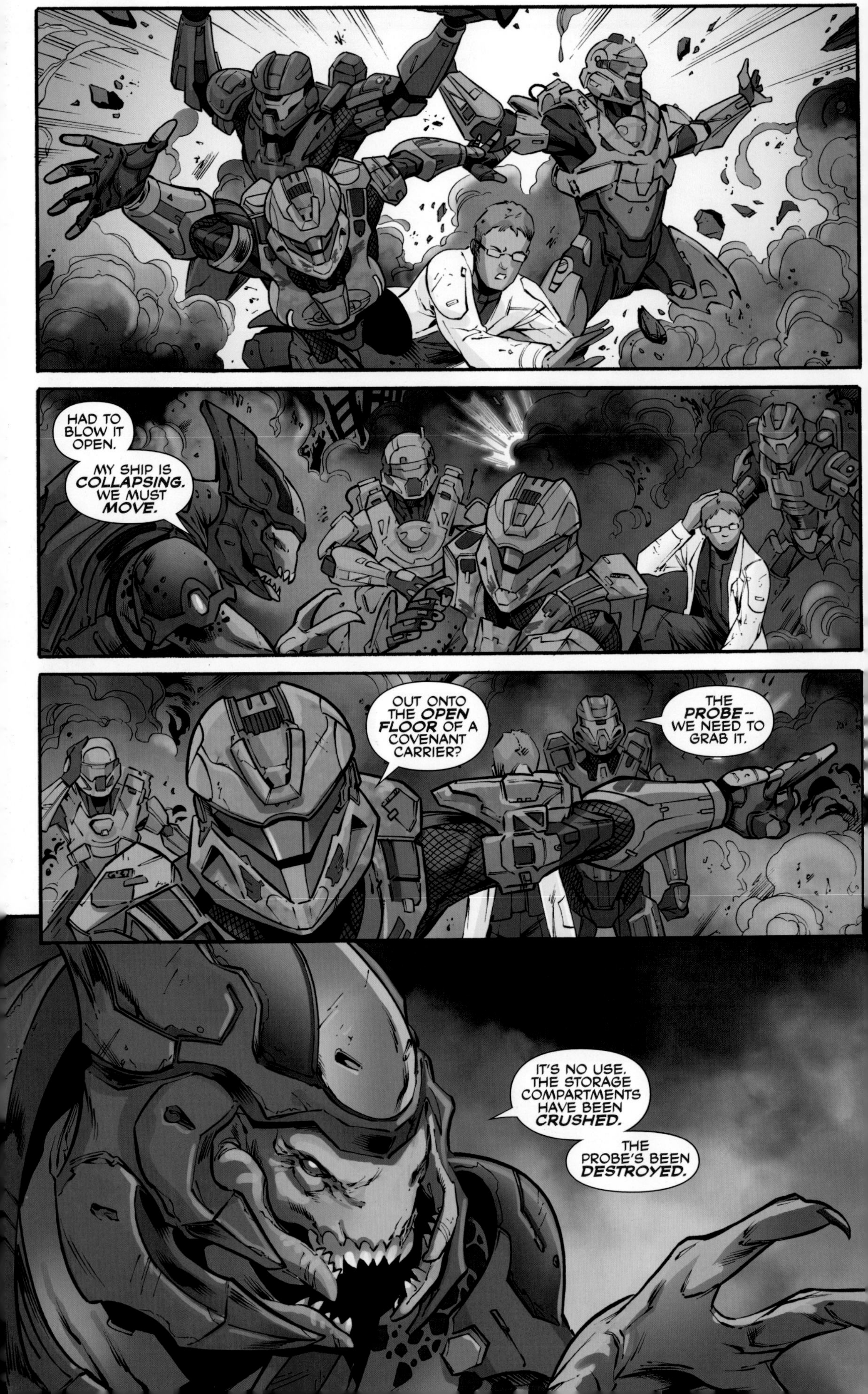
HAD TO BLOW IT OPEN.
MY SHIP IS COLLAPSING. WE MUST MOVE.
OUT ONTO THE OPEN FLOOR OF A COVENANT CARRIER?
THE PROBE-- WE NEED TO GRAB IT.
IT'S NO USE. THE STORAGE COMPARTMENTS HAVE BEEN CRUSHED.
THE PROBE'S BEEN DESTROYED.

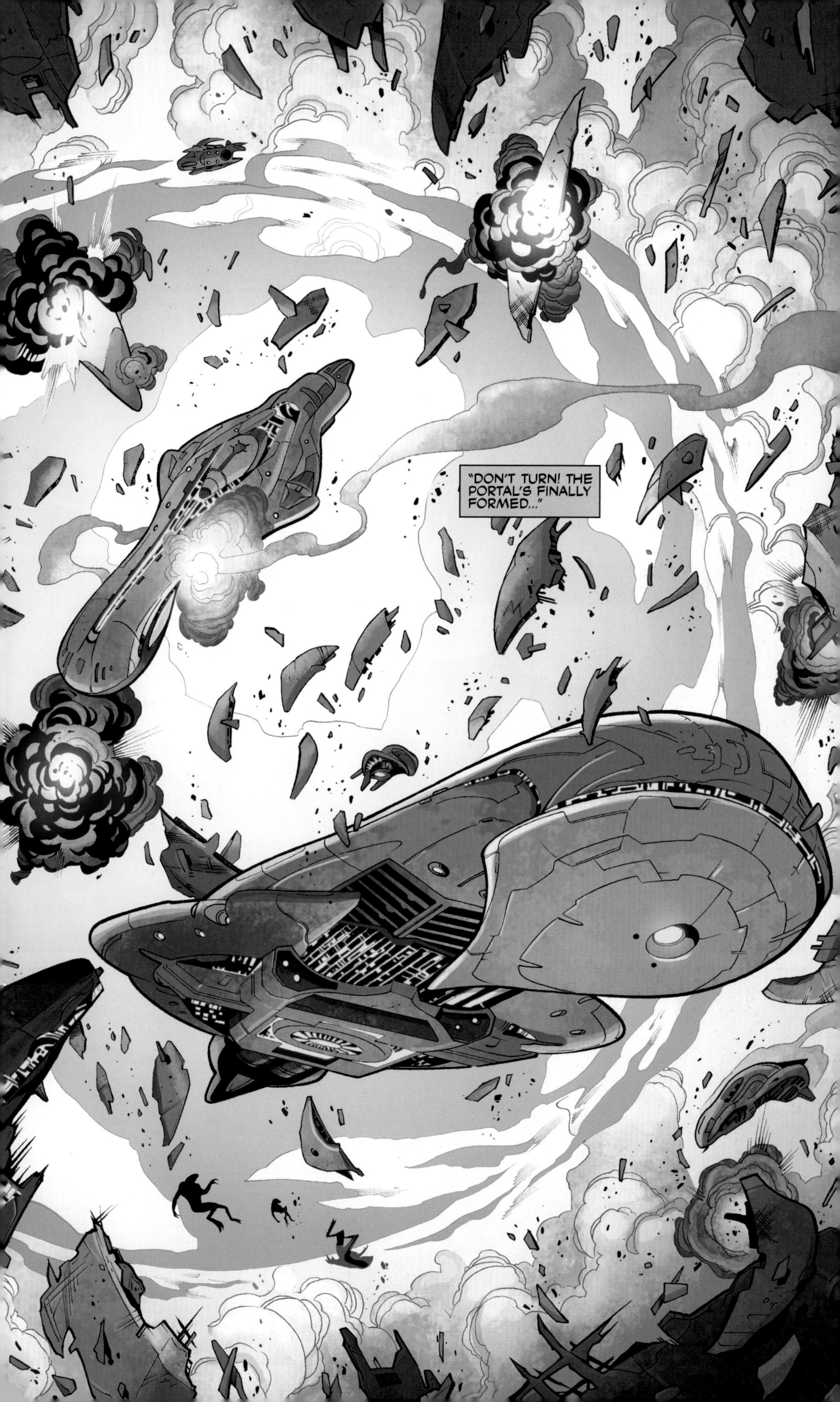
"DON'T TURN! THE PORTAL'S FINALLY FORMED..."

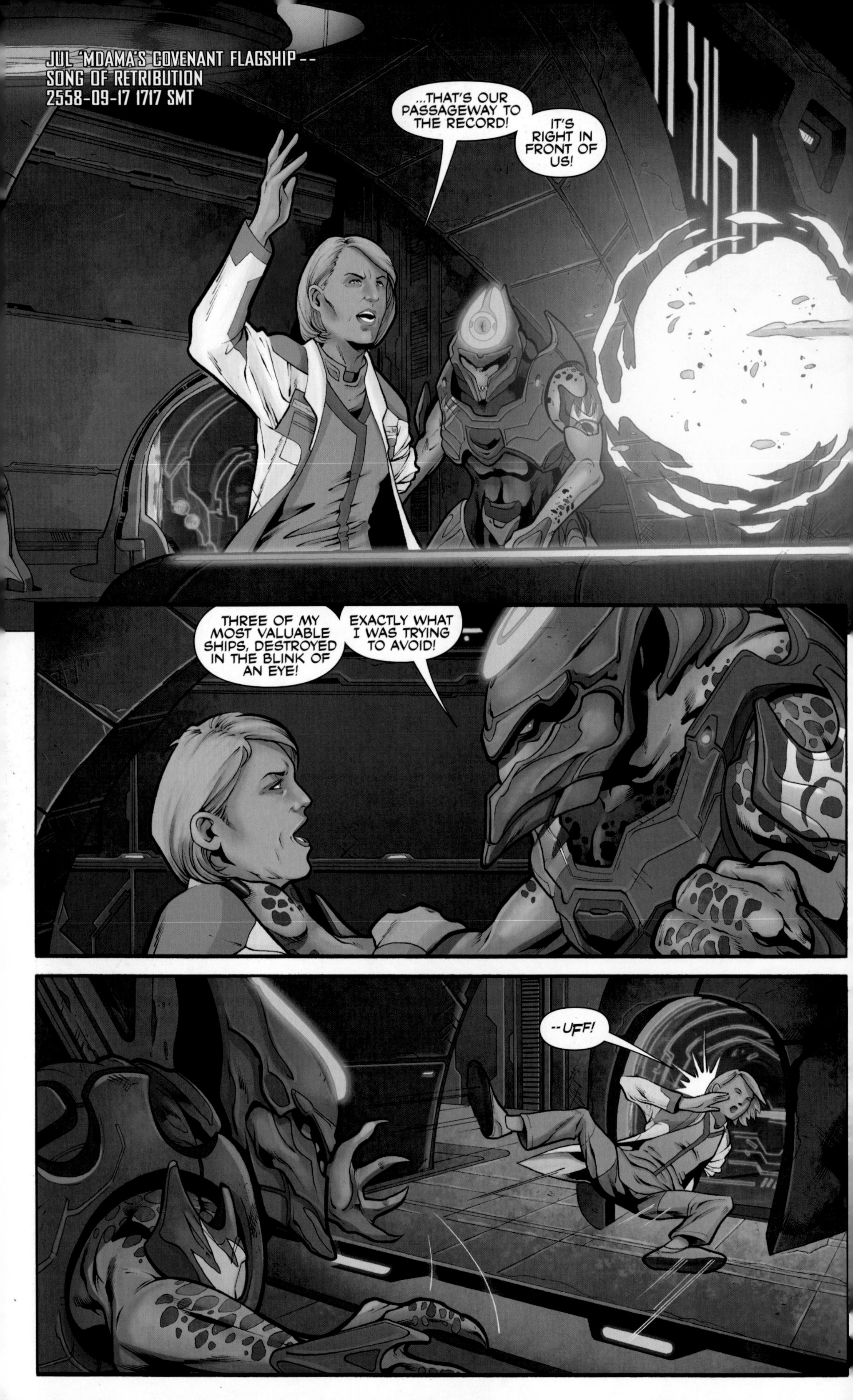
JUL 'MDAMA'S COVENANT FLAGSHIP --
SONG OF RETRIBUTION
2558-09-17 1717 SMT
...THAT'S OUR PASSAGEWAY TO THE RECORD!
IT'S RIGHT IN FRONT OF US!
THREE OF MY MOST VALUABLE SHIPS, DESTROYED IN THE BLINK OF AN EYE!
EXACTLY WHAT I WAS TRYING TO AVOID!
--UFF!

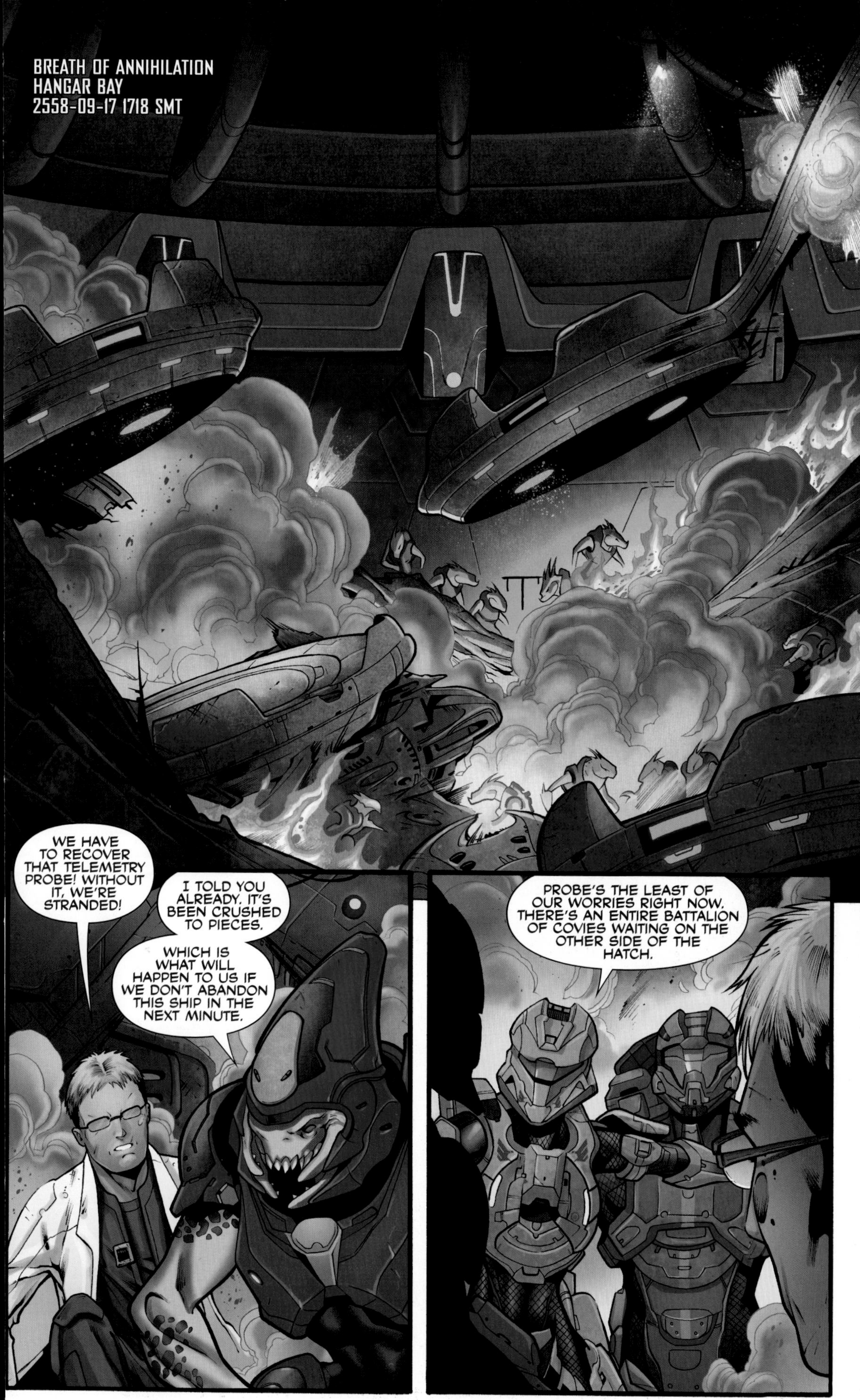
BREATH OF ANNIHILATION
HANGAR BAY
2558-09-17 1718 SMT
WE HAVE TO RECOVER THAT TELEMETRY PROBE! WITHOUT IT, WE'RE STRANDED!
I TOLD YOU ALREADY. IT'S BEEN CRUSHED TO PIECES.
WHICH IS WHAT WILL HAPPEN TO US IF WE DON'T ABANDON THIS SHIP IN THE NEXT MINUTE.
PROBE'S THE LEAST OF OUR WORRIES RIGHT NOW. THERE'S AN ENTIRE BATTALION OF COVIES WAITING ON THE OTHER SIDE OF THE HATCH.

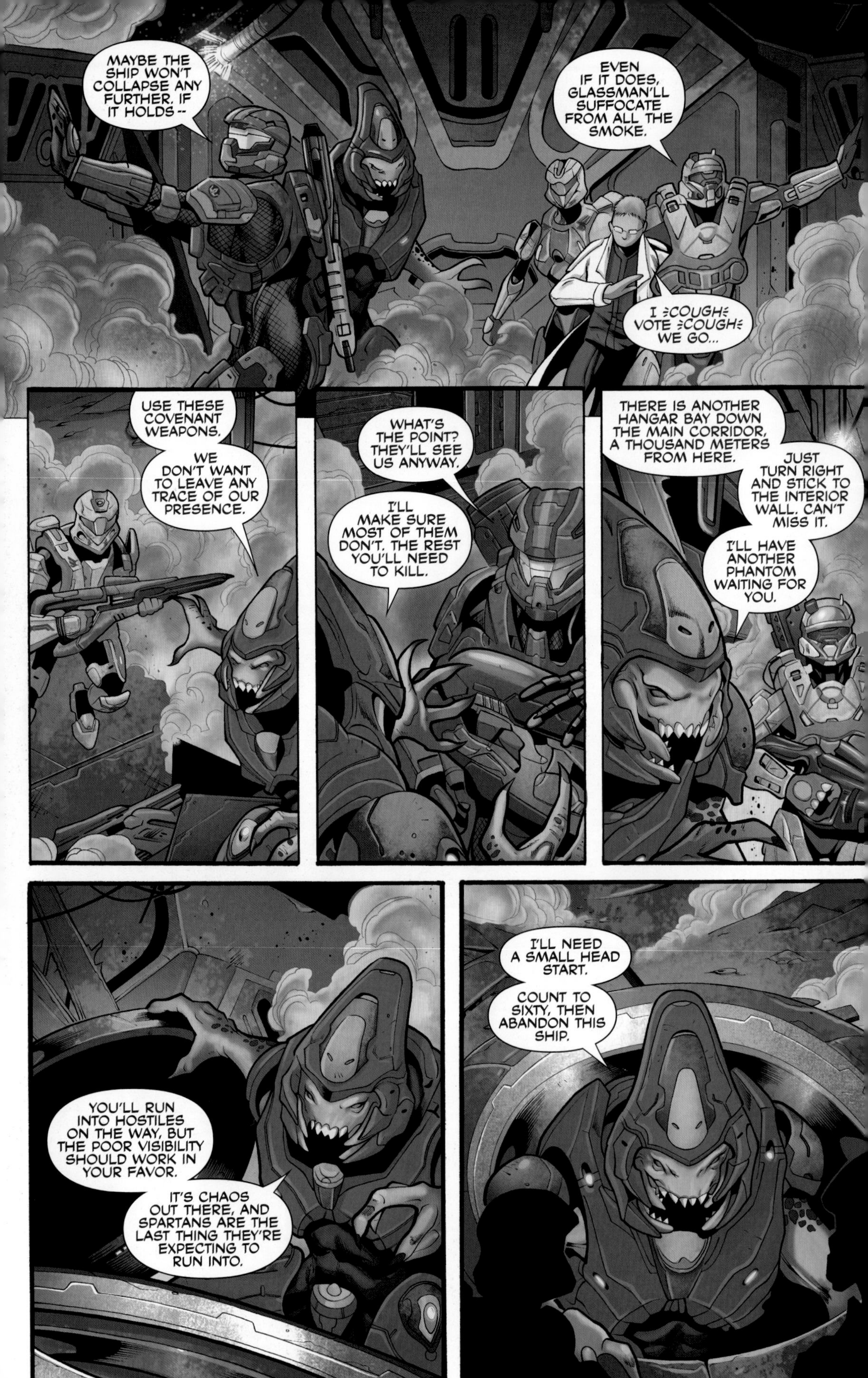
MAYBE THE SHIP WON'T COLLAPSE ANY FURTHER. IF IT HOLDS --
EVEN IF IT DOES, GLASSMAN'LL SUFFOCATE FROM ALL THE SMOKE.
I ≈COUGH≈ VOTE ≈COUGH≈ WE GO...
USE THESE COVENANT WEAPONS.
WE DON'T WANT TO LEAVE ANY TRACE OF OUR PRESENCE.
WHAT'S THE POINT? THEY'LL SEE US ANYWAY.
I'LL MAKE SURE MOST OF THEM DON'T. THE REST YOU'LL NEED TO KILL.
THERE IS ANOTHER HANGAR BAY DOWN THE MAIN CORRIDOR, A THOUSAND METERS FROM HERE.
JUST TURN RIGHT AND STICK TO THE INTERIOR WALL. CAN'T MISS IT.
I'LL HAVE ANOTHER PHANTOM WAITING FOR YOU.
YOU'LL RUN INTO HOSTILES ON THE WAY, BUT THE POOR VISIBILITY SHOULD WORK IN YOUR FAVOR.
IT'S CHAOS OUT THERE, AND SPARTANS ARE THE LAST THING THEY'RE EXPECTING TO RUN INTO.
I'LL NEED A SMALL HEAD START.
COUNT TO SIXTY, THEN ABANDON THIS SHIP.

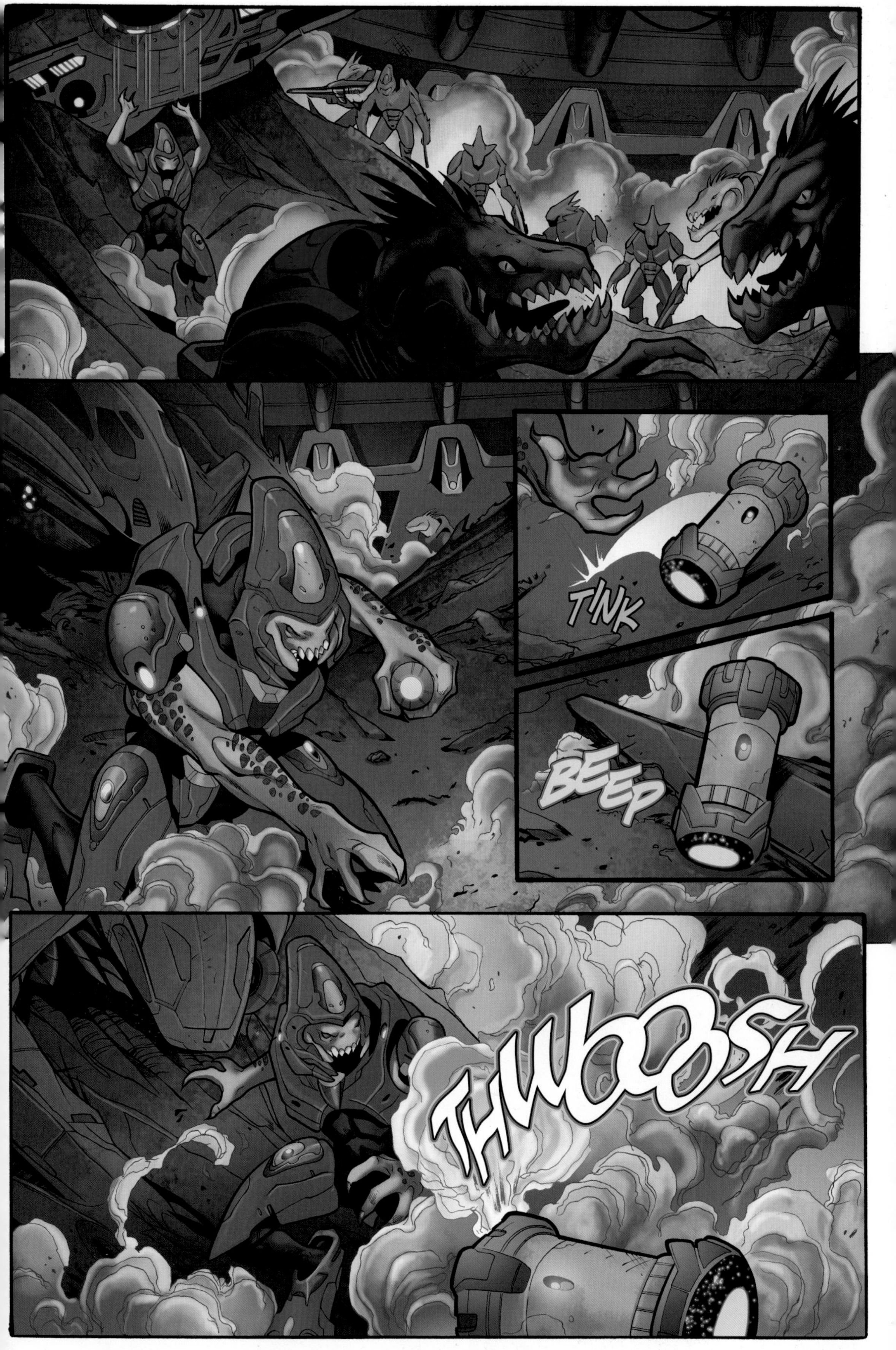
TINK
BEEP
THWOOSH

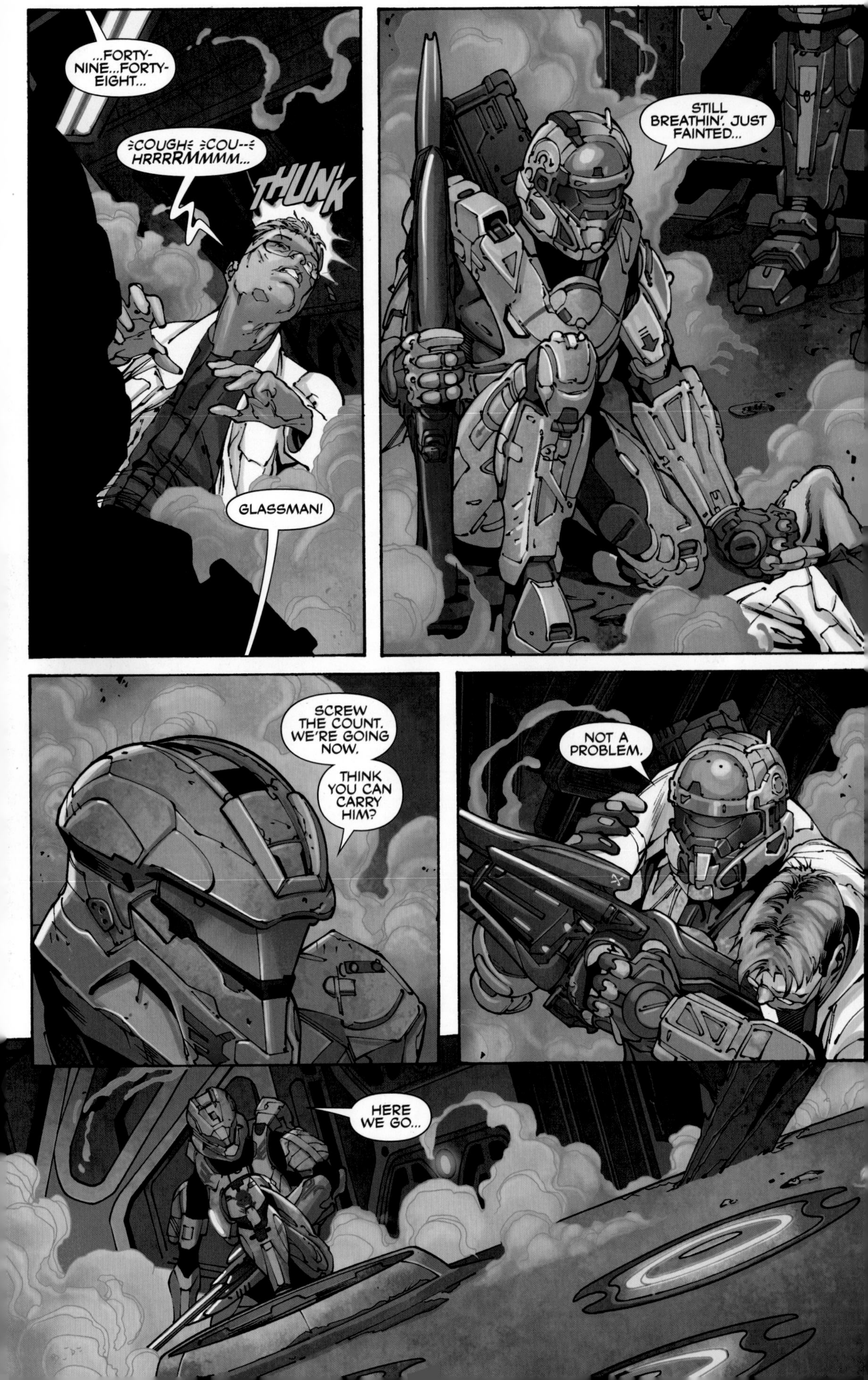
...FORTY-NINE...FORTY-EIGHT...
≷COUGH≶ ≷COU--≶ HRRRRMMMM...
THUNK
GLASSMAN!
STILL BREATHIN'. JUST FAINTED...
SCREW THE COUNT. WE'RE GOING NOW.
THINK YOU CAN CARRY HIM?
NOT A PROBLEM.
HERE WE GO...

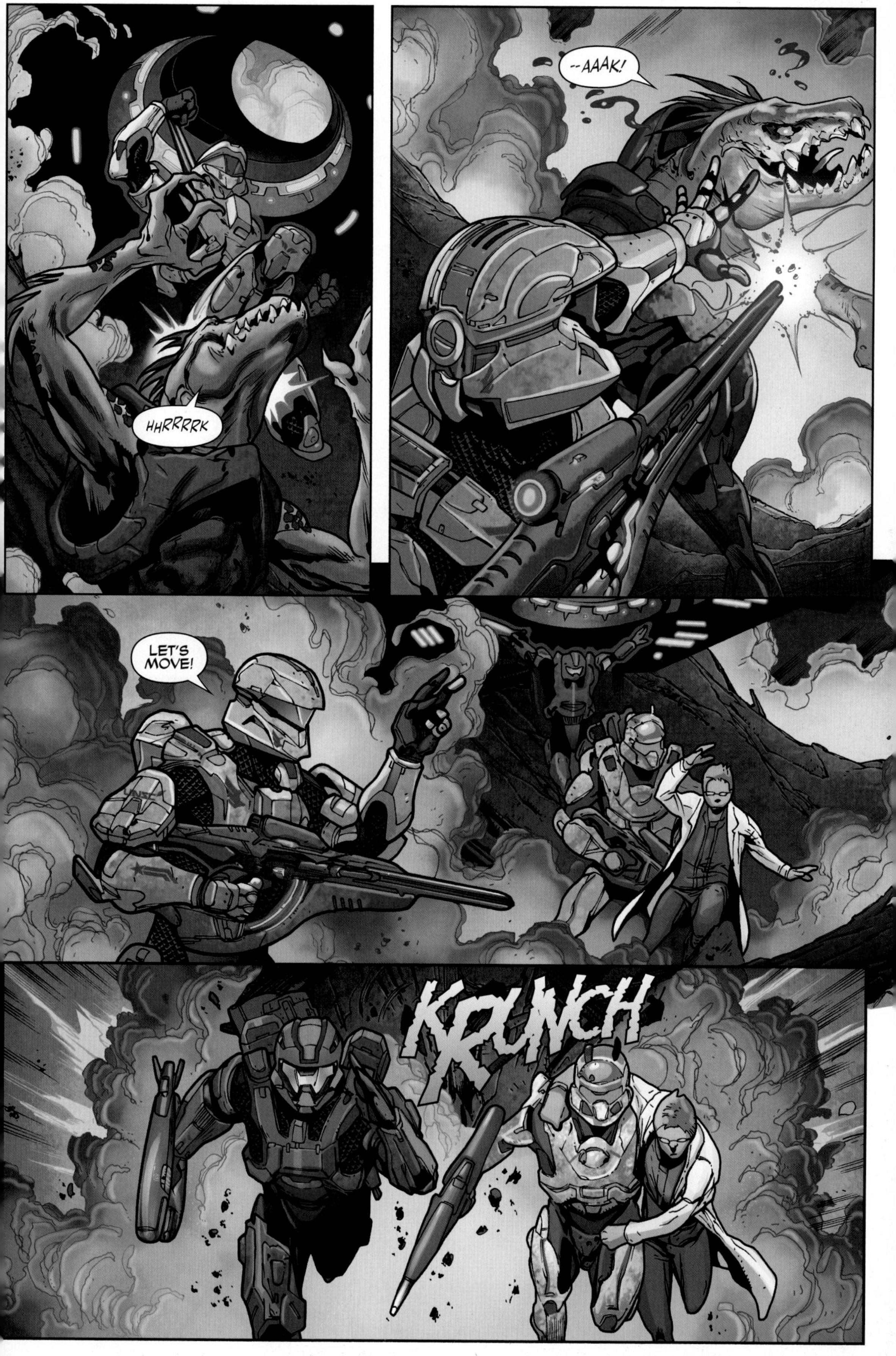
HHRRRRK
--AAAK!
LET'S MOVE!
KRUNCH

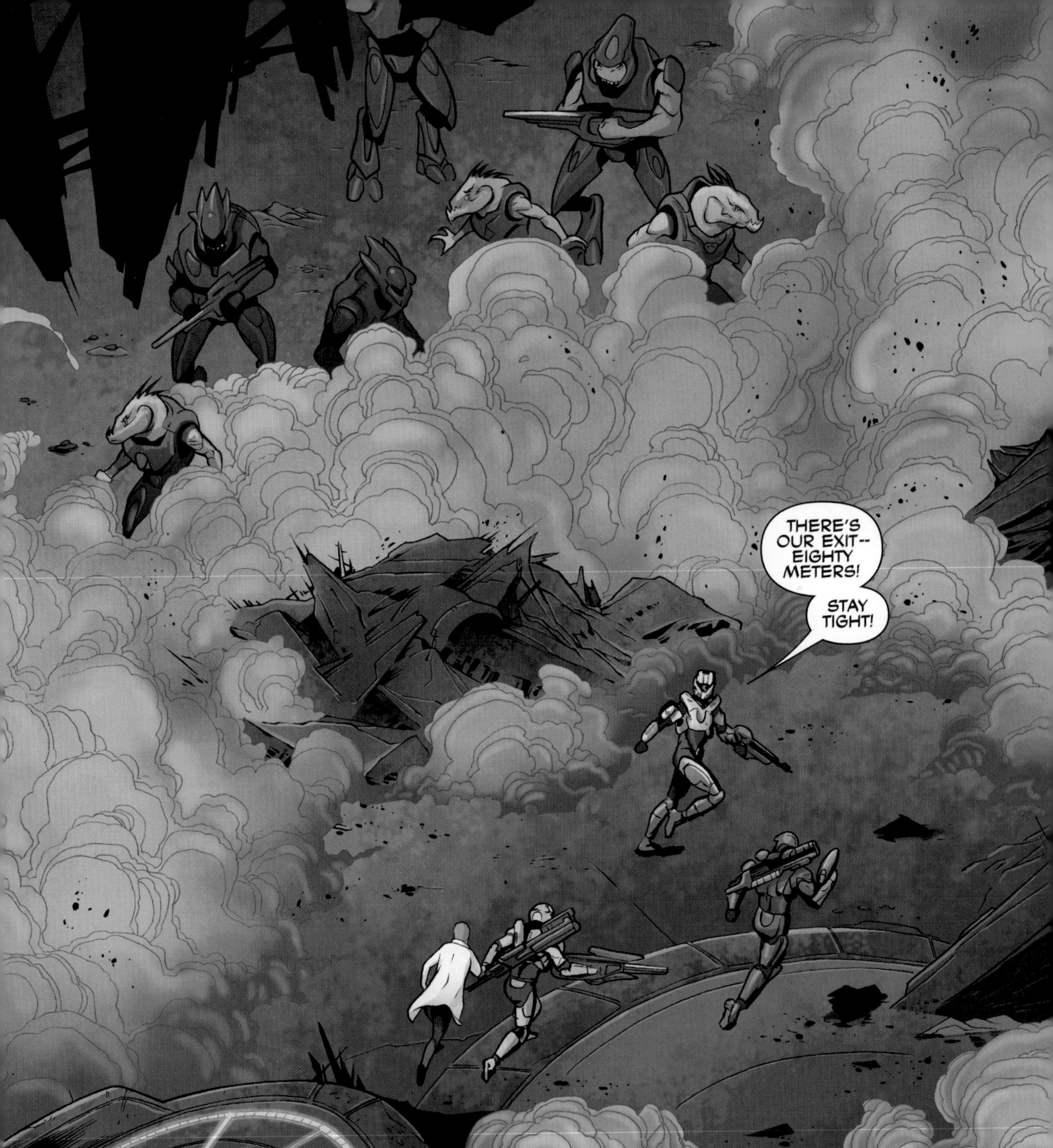
THERE'S OUR EXIT-- EIGHTY METERS!
STAY TIGHT!

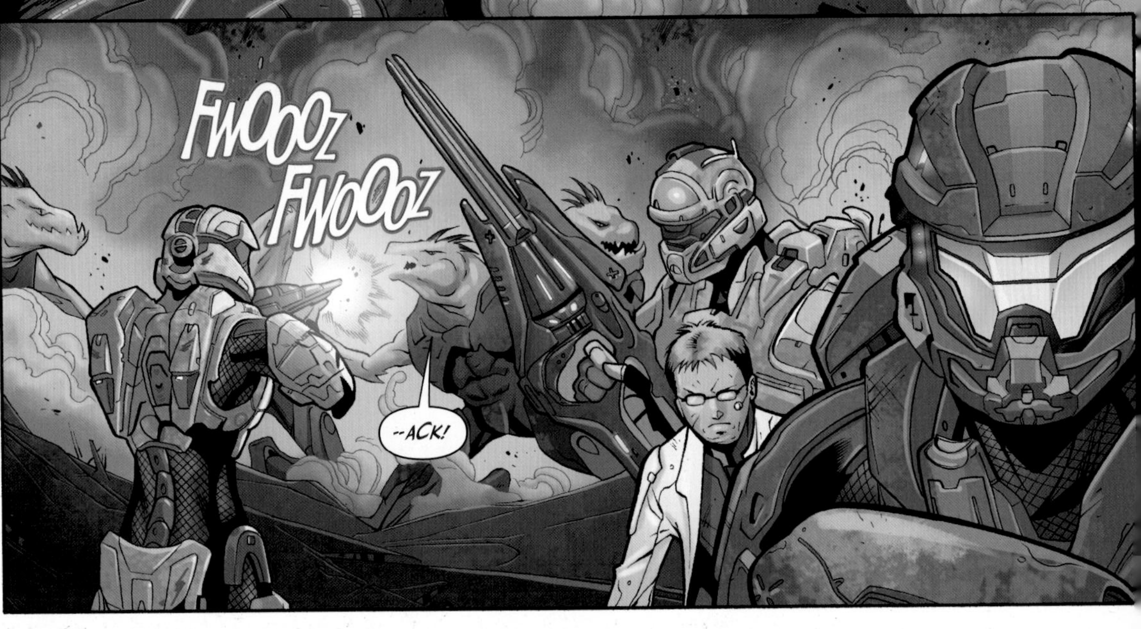
FWOOOZ
FWOOOZ
--ACK!

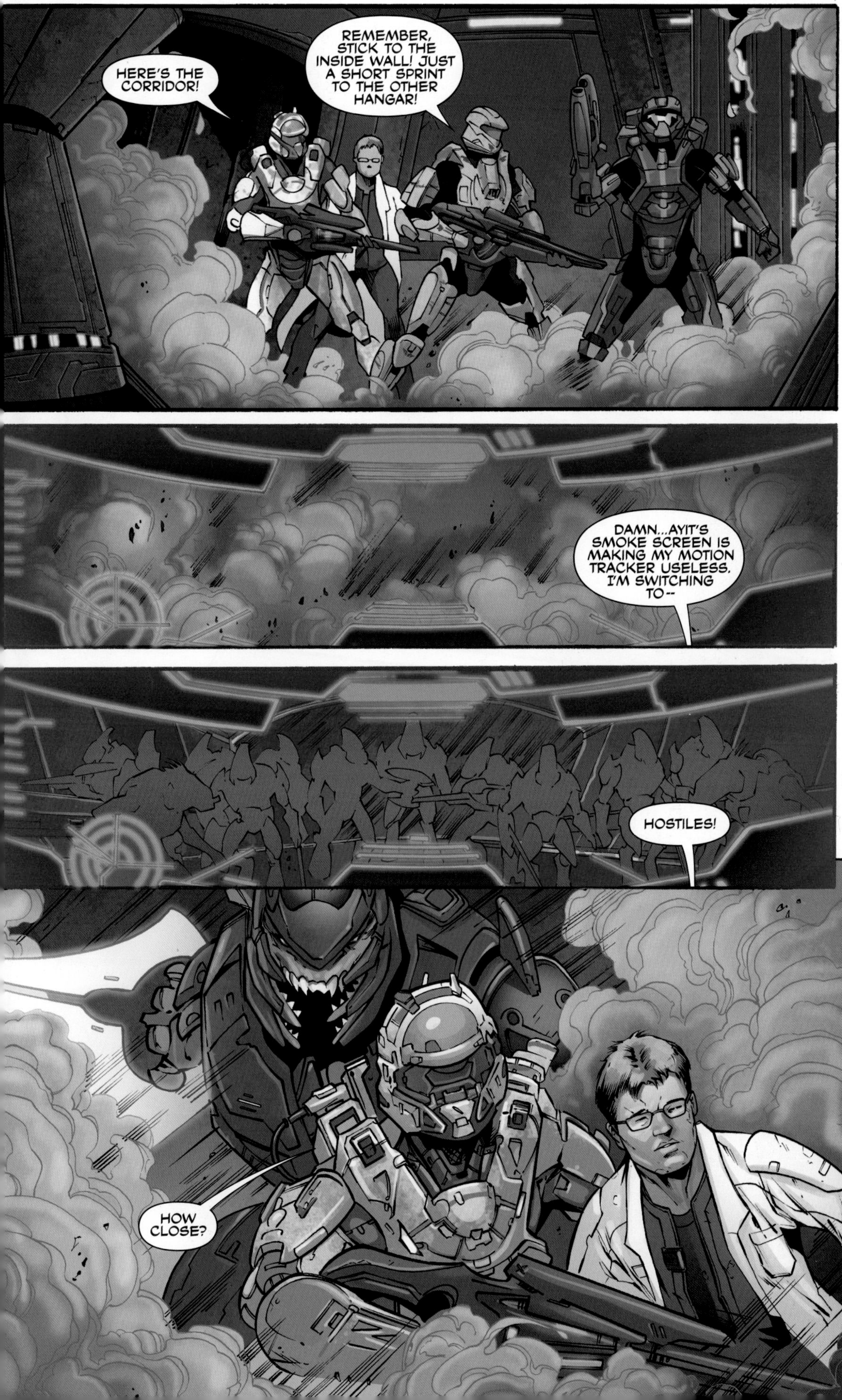
HERE'S THE CORRIDOR!
REMEMBER, STICK TO THE INSIDE WALL! JUST A SHORT SPRINT TO THE OTHER HANGAR!
DAMN...AYIT'S SMOKE SCREEN IS MAKING MY MOTION TRACKER USELESS. I'M SWITCHING TO--
HOSTILES!
HOW CLOSE?

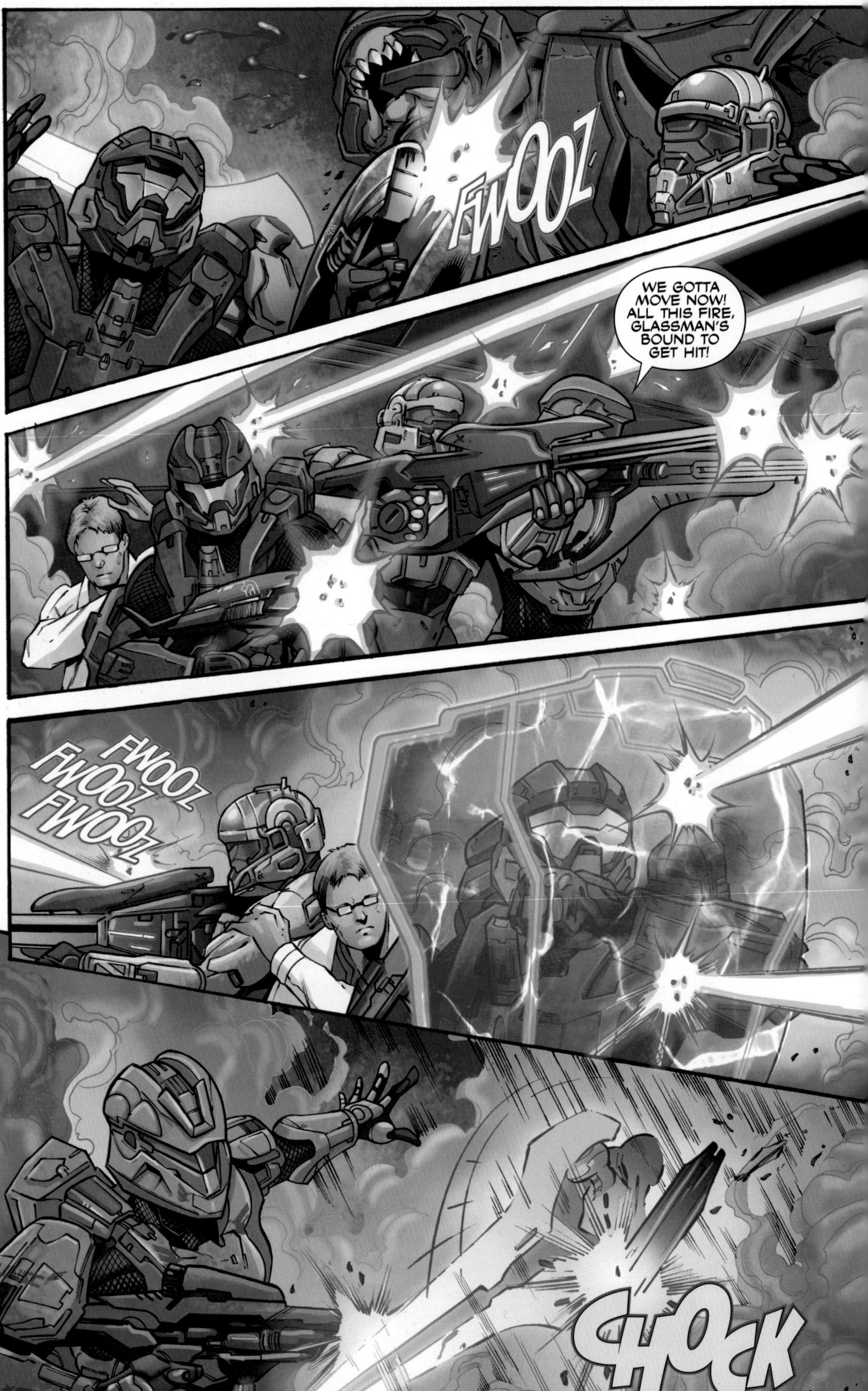
FWOOZ
WE GOTTA MOVE NOW! ALL THIS FIRE, GLASSMAN'S BOUND TO GET HIT!
FWOOZ
FWOOZ
FWOOZ
CHOCK

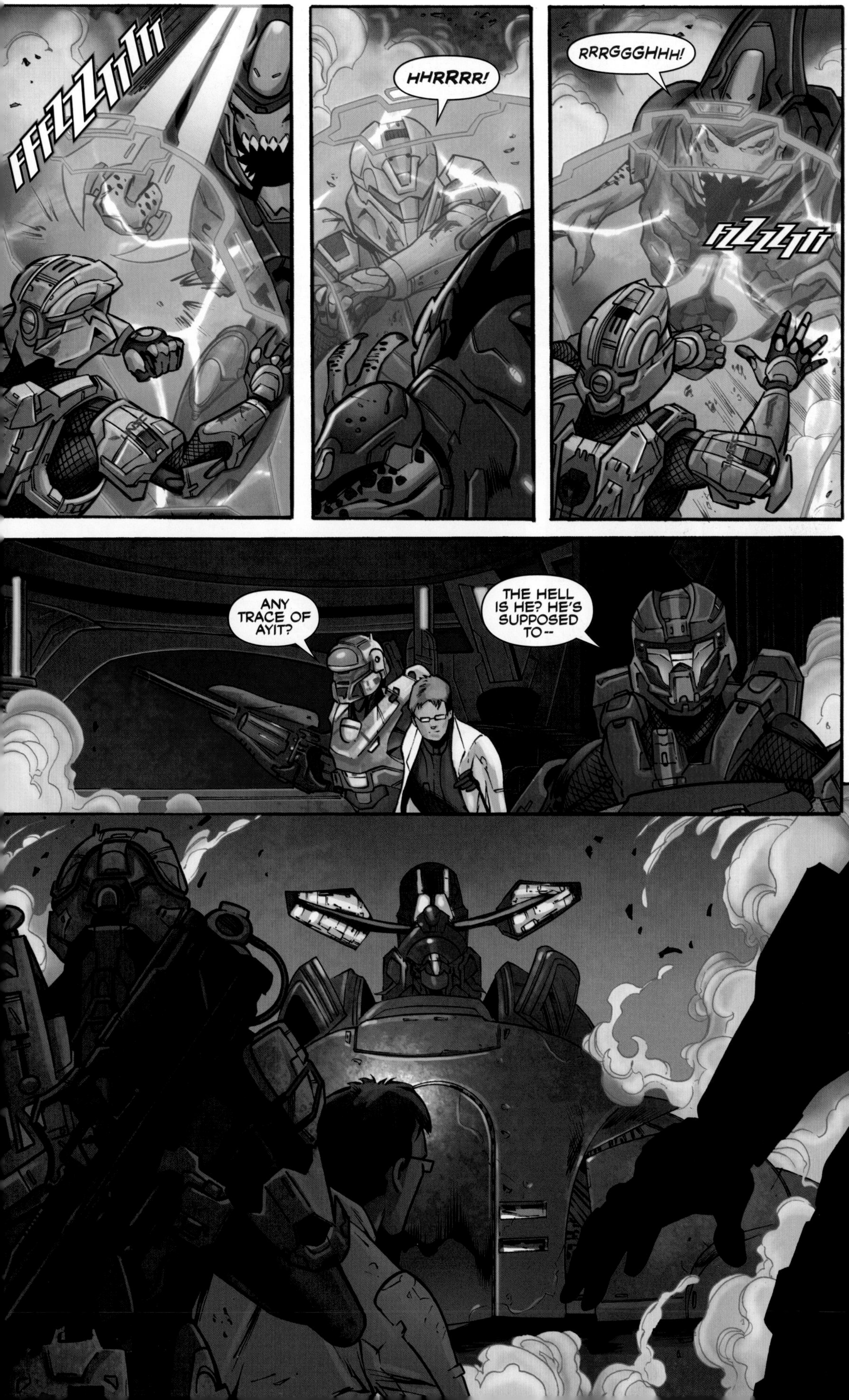
FFFZZZTTTTT
HHRRRR!
RRRGGGHHH!
FZZZZTTT
ANY TRACE OF AYIT?
THE HELL IS HE? HE'S SUPPOSED TO--

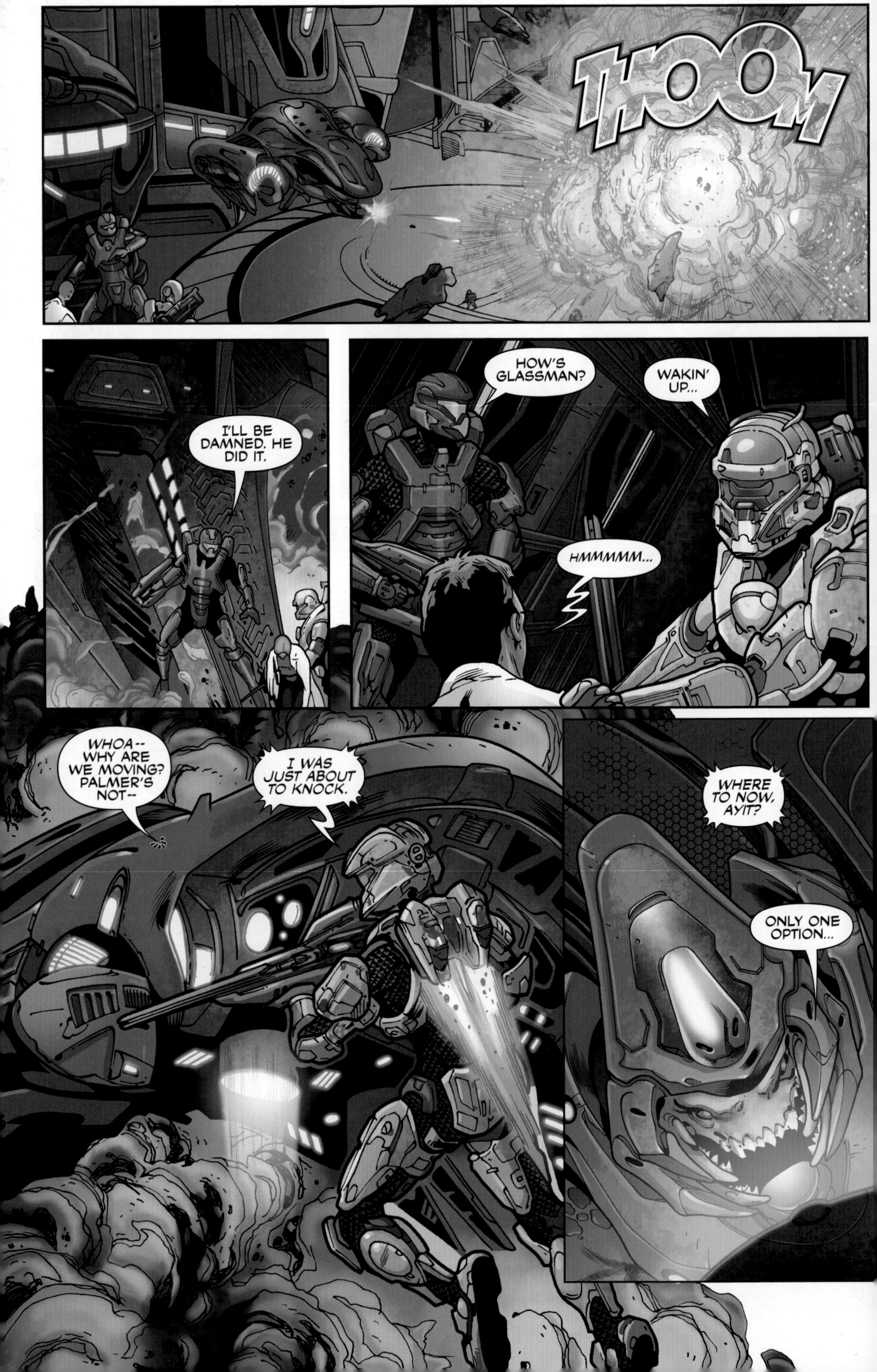
THOOM
I'LL BE DAMNED. HE DID IT.
HOW'S GLASSMAN?
WAKIN' UP...
HMMMMM...
WHOA-- WHY ARE WE MOVING? PALMER'S NOT--
I WAS JUST ABOUT TO KNOCK.
WHERE TO NOW, AYIT?
ONLY ONE OPTION...

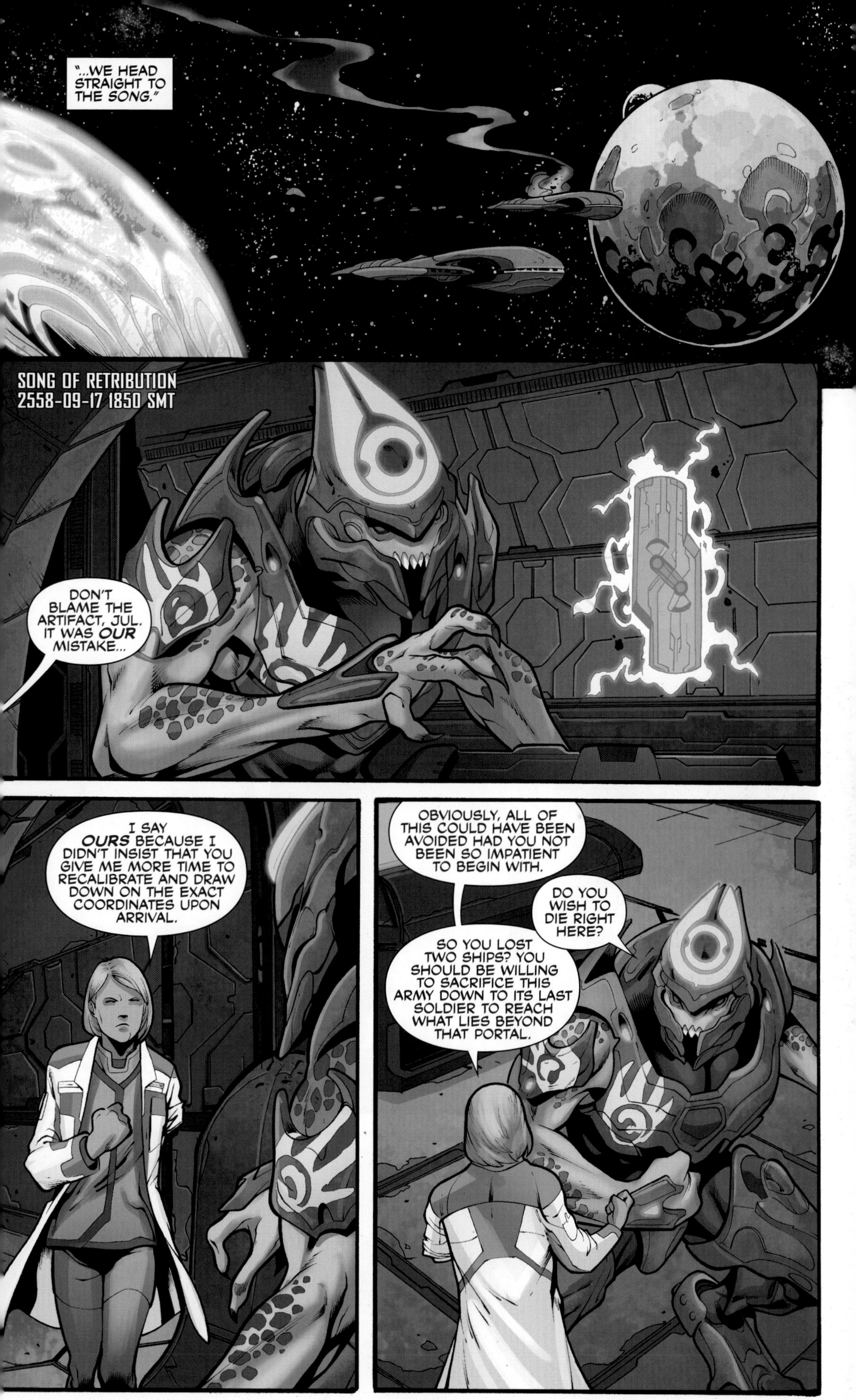
"...WE HEAD STRAIGHT TO THE SONG."
SONG OF RETRIBUTION
2558-09-17 1850 SMT
DON'T BLAME THE ARTIFACT, JUL. IT WAS *OUR* MISTAKE...
I SAY *OURS* BECAUSE I DIDN'T INSIST THAT YOU GIVE ME MORE TIME TO RECALIBRATE AND DRAW DOWN ON THE EXACT COORDINATES UPON ARRIVAL.
OBVIOUSLY, ALL OF THIS COULD HAVE BEEN AVOIDED HAD YOU NOT BEEN SO IMPATIENT TO BEGIN WITH.
DO YOU WISH TO DIE RIGHT HERE?
SO YOU LOST TWO SHIPS? YOU SHOULD BE WILLING TO SACRIFICE THIS ARMY DOWN TO ITS LAST SOLDIER TO REACH WHAT LIES BEYOND THAT PORTAL.

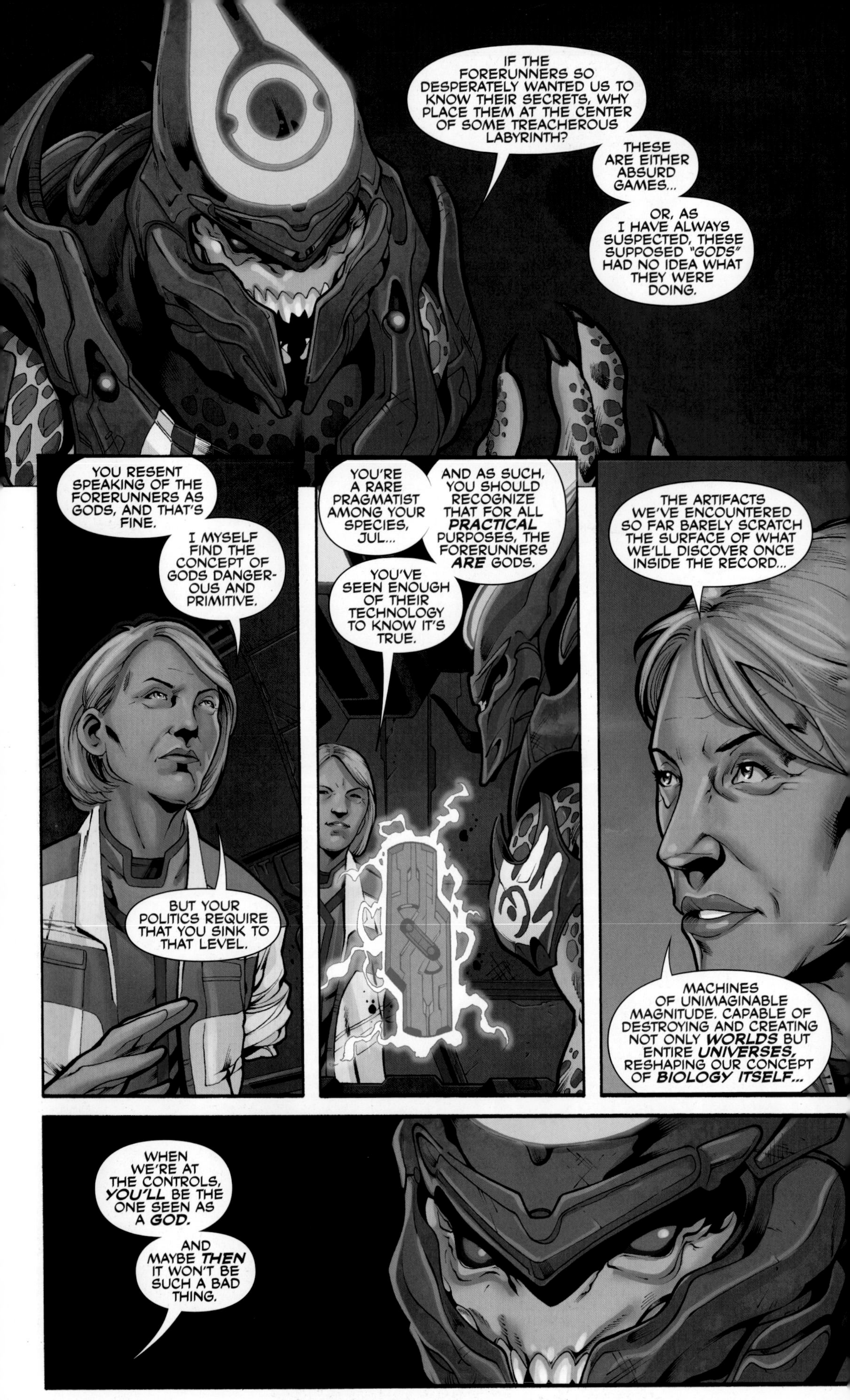

IF THE FORERUNNERS SO DESPERATELY WANTED US TO KNOW THEIR SECRETS, WHY PLACE THEM AT THE CENTER OF SOME TREACHEROUS LABYRINTH?
THESE ARE EITHER ABSURD GAMES...
OR, AS I HAVE ALWAYS SUSPECTED, THESE SUPPOSED "GODS" HAD NO IDEA WHAT THEY WERE DOING.
YOU RESENT SPEAKING OF THE FORERUNNERS AS GODS, AND THAT'S FINE.
I MYSELF FIND THE CONCEPT OF GODS DANGEROUS AND PRIMITIVE.
BUT YOUR POLITICS REQUIRE THAT YOU SINK TO THAT LEVEL.
YOU'RE A RARE PRAGMATIST AMONG YOUR SPECIES, JUL...
AND AS SUCH, YOU SHOULD RECOGNIZE THAT FOR ALL PRACTICAL PURPOSES, THE FORERUNNERS ARE GODS.
YOU'VE SEEN ENOUGH OF THEIR TECHNOLOGY TO KNOW IT'S TRUE.
THE ARTIFACTS WE'VE ENCOUNTERED SO FAR BARELY SCRATCH THE SURFACE OF WHAT WE'LL DISCOVER ONCE INSIDE THE RECORD...
MACHINES OF UNIMAGINABLE MAGNITUDE, CAPABLE OF DESTROYING AND CREATING NOT ONLY WORLDS BUT ENTIRE UNIVERSES, RESHAPING OUR CONCEPT OF BIOLOGY ITSELF...
WHEN WE'RE AT THE CONTROLS, YOU'LL BE THE ONE SEEN AS A GOD.
AND MAYBE THEN IT WON'T BE SUCH A BAD THING.

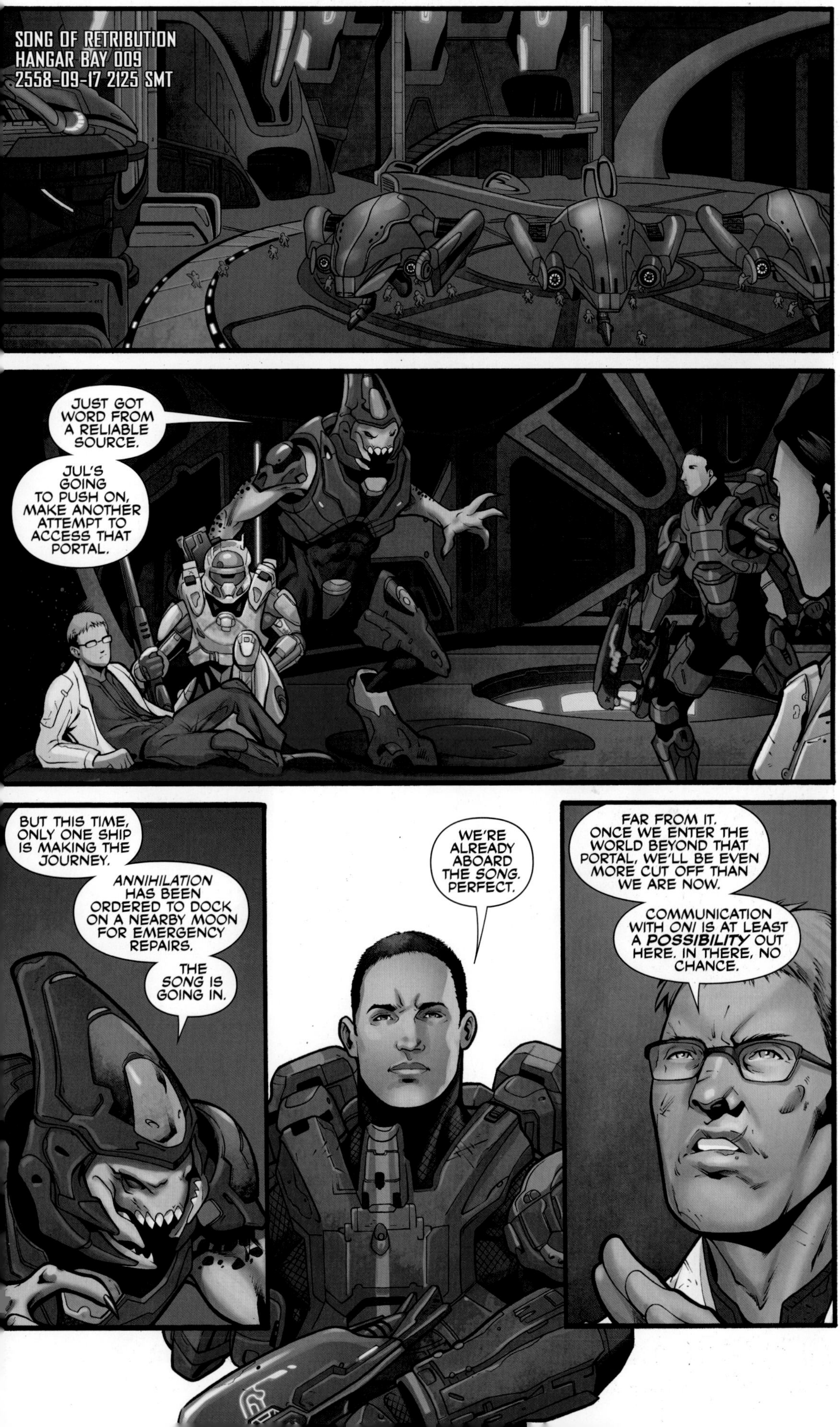
SONG OF RETRIBUTION
HANGAR BAY 009
2558-09-17 2125 SMT
JUST GOT WORD FROM A RELIABLE SOURCE.
JUL'S GOING TO PUSH ON, MAKE ANOTHER ATTEMPT TO ACCESS THAT PORTAL.
BUT THIS TIME, ONLY ONE SHIP IS MAKING THE JOURNEY.
ANNIHILATION HAS BEEN ORDERED TO DOCK ON A NEARBY MOON FOR EMERGENCY REPAIRS.
THE SONG IS GOING IN.
WE'RE ALREADY ABOARD THE SONG. PERFECT.
FAR FROM IT. ONCE WE ENTER THE WORLD BEYOND THAT PORTAL, WE'LL BE EVEN MORE CUT OFF THAN WE ARE NOW.
COMMUNICATION WITH ONI IS AT LEAST A POSSIBILITY OUT HERE. IN THERE, NO CHANCE.

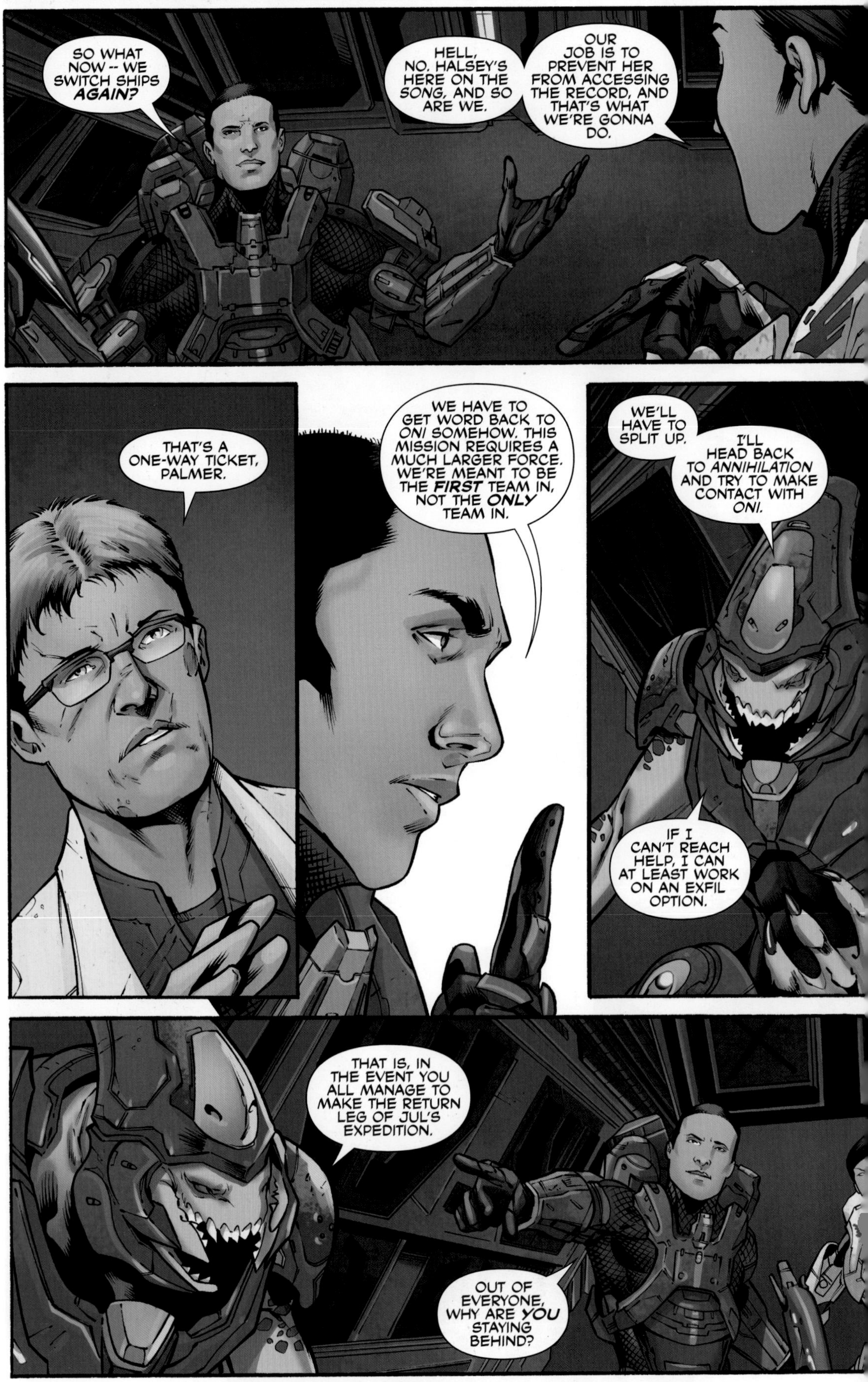
SO WHAT NOW -- WE SWITCH SHIPS AGAIN?
HELL, NO. HALSEY'S HERE ON THE SONG, AND SO ARE WE.
OUR JOB IS TO PREVENT HER FROM ACCESSING THE RECORD, AND THAT'S WHAT WE'RE GONNA DO.
THAT'S A ONE-WAY TICKET, PALMER.
WE HAVE TO GET WORD BACK TO ONI SOMEHOW. THIS MISSION REQUIRES A MUCH LARGER FORCE. WE'RE MEANT TO BE THE FIRST TEAM IN, NOT THE ONLY TEAM IN.
WE'LL HAVE TO SPLIT UP.
I'LL HEAD BACK TO ANNIHILATION AND TRY TO MAKE CONTACT WITH ONI.
IF I CAN'T REACH HELP, I CAN AT LEAST WORK ON AN EXFIL OPTION.
THAT IS, IN THE EVENT YOU ALL MANAGE TO MAKE THE RETURN LEG OF JUL'S EXPEDITION.
OUT OF EVERYONE, WHY ARE YOU STAYING BEHIND?

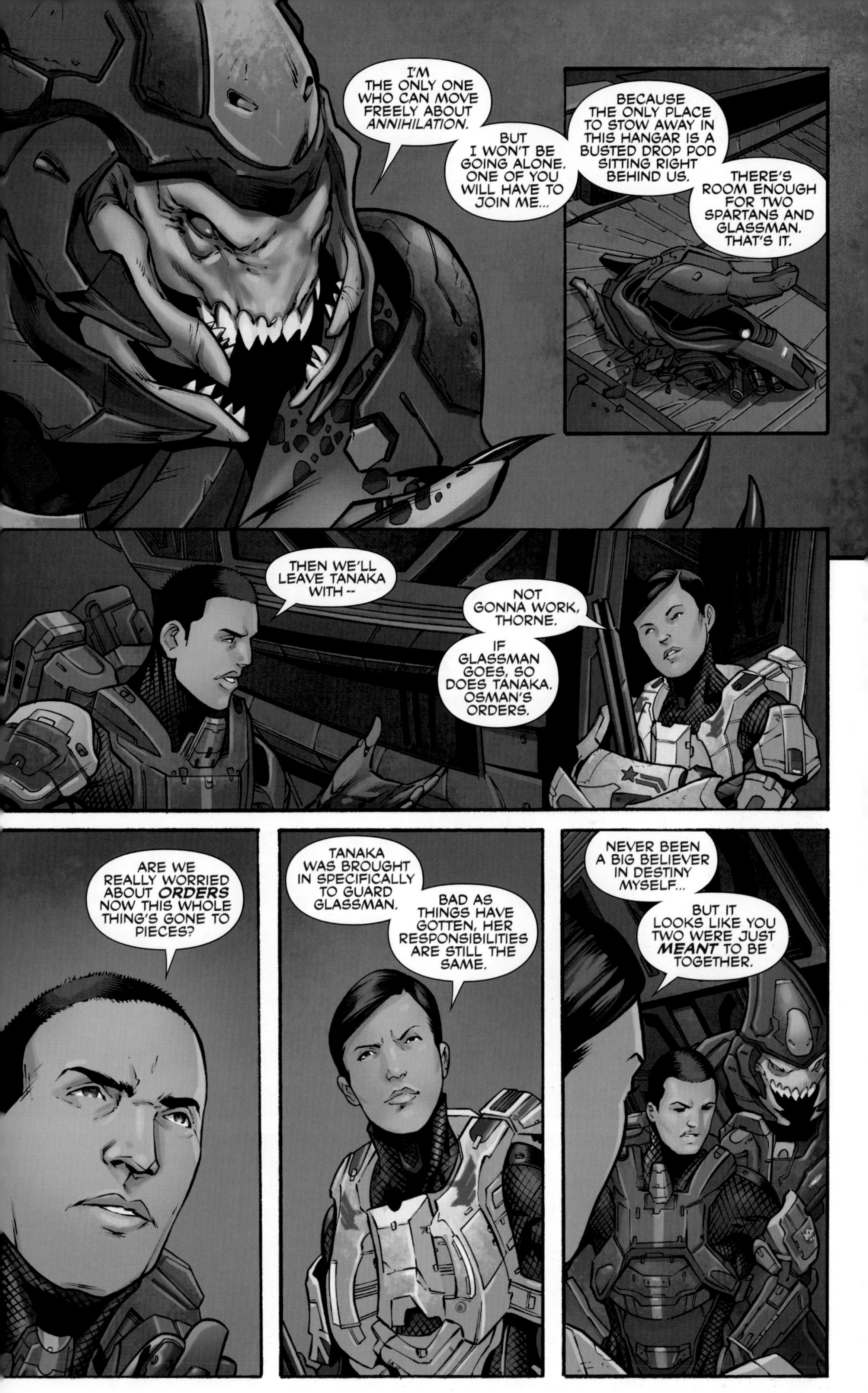

I'M THE ONLY ONE WHO CAN MOVE FREELY ABOUT *ANNIHILATION.*
BUT I WON'T BE GOING ALONE. ONE OF YOU WILL HAVE TO JOIN ME...
BECAUSE THE ONLY PLACE TO STOW AWAY IN THIS HANGAR IS A BUSTED DROP POD SITTING RIGHT BEHIND US.
THERE'S ROOM ENOUGH FOR TWO SPARTANS AND GLASSMAN. THAT'S IT.
THEN WE'LL LEAVE TANAKA WITH --
NOT GONNA WORK, THORNE.
IF GLASSMAN GOES, SO DOES TANAKA. OSMAN'S ORDERS.
ARE WE REALLY WORRIED ABOUT ***ORDERS*** NOW THIS WHOLE THING'S GONE TO PIECES?
TANAKA WAS BROUGHT IN SPECIFICALLY TO GUARD GLASSMAN.
BAD AS THINGS HAVE GOTTEN, HER RESPONSIBILITIES ARE STILL THE SAME.
NEVER BEEN A BIG BELIEVER IN DESTINY MYSELF...
BUT IT LOOKS LIKE YOU TWO WERE JUST ***MEANT*** TO BE TOGETHER.

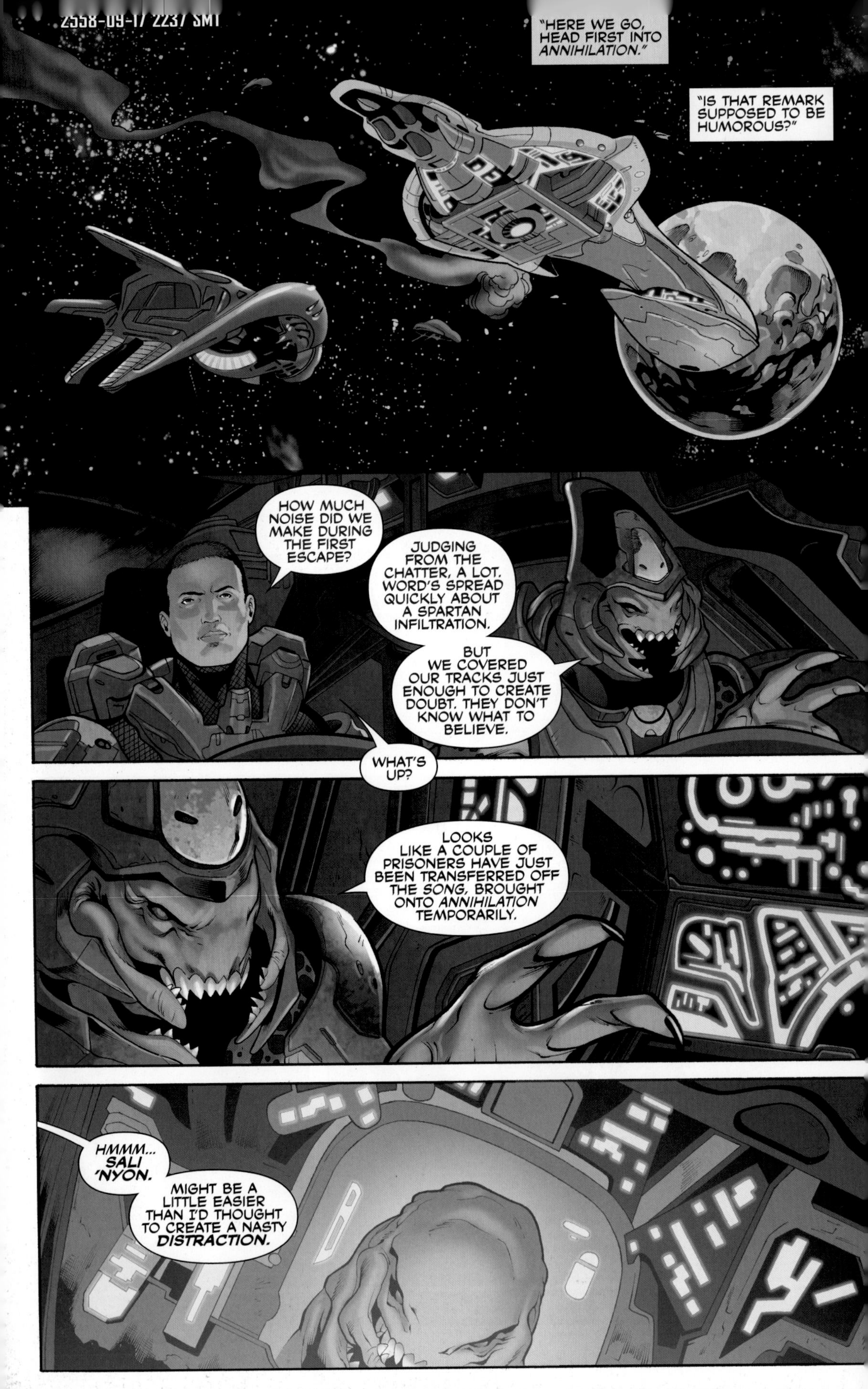
2558-09-17 2237 SMT
"HERE WE GO, HEAD FIRST INTO ANNIHILATION."
"IS THAT REMARK SUPPOSED TO BE HUMOROUS?"
HOW MUCH NOISE DID WE MAKE DURING THE FIRST ESCAPE?
JUDGING FROM THE CHATTER, A LOT. WORD'S SPREAD QUICKLY ABOUT A SPARTAN INFILTRATION.
BUT WE COVERED OUR TRACKS JUST ENOUGH TO CREATE DOUBT. THEY DON'T KNOW WHAT TO BELIEVE.
WHAT'S UP?
LOOKS LIKE A COUPLE OF PRISONERS HAVE JUST BEEN TRANSFERRED OFF THE SONG, BROUGHT ONTO ANNIHILATION TEMPORARILY.
HMMM... SALI 'NYON.
MIGHT BE A LITTLE EASIER THAN I'D THOUGHT TO CREATE A NASTY DISTRACTION.

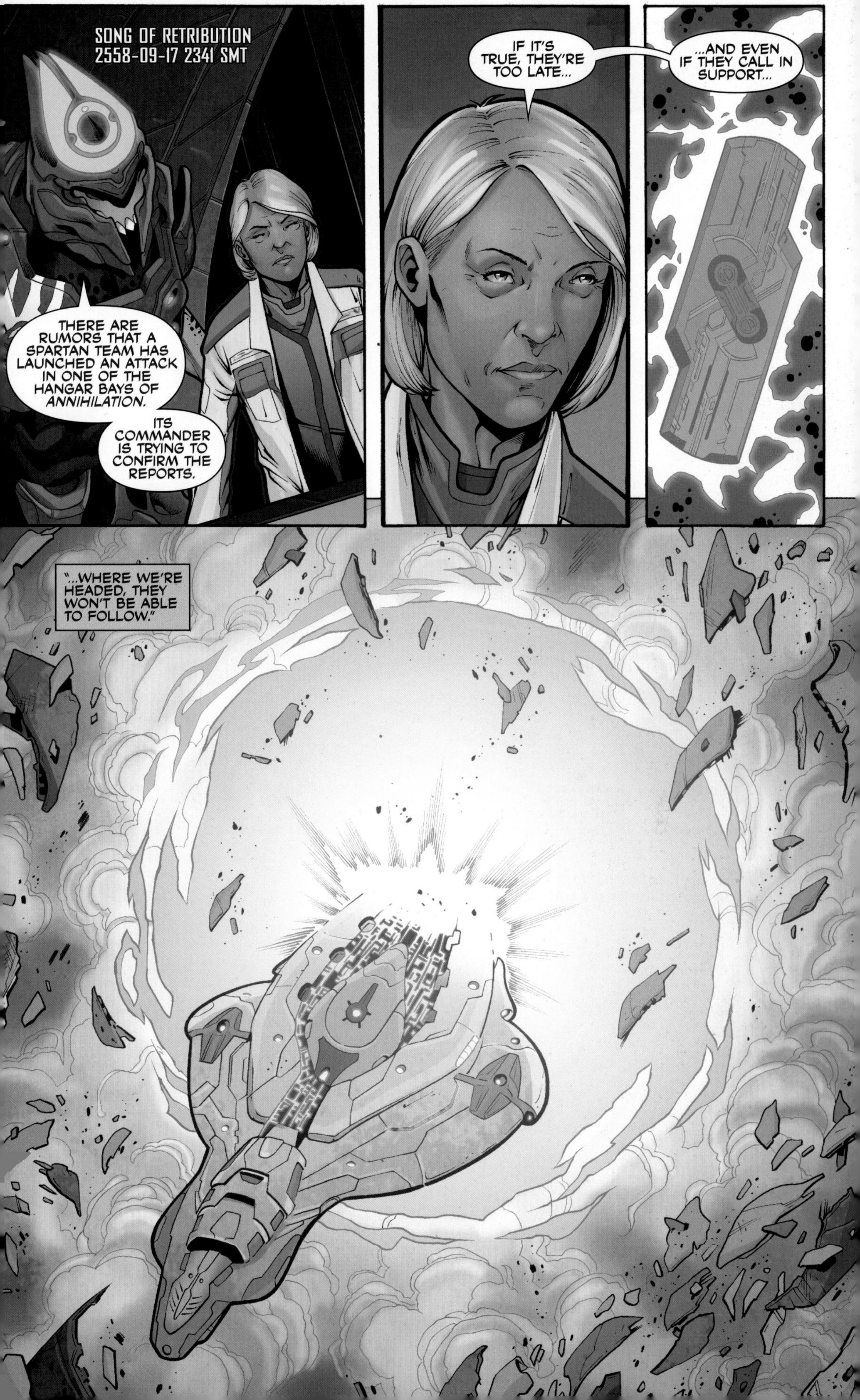
SONG OF RETRIBUTION
2558-09-17 2341 SMT
THERE ARE RUMORS THAT A SPARTAN TEAM HAS LAUNCHED AN ATTACK IN ONE OF THE HANGAR BAYS OF *ANNIHILATION.*
ITS COMMANDER IS TRYING TO CONFIRM THE REPORTS.
IF IT'S TRUE, THEY'RE TOO LATE...
...AND EVEN IF THEY CALL IN SUPPORT...
"...WHERE WE'RE HEADED, THEY WON'T BE ABLE TO FOLLOW."

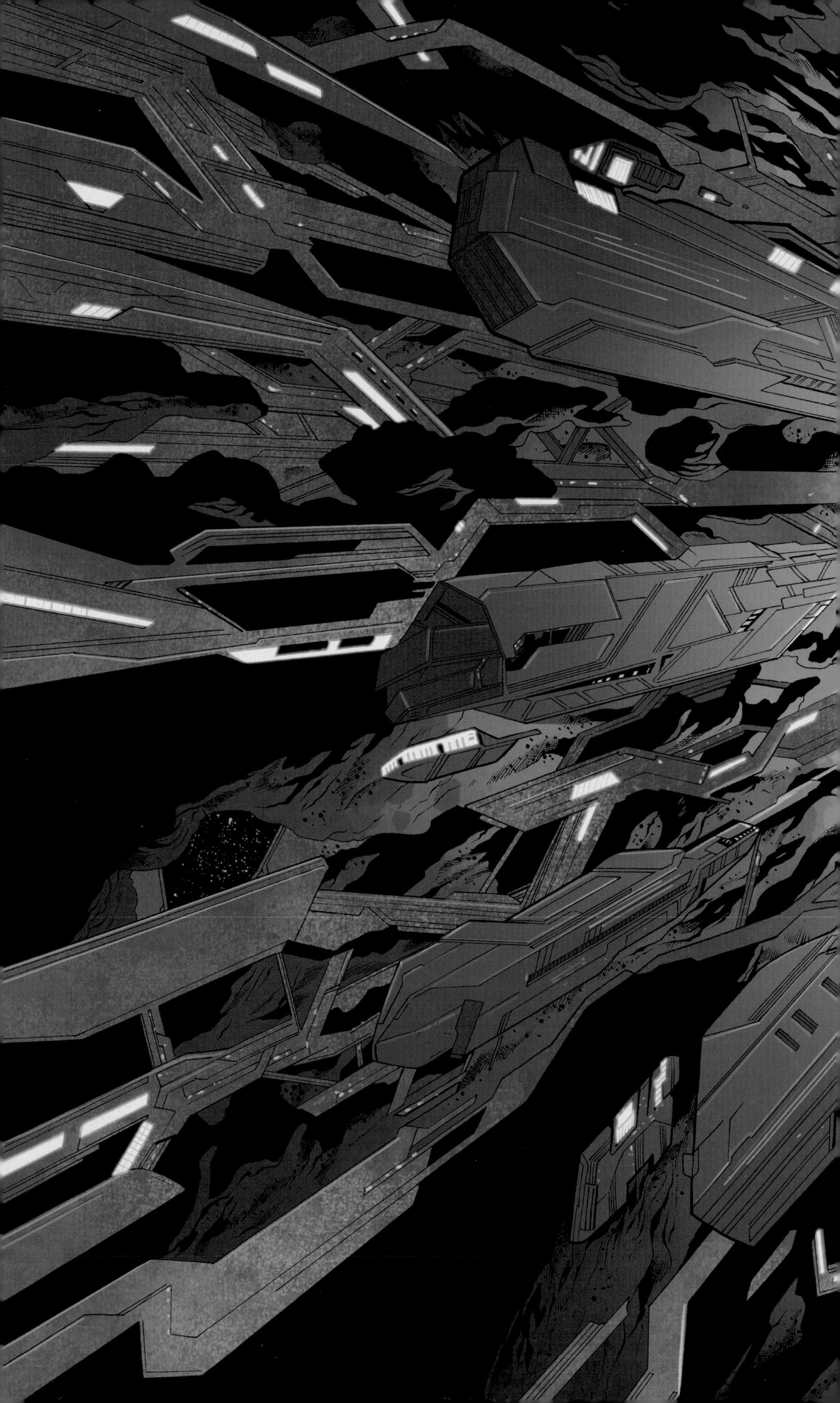

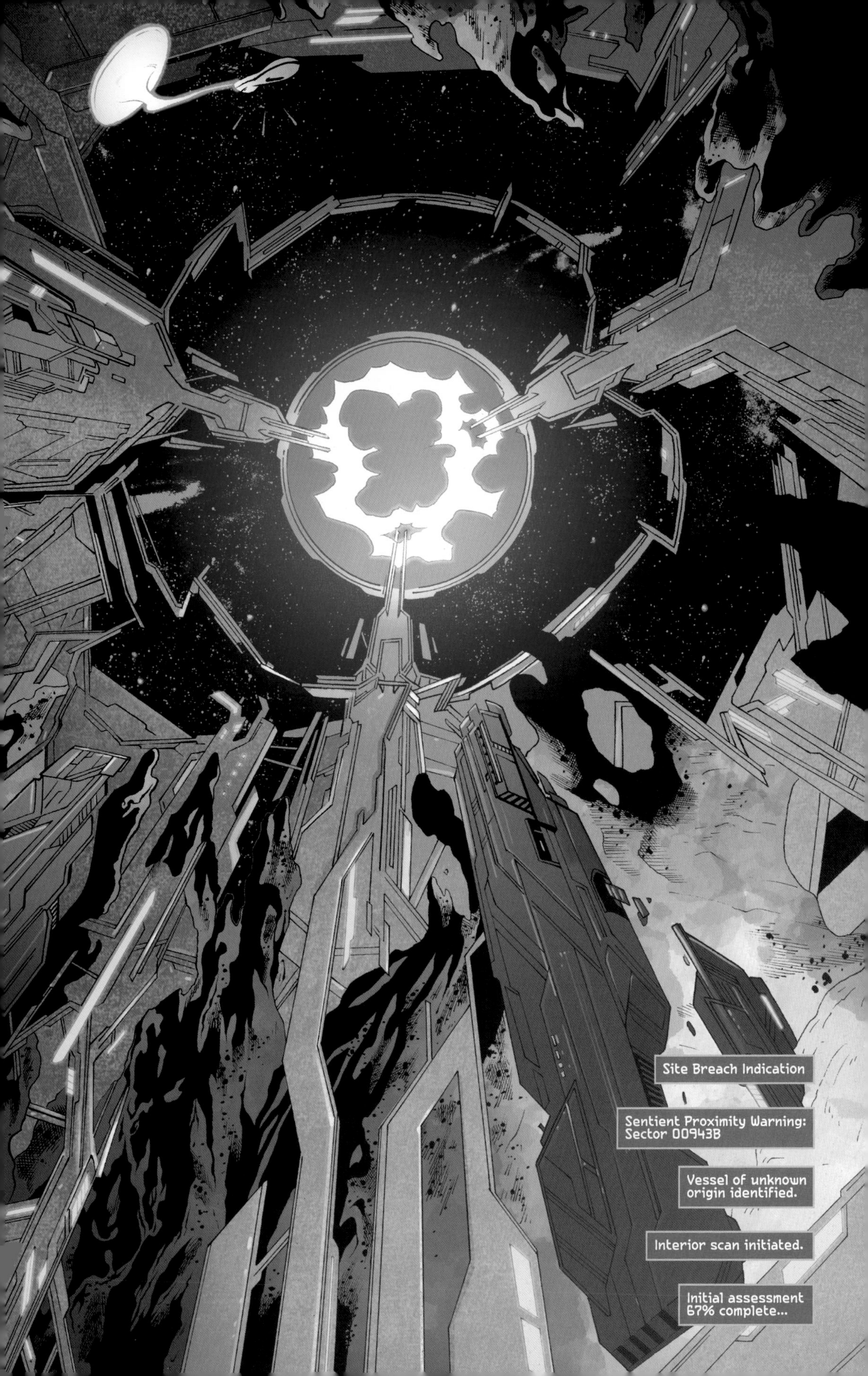
Site Breach Indication
Sentient Proximity Warning: Sector 00943B
Vessel of unknown origin identified.
Interior scan initiated.
Initial assessment 67% complete...

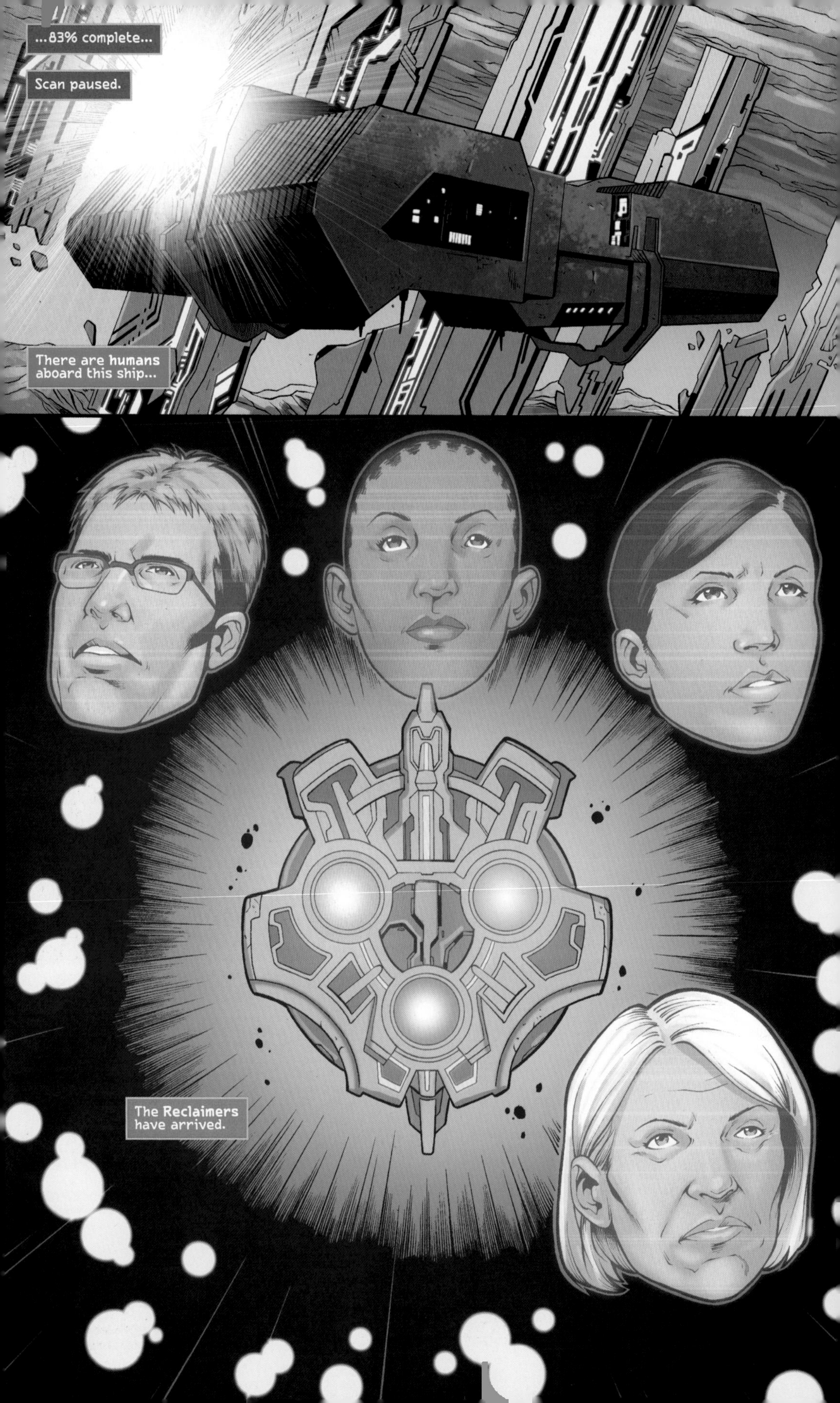
...83% complete...
Scan paused.
There are humans aboard this ship...
The Reclaimers have arrived.

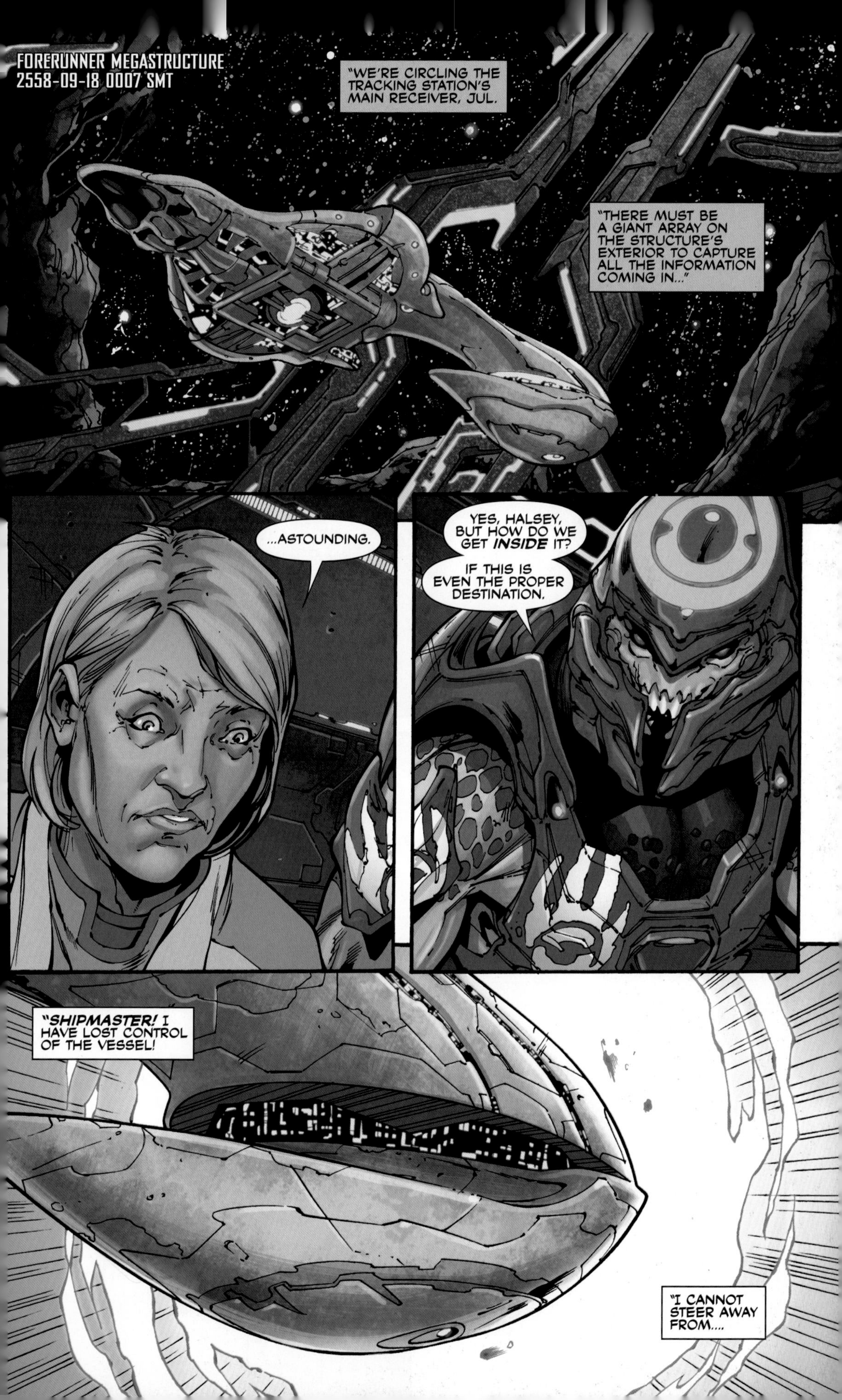
FORERUNNER MEGASTRUCTURE
2558-09-18 0007 SMT
"WE'RE CIRCLING THE TRACKING STATION'S MAIN RECEIVER, JUL.
"THERE MUST BE A GIANT ARRAY ON THE STRUCTURE'S EXTERIOR TO CAPTURE ALL THE INFORMATION COMING IN..."
...ASTOUNDING.
YES, HALSEY, BUT HOW DO WE GET *INSIDE* IT?
IF THIS IS EVEN THE PROPER DESTINATION.
"*SHIPMASTER!* I HAVE LOST CONTROL OF THE VESSEL!
"I CANNOT STEER AWAY FROM....

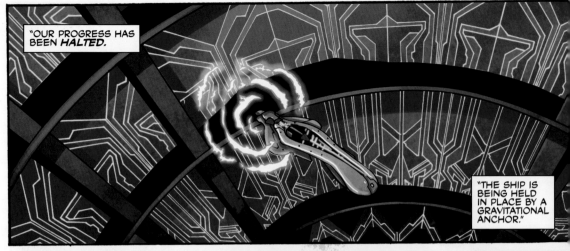

"OUR PROGRESS HAS BEEN *HALTED.*"

"THE SHIP IS BEING HELD IN PLACE BY A GRAVITATIONAL ANCHOR."

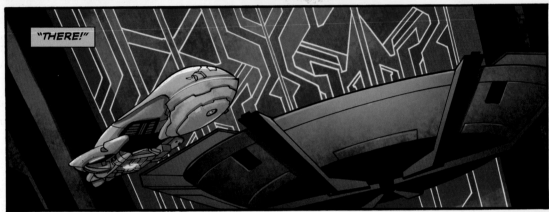

"*THERE!*"

OUR CUE TO HEAD DOWN AND MAKE CONTACT...

"...TIME FOR A FORMAL RECEPTION."

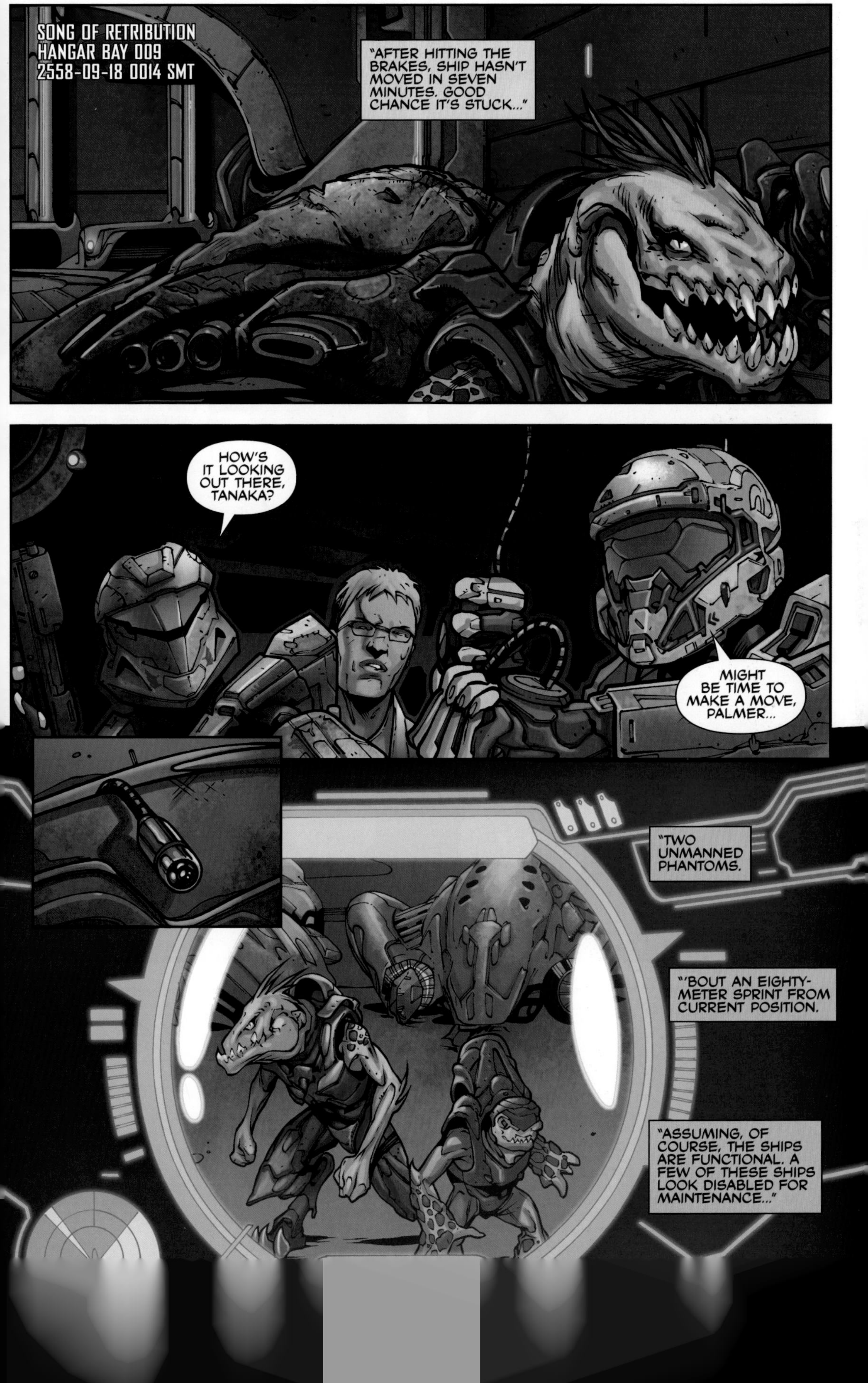
SONG OF RETRIBUTION
HANGAR BAY 009
2558-09-18 0014 SMT
"AFTER HITTING THE BRAKES, SHIP HASN'T MOVED IN SEVEN MINUTES. GOOD CHANCE IT'S STUCK..."
HOW'S IT LOOKING OUT THERE, TANAKA?
MIGHT BE TIME TO MAKE A MOVE, PALMER...
"TWO UNMANNED PHANTOMS.
"'BOUT AN EIGHTY-METER SPRINT FROM CURRENT POSITION.
"ASSUMING, OF COURSE, THE SHIPS ARE FUNCTIONAL. A FEW OF THESE SHIPS LOOK DISABLED FOR MAINTENANCE..."

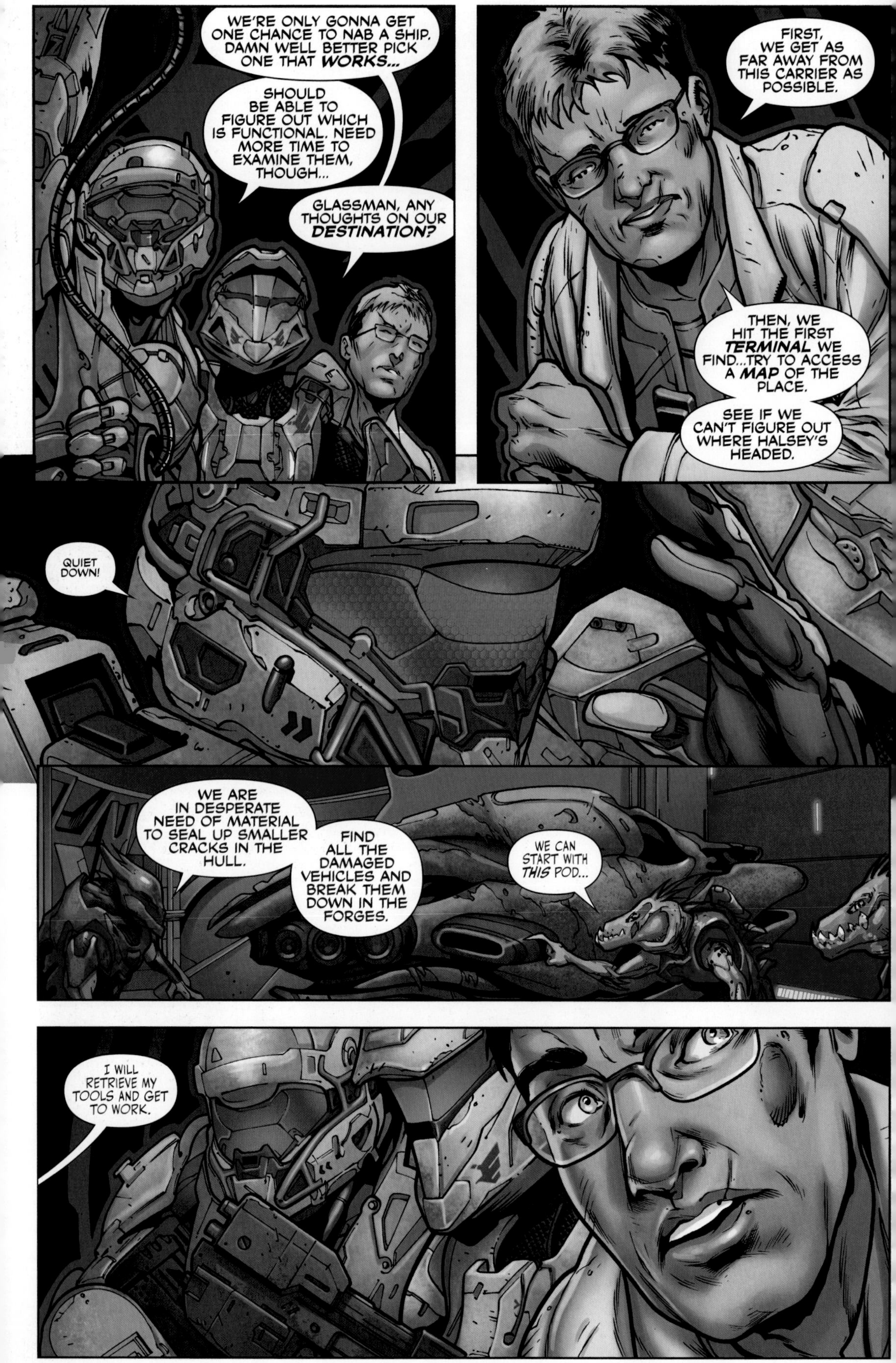
WE'RE ONLY GONNA GET ONE CHANCE TO NAB A SHIP. DAMN WELL BETTER PICK ONE THAT WORKS...
SHOULD BE ABLE TO FIGURE OUT WHICH IS FUNCTIONAL. NEED MORE TIME TO EXAMINE THEM, THOUGH...
GLASSMAN, ANY THOUGHTS ON OUR DESTINATION?
FIRST, WE GET AS FAR AWAY FROM THIS CARRIER AS POSSIBLE.
THEN, WE HIT THE FIRST TERMINAL WE FIND...TRY TO ACCESS A MAP OF THE PLACE.
SEE IF WE CAN'T FIGURE OUT WHERE HALSEY'S HEADED.
QUIET DOWN!
WE ARE IN DESPERATE NEED OF MATERIAL TO SEAL UP SMALLER CRACKS IN THE HULL.
FIND ALL THE DAMAGED VEHICLES AND BREAK THEM DOWN IN THE FORGES.
WE CAN START WITH THIS POD...
I WILL RETRIEVE MY TOOLS AND GET TO WORK.

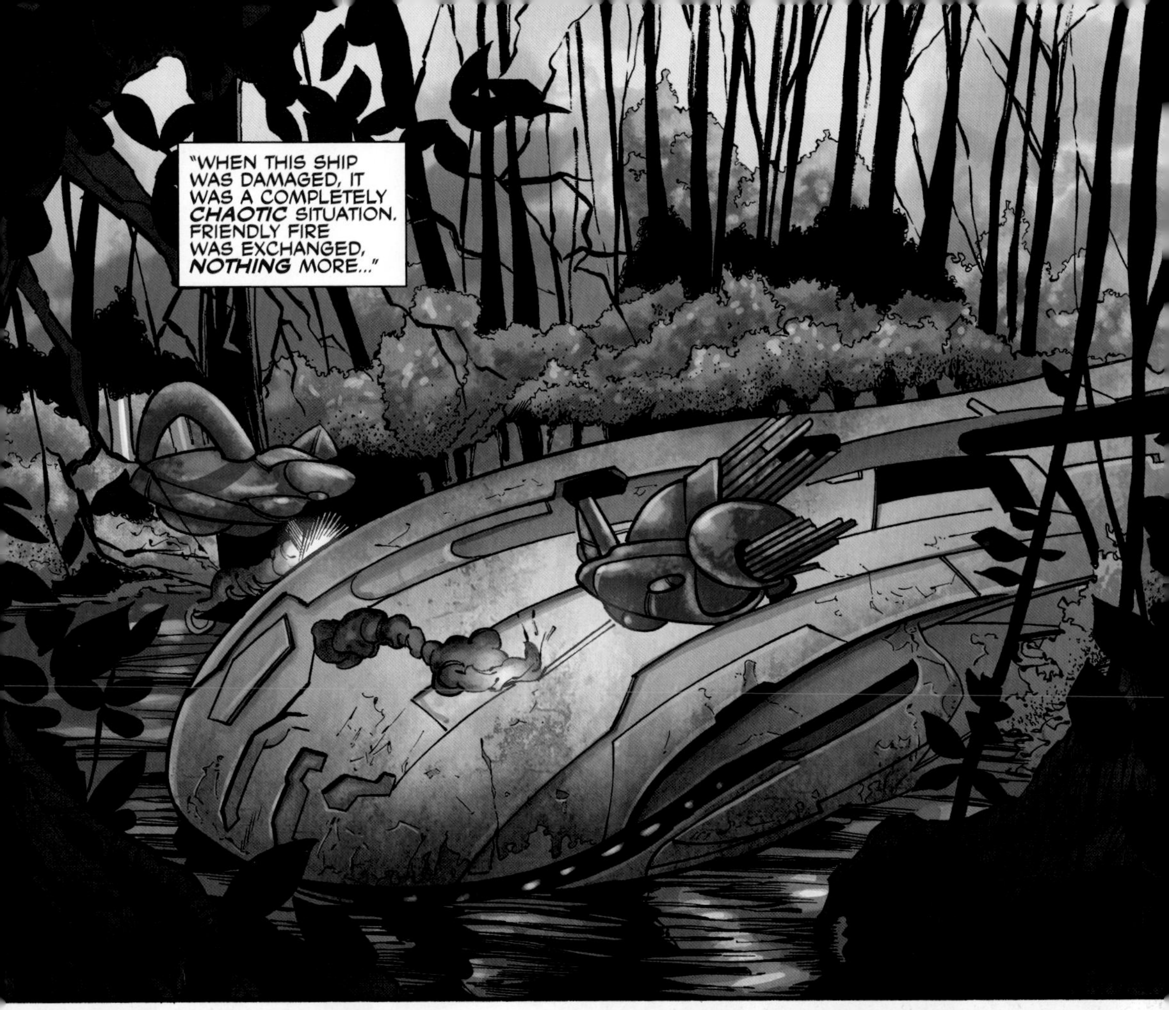
"WHEN THIS SHIP WAS DAMAGED, IT WAS A COMPLETELY *CHAOTIC* SITUATION. FRIENDLY FIRE WAS EXCHANGED, *NOTHING* MORE..."

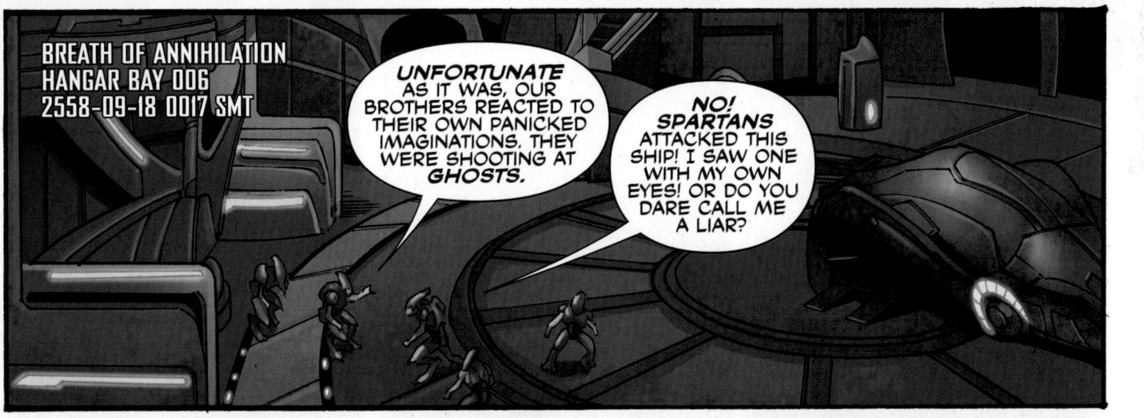
BREATH OF ANNIHILATION
HANGAR BAY 006
2558-09-18 0017 SMT
UNFORTUNATE AS IT WAS, OUR BROTHERS REACTED TO THEIR OWN PANICKED IMAGINATIONS. THEY WERE SHOOTING AT *GHOSTS.*
NO! SPARTANS ATTACKED THIS SHIP! I SAW ONE WITH MY OWN EYES! OR DO YOU DARE CALL ME A LIAR?

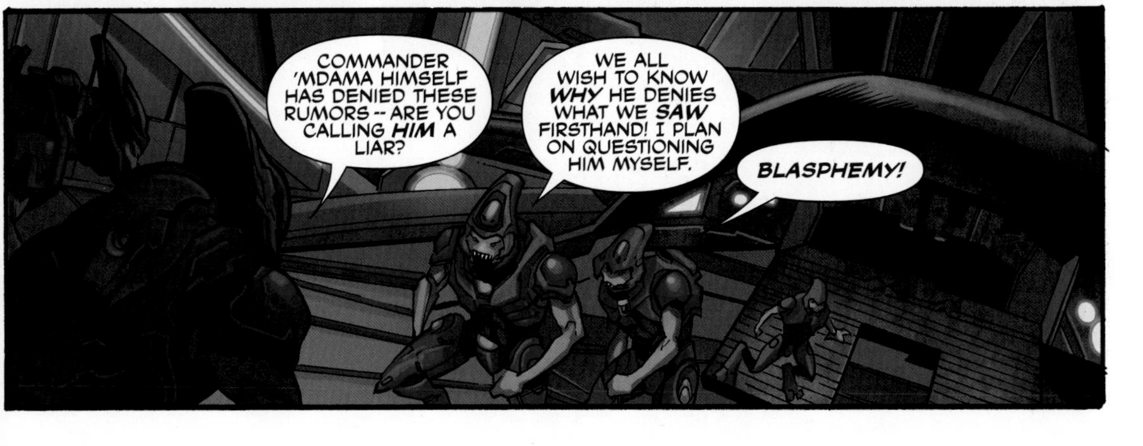
COMMANDER 'MDAMA HIMSELF HAS DENIED THESE RUMORS -- ARE YOU CALLING *HIM* A LIAR?
WE ALL WISH TO KNOW *WHY* HE DENIES WHAT WE *SAW* FIRSTHAND! I PLAN ON QUESTIONING HIM MYSELF.
BLASPHEMY!

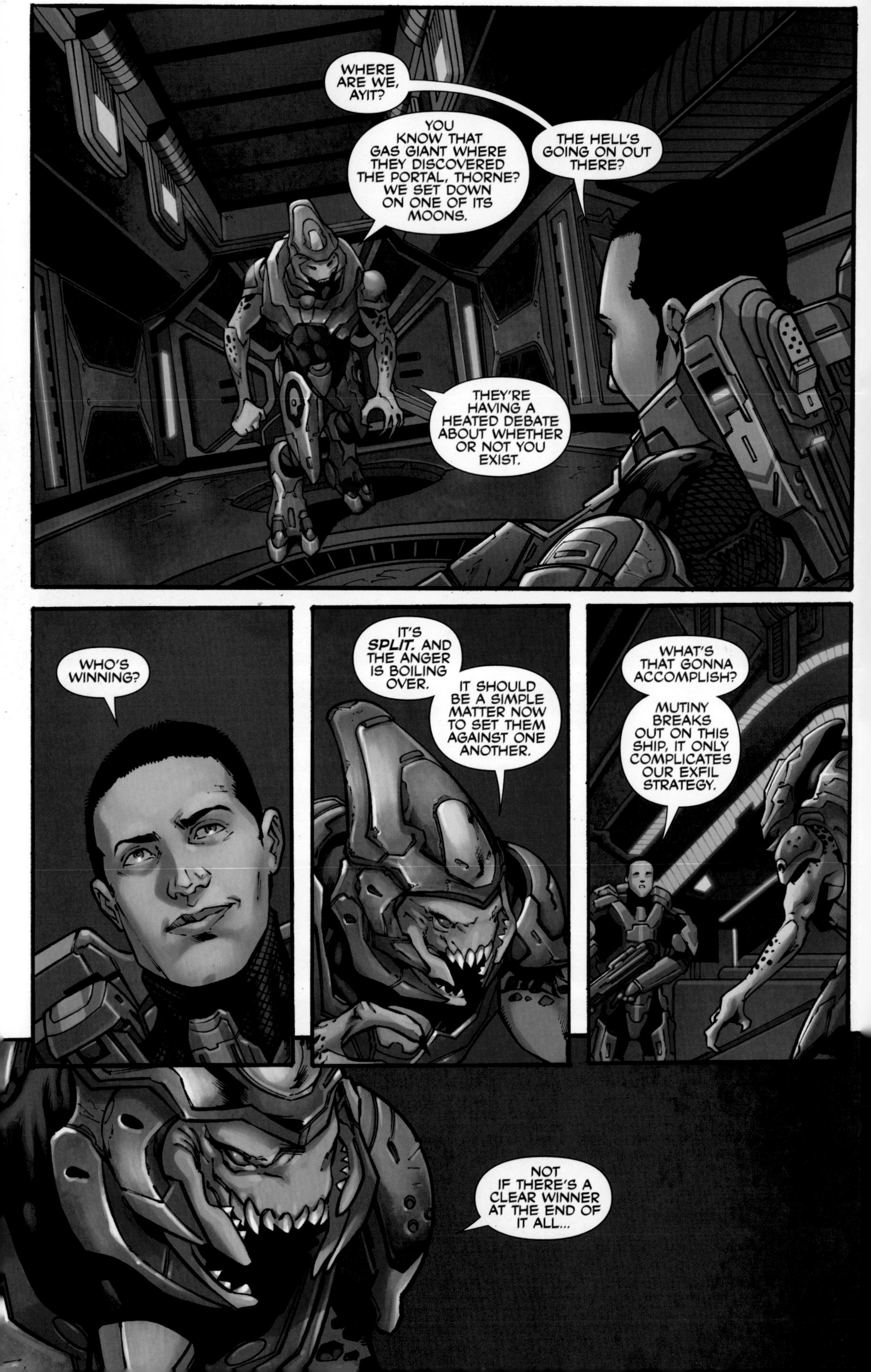
WHERE ARE WE, AYIT?
THE HELL'S GOING ON OUT THERE?
YOU KNOW THAT GAS GIANT WHERE THEY DISCOVERED THE PORTAL, THORNE? WE SET DOWN ON ONE OF ITS MOONS.
THEY'RE HAVING A HEATED DEBATE ABOUT WHETHER OR NOT YOU EXIST.
WHO'S WINNING?
IT'S *SPLIT.* AND THE ANGER IS BOILING OVER.
IT SHOULD BE A SIMPLE MATTER NOW TO SET THEM AGAINST ONE ANOTHER.
WHAT'S THAT GONNA ACCOMPLISH?
MUTINY BREAKS OUT ON THIS SHIP, IT ONLY COMPLICATES OUR EXFIL STRATEGY.
NOT IF THERE'S A CLEAR WINNER AT THE END OF IT ALL...

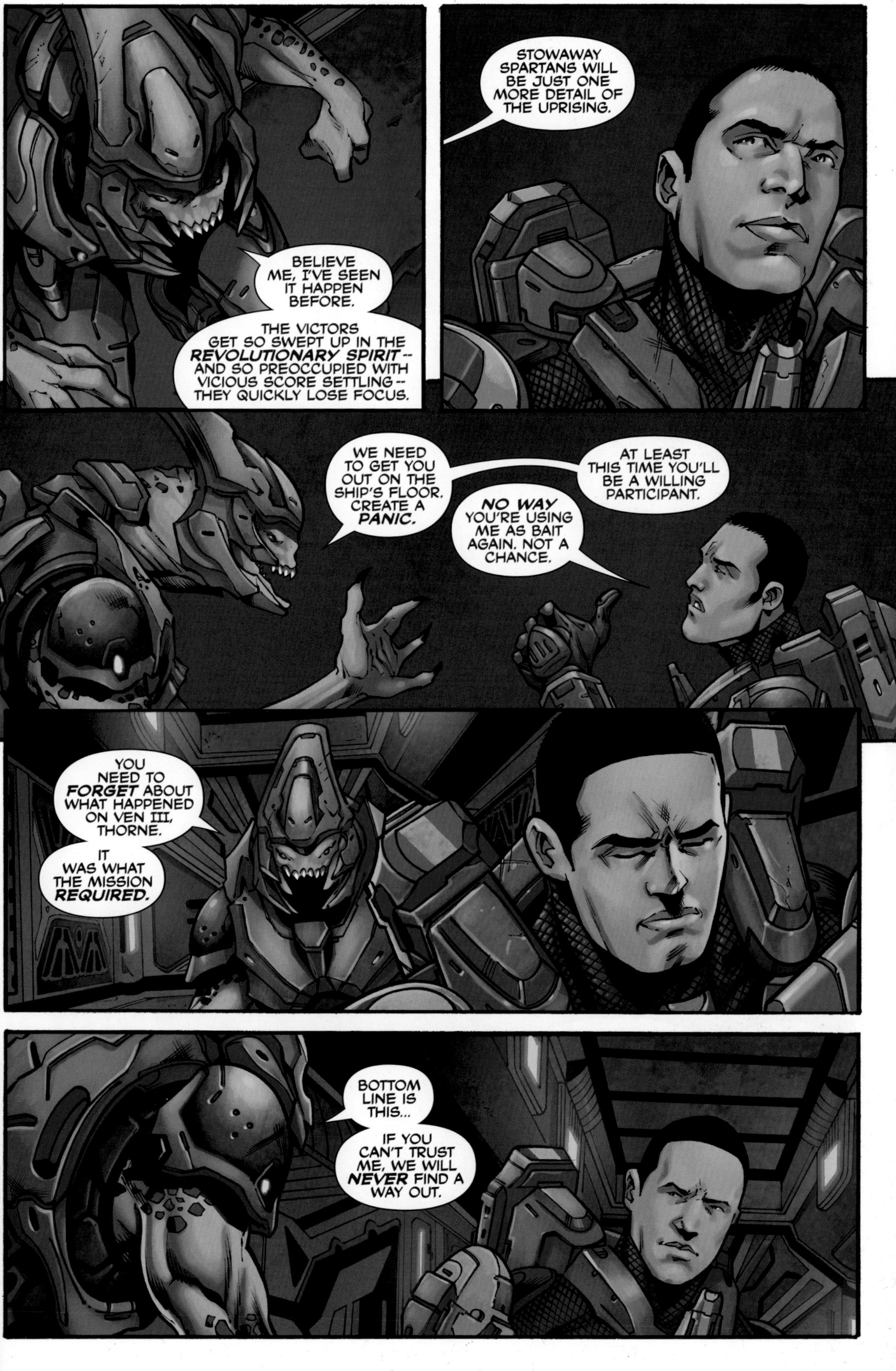
BELIEVE ME, I'VE SEEN IT HAPPEN BEFORE.
THE VICTORS GET SO SWEPT UP IN THE *REVOLUTIONARY SPIRIT*-- AND SO PREOCCUPIED WITH VICIOUS SCORE SETTLING-- THEY QUICKLY LOSE FOCUS.
STOWAWAY SPARTANS WILL BE JUST ONE MORE DETAIL OF THE UPRISING.
WE NEED TO GET YOU OUT ON THE SHIP'S FLOOR. CREATE A *PANIC.*
NO WAY YOU'RE USING ME AS BAIT AGAIN. NOT A CHANCE.
AT LEAST THIS TIME YOU'LL BE A WILLING PARTICIPANT.
YOU NEED TO *FORGET* ABOUT WHAT HAPPENED ON VEN III, THORNE.
IT WAS WHAT THE MISSION *REQUIRED.*
BOTTOM LINE IS THIS...
IF YOU CAN'T TRUST ME, WE WILL *NEVER* FIND A WAY OUT.

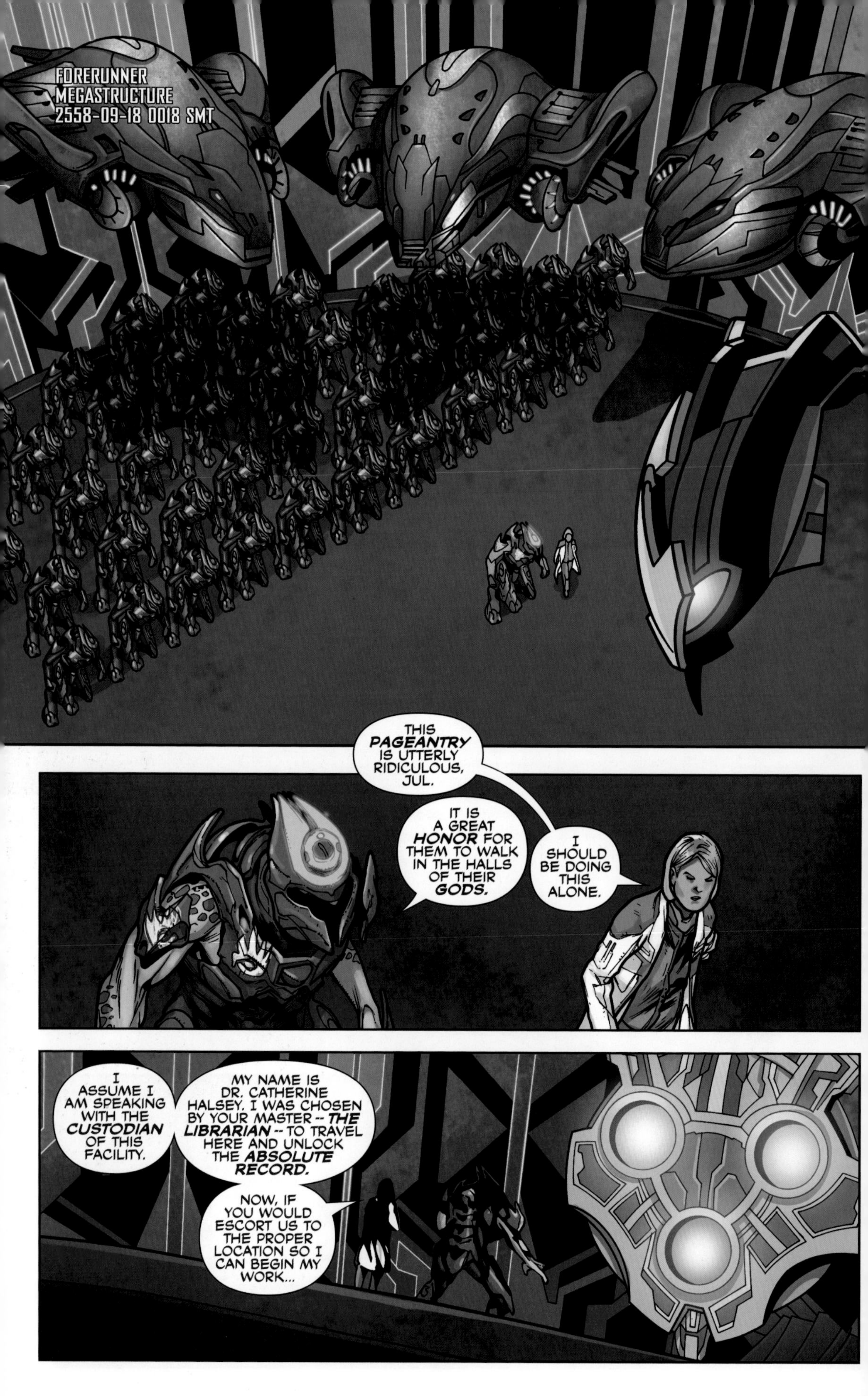
FORERUNNER MEGASTRUCTURE 2558-09-18 0018 SMT
THIS PAGEANTRY IS UTTERLY RIDICULOUS, JUL.
I SHOULD BE DOING THIS ALONE.
IT IS A GREAT HONOR FOR THEM TO WALK IN THE HALLS OF THEIR GODS.
I ASSUME I AM SPEAKING WITH THE CUSTODIAN OF THIS FACILITY.
MY NAME IS DR. CATHERINE HALSEY. I WAS CHOSEN BY YOUR MASTER -- THE LIBRARIAN -- TO TRAVEL HERE AND UNLOCK THE ABSOLUTE RECORD.
NOW, IF YOU WOULD ESCORT US TO THE PROPER LOCATION SO I CAN BEGIN MY WORK...

DO YOU NOT **UNDER-STAND** ME? THE LIBRARIAN -- **YOUR MASTER** -- GAVE ME THIS!

SHE TOLD ME TO COME **HERE**!

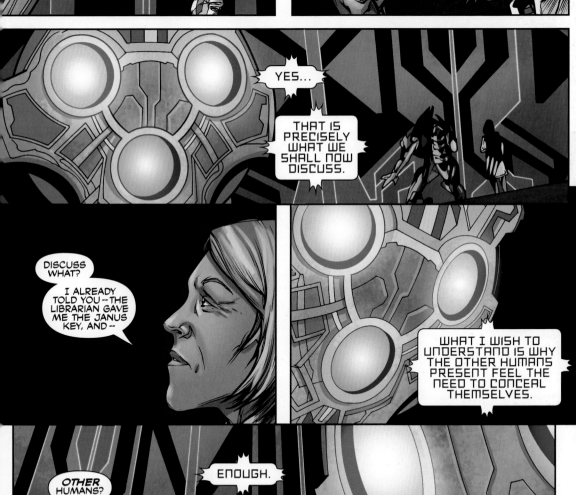

YES...

THAT IS PRECISELY WHAT WE SHALL NOW DISCUSS.

DISCUSS WHAT? I ALREADY TOLD YOU -- THE LIBRARIAN GAVE ME THE JANUS KEY, AND --

WHAT I WISH TO UNDERSTAND IS WHY THE OTHER HUMANS PRESENT FEEL THE NEED TO CONCEAL THEMSELVES.

OTHER HUMANS?

ENOUGH.

LET US SPEAK WITH THEM DIRECTLY...

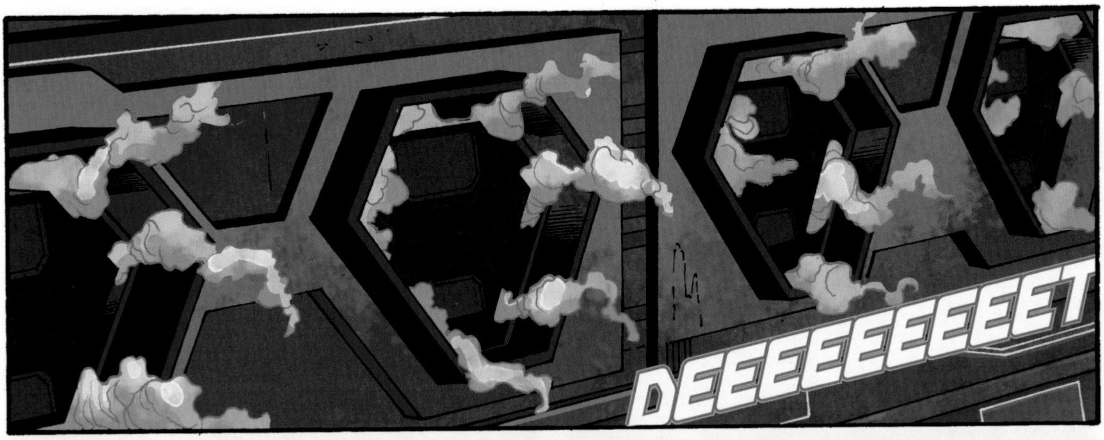
DEEEEEEEEET

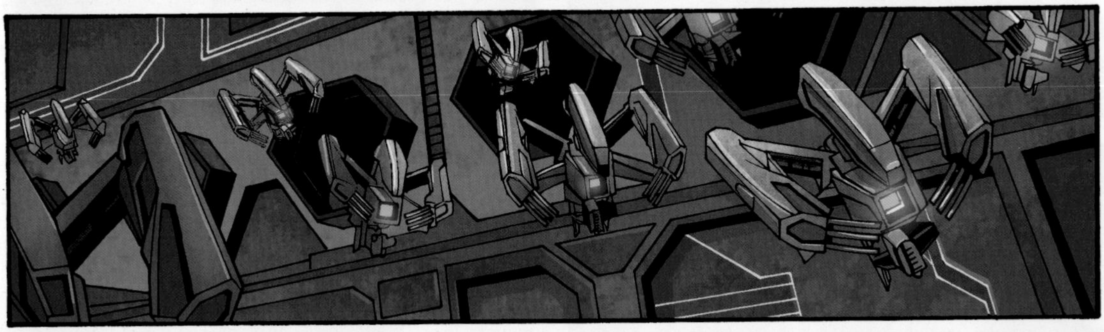

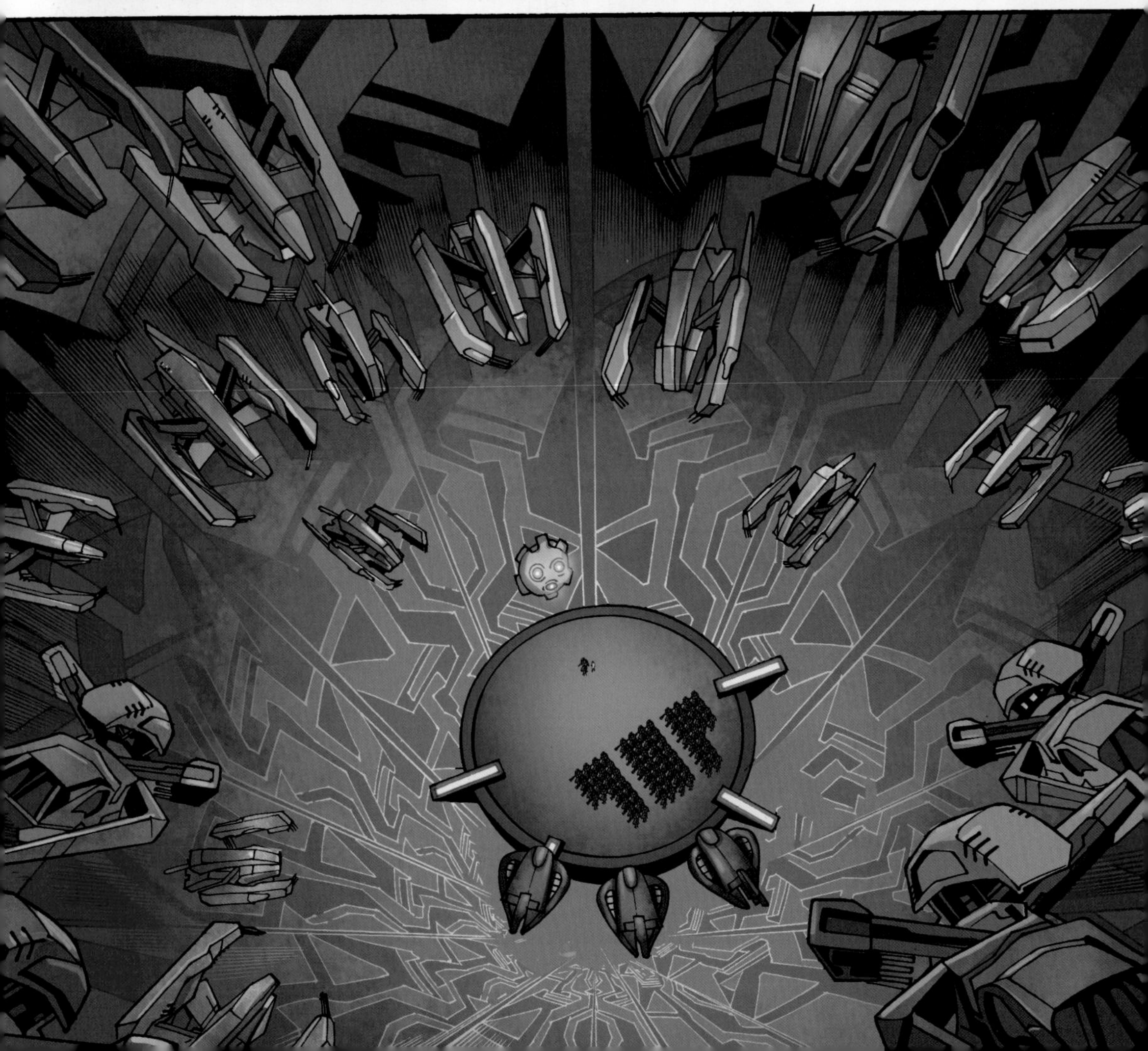

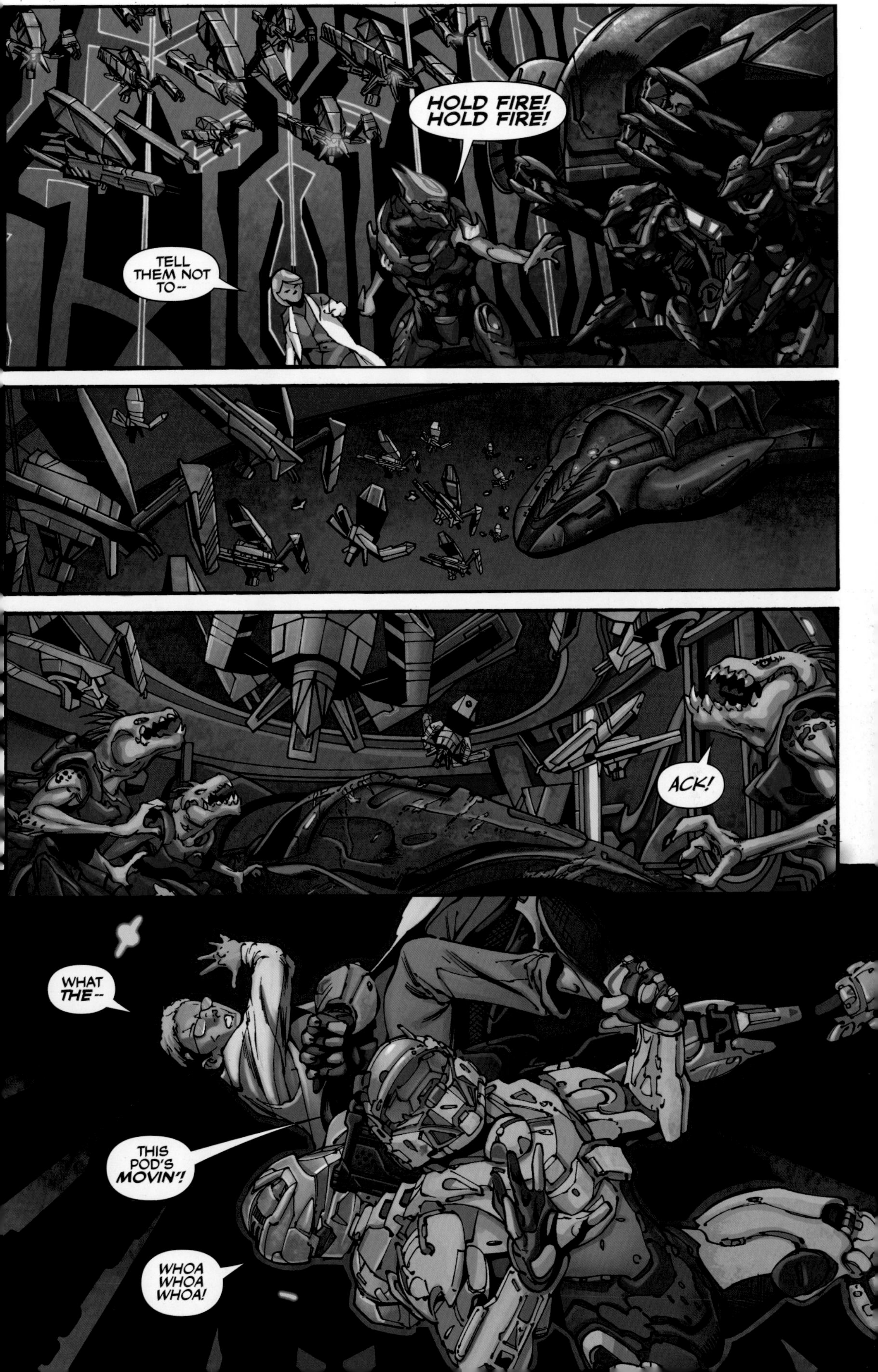
HOLD FIRE! HOLD FIRE!
TELL THEM NOT TO--
ACK!
WHAT THE--
THIS POD'S MOVIN'!
WHOA WHOA WHOA!

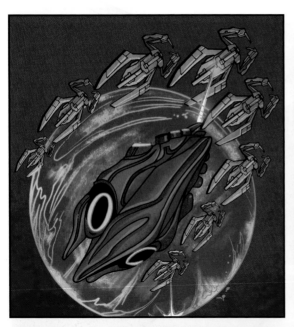

STAND *DOWN!* I *ORDER* YOU!

HOW....?

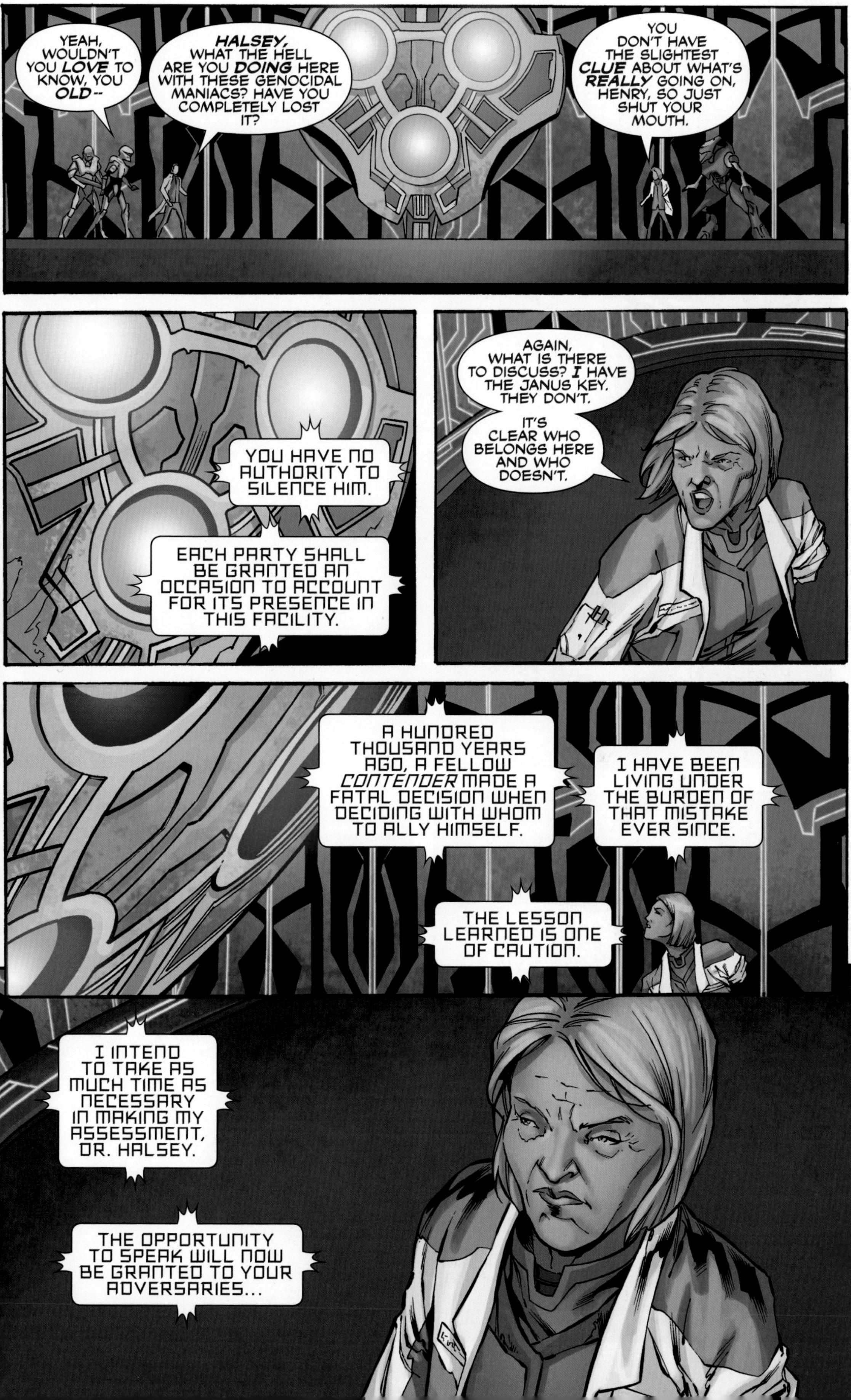
YEAH, WOULDN'T YOU LOVE TO KNOW, YOU OLD--
HALSEY, WHAT THE HELL ARE YOU DOING HERE WITH THESE GENOCIDAL MANIACS? HAVE YOU COMPLETELY LOST IT?
YOU DON'T HAVE THE SLIGHTEST CLUE ABOUT WHAT'S REALLY GOING ON, HENRY, SO JUST SHUT YOUR MOUTH.
YOU HAVE NO AUTHORITY TO SILENCE HIM.
EACH PARTY SHALL BE GRANTED AN OCCASION TO ACCOUNT FOR ITS PRESENCE IN THIS FACILITY.
AGAIN, WHAT IS THERE TO DISCUSS? I HAVE THE JANUS KEY. THEY DON'T.
IT'S CLEAR WHO BELONGS HERE AND WHO DOESN'T.
A HUNDRED THOUSAND YEARS AGO, A FELLOW CONTENDER MADE A FATAL DECISION WHEN DECIDING WITH WHOM TO ALLY HIMSELF.
I HAVE BEEN LIVING UNDER THE BURDEN OF THAT MISTAKE EVER SINCE.
THE LESSON LEARNED IS ONE OF CAUTION.
I INTEND TO TAKE AS MUCH TIME AS NECESSARY IN MAKING MY ASSESSMENT, DR. HALSEY.
THE OPPORTUNITY TO SPEAK WILL NOW BE GRANTED TO YOUR ADVERSARIES...

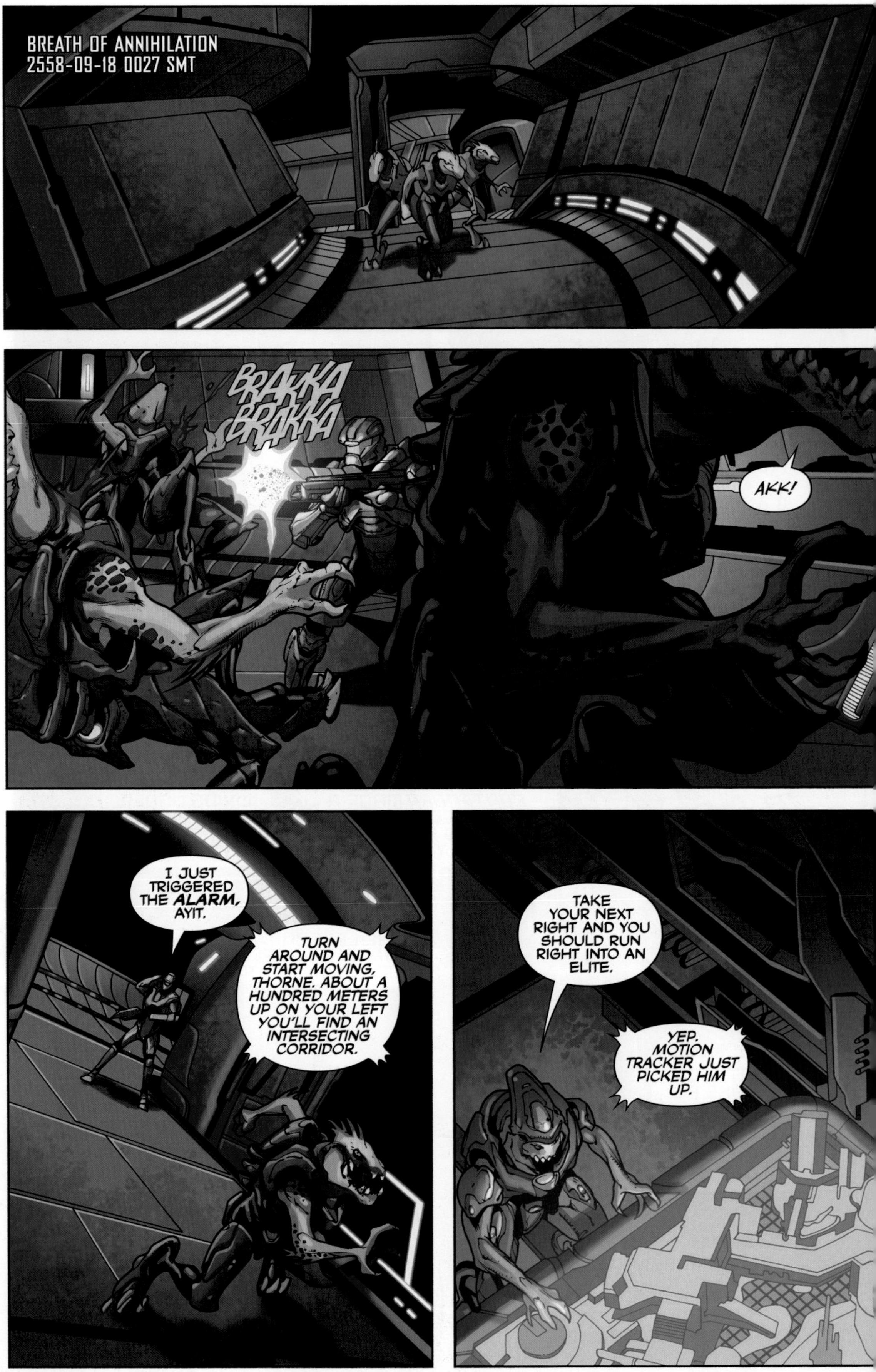
BREATH OF ANNIHILATION
2558-09-18 0027 SMT
BRAKKA BRAKKA
AKK!
I JUST TRIGGERED THE ALARM, AYIT.
TURN AROUND AND START MOVING, THORNE. ABOUT A HUNDRED METERS UP ON YOUR LEFT YOU'LL FIND AN INTERSECTING CORRIDOR.
TAKE YOUR NEXT RIGHT AND YOU SHOULD RUN RIGHT INTO AN ELITE.
YEP. MOTION TRACKER JUST PICKED HIM UP.

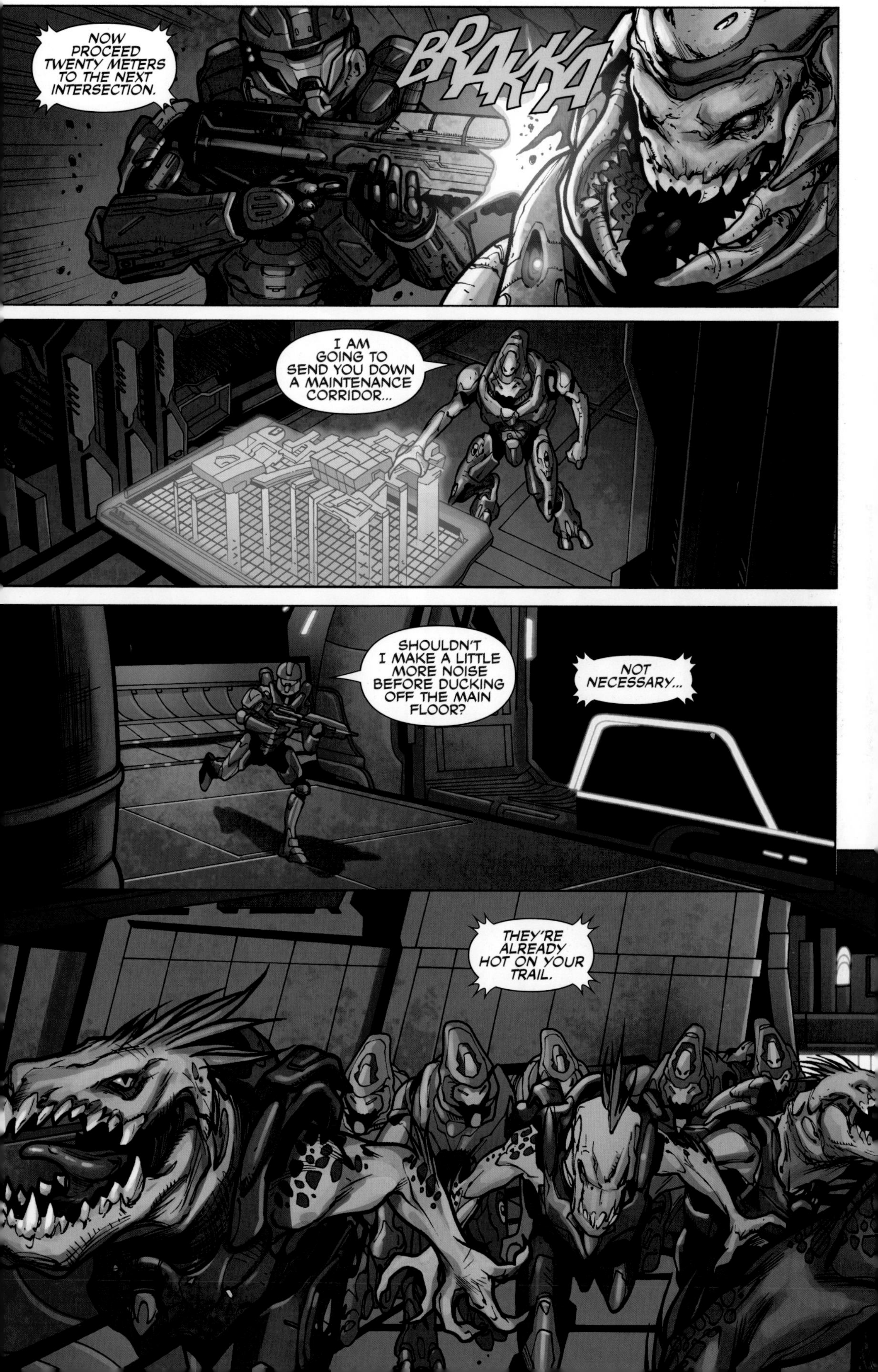
NOW PROCEED TWENTY METERS TO THE NEXT INTERSECTION.
BRAKKA
I AM GOING TO SEND YOU DOWN A MAINTENANCE CORRIDOR...
SHOULDN'T I MAKE A LITTLE MORE NOISE BEFORE DUCKING OFF THE MAIN FLOOR?
NOT NECESSARY...
THEY'RE ALREADY HOT ON YOUR TRAIL.

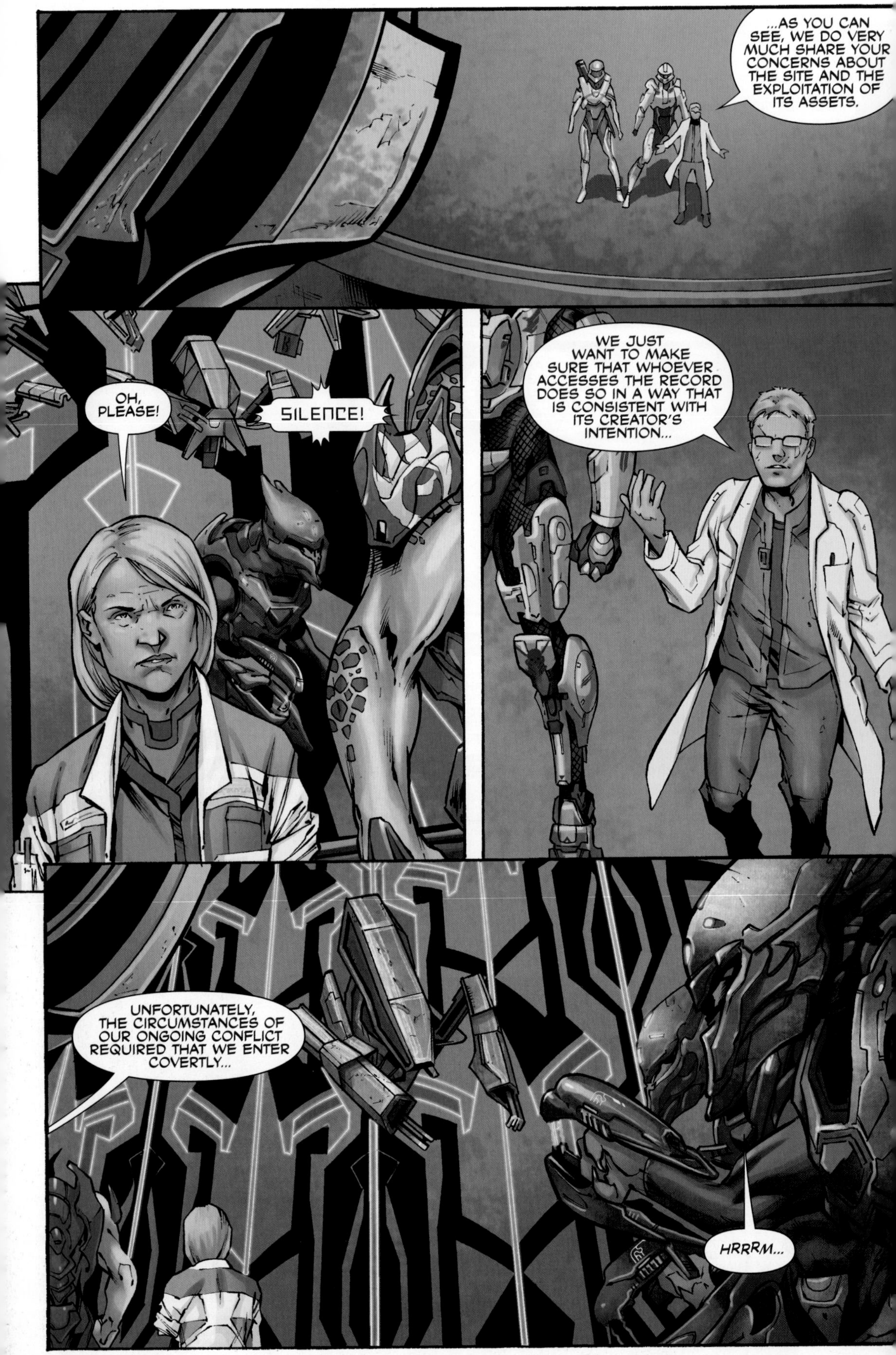
...AS YOU CAN SEE, WE DO VERY MUCH SHARE YOUR CONCERNS ABOUT THE SITE AND THE EXPLOITATION OF ITS ASSETS.
OH, PLEASE!
SILENCE!
WE JUST WANT TO MAKE SURE THAT WHOEVER ACCESSES THE RECORD DOES SO IN A WAY THAT IS CONSISTENT WITH ITS CREATOR'S INTENTION...
UNFORTUNATELY, THE CIRCUMSTANCES OF OUR ONGOING CONFLICT REQUIRED THAT WE ENTER COVERTLY...
HRRRM...

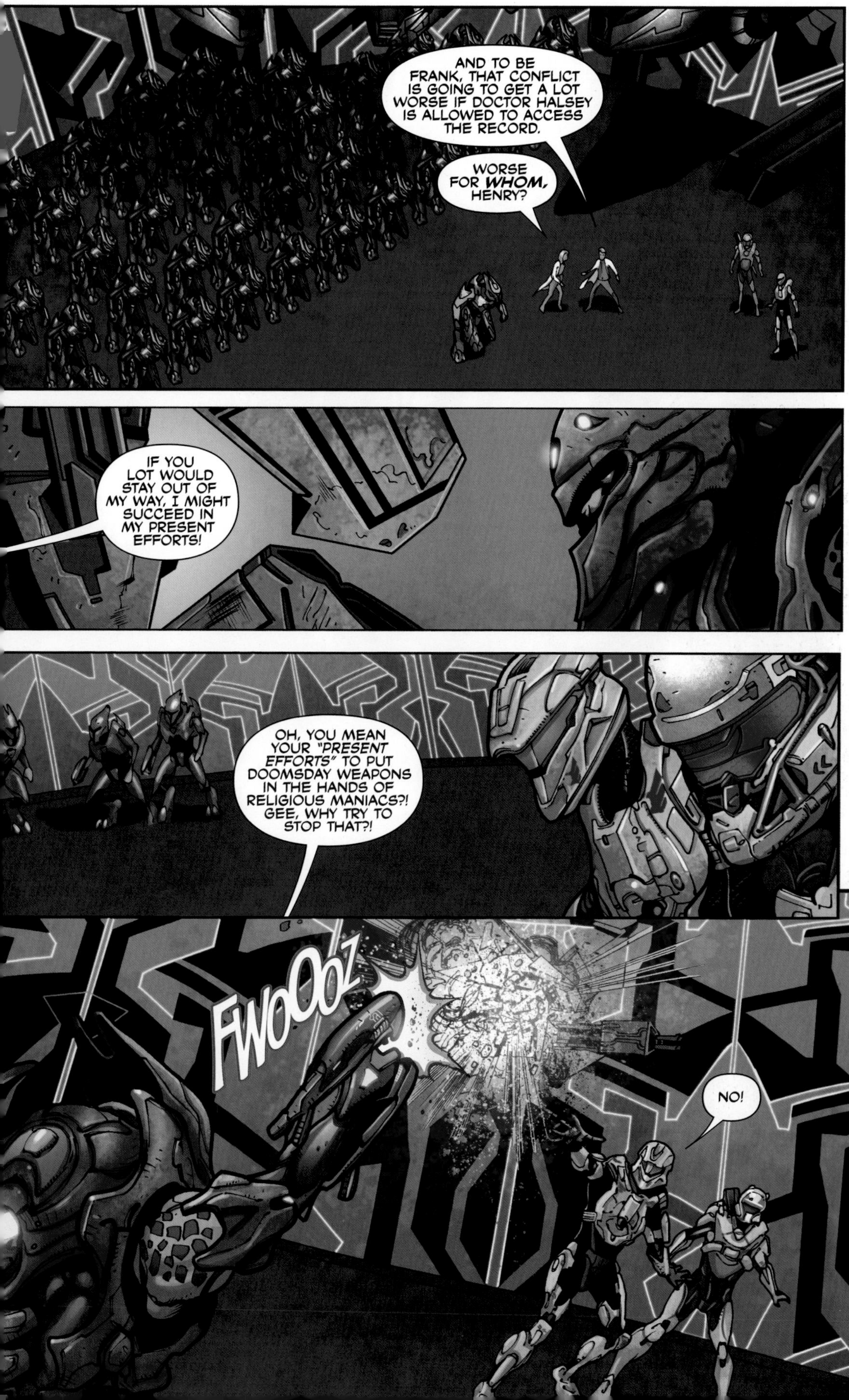
AND TO BE FRANK, THAT CONFLICT IS GOING TO GET A LOT WORSE IF DOCTOR HALSEY IS ALLOWED TO ACCESS THE RECORD.
WORSE FOR *WHOM,* HENRY?
IF YOU LOT WOULD STAY OUT OF MY WAY, I MIGHT SUCCEED IN MY PRESENT EFFORTS!
OH, YOU MEAN YOUR *"PRESENT EFFORTS"* TO PUT DOOMSDAY WEAPONS IN THE HANDS OF RELIGIOUS MANIACS?! GEE, WHY TRY TO STOP THAT?!
FWOOOZ
NO!

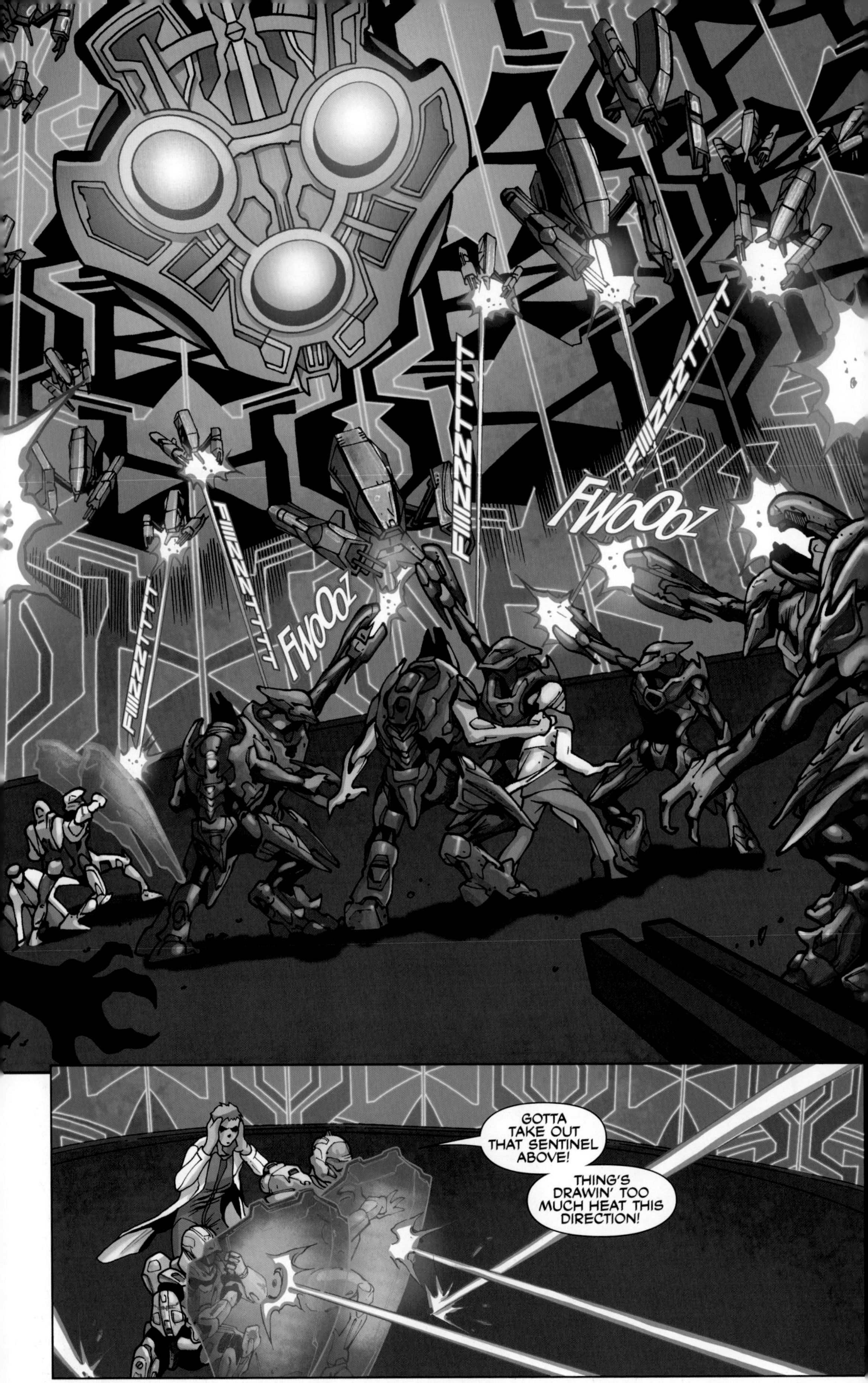
FIIIIZZZZTTTTT
FIIIIZZZZTTTTTT
FWOOOZ
FIIIIZZZZTTTTT
FIIIIZZZZTTTTT
FWOOOZ
GOTTA TAKE OUT THAT SENTINEL ABOVE!
THING'S DRAWIN' TOO MUCH HEAT THIS DIRECTION!

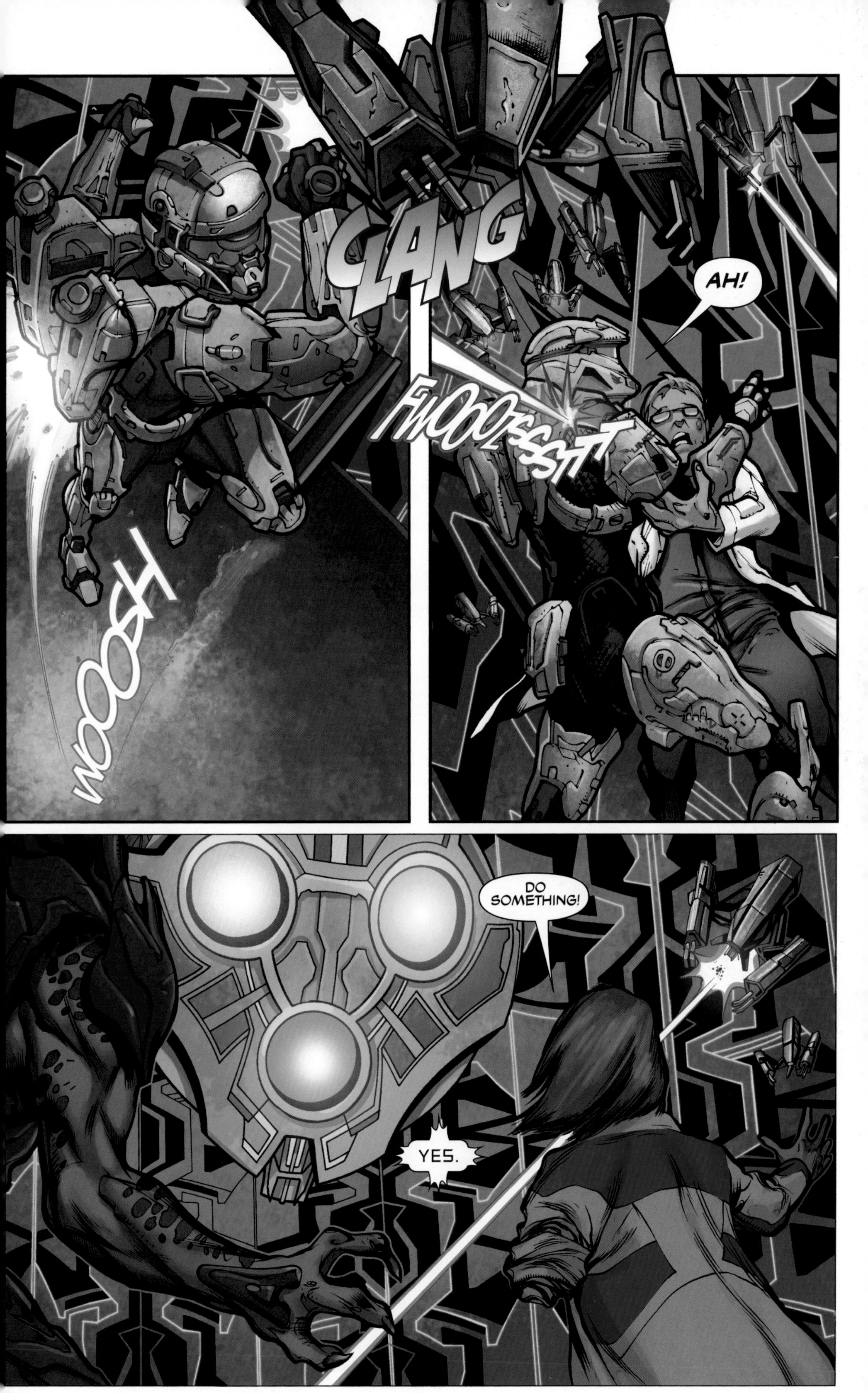
CLANG
AH!
FWOOOSSSTTT
WOOOSH
DO SOMETHING!
YES.

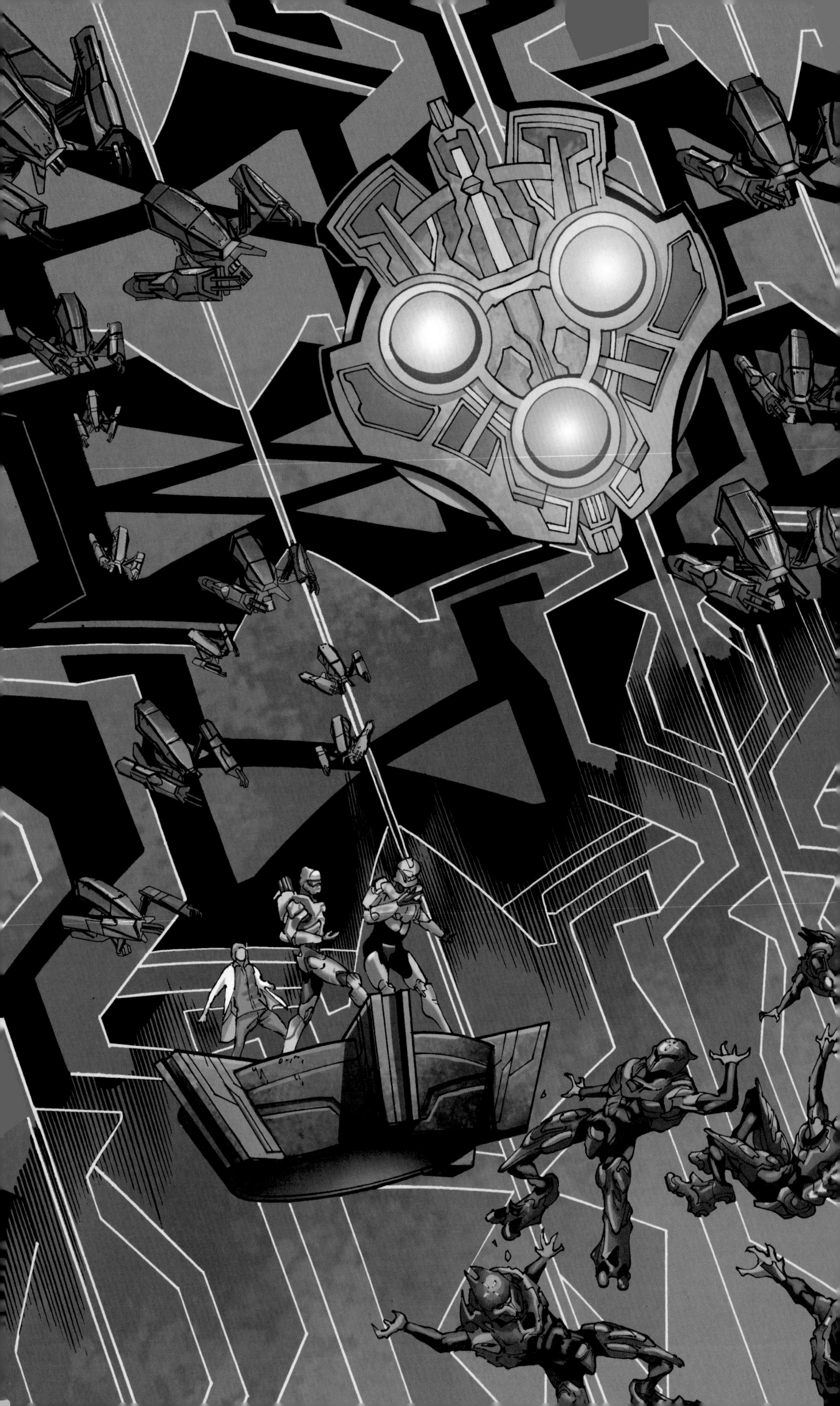

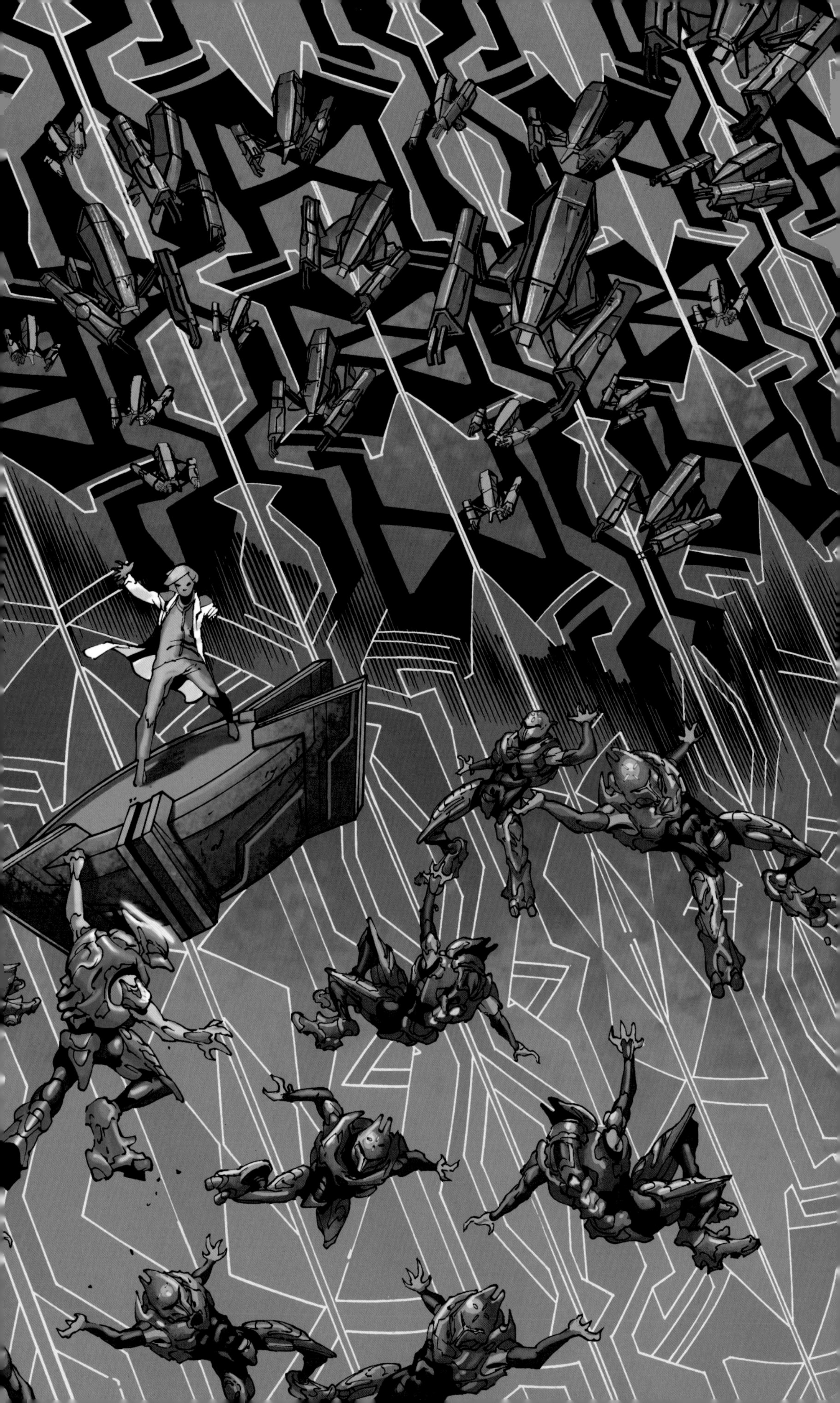

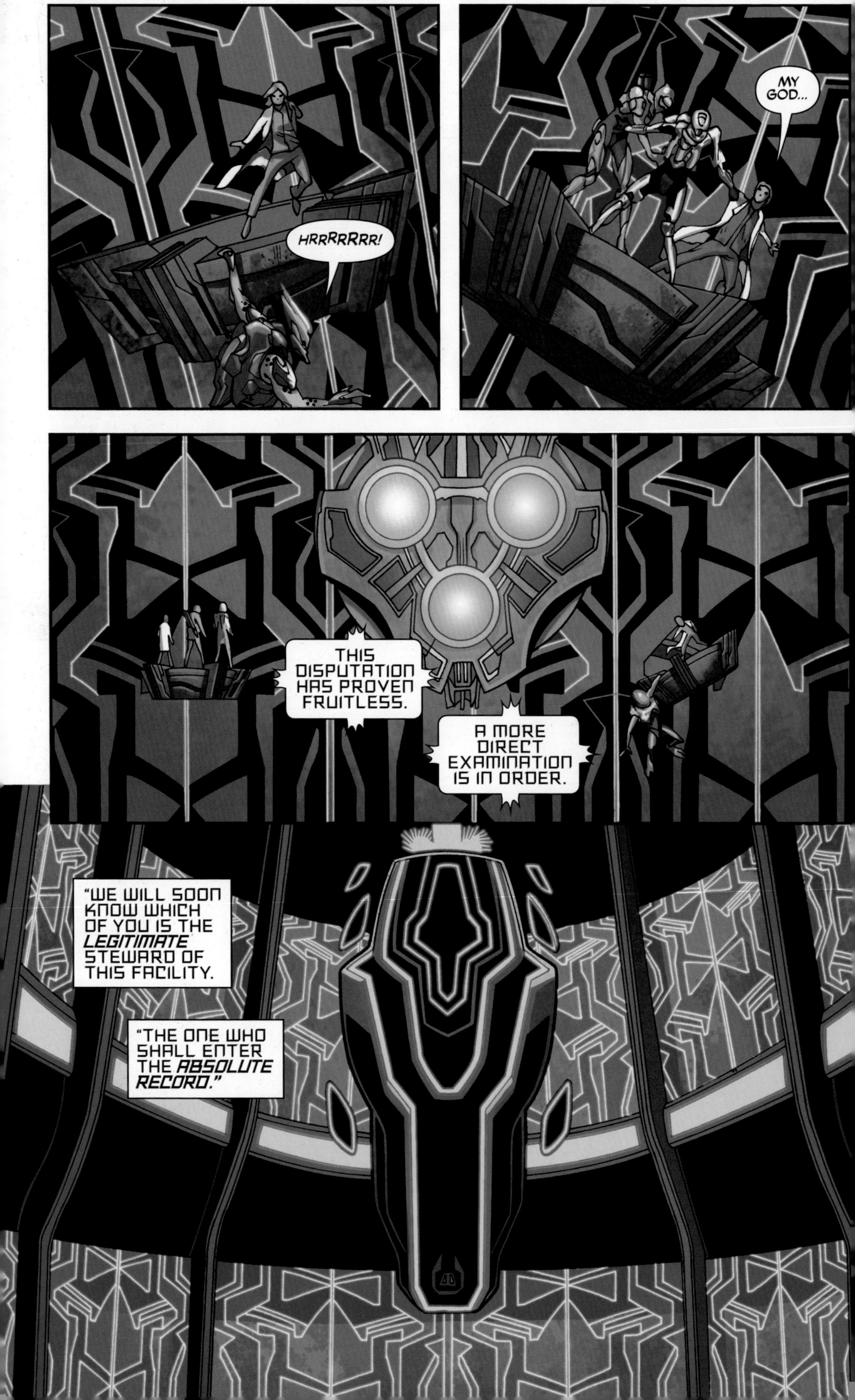

HRRRRRRR!
MY GOD...
THIS DISPUTATION HAS PROVEN FRUITLESS.
A MORE DIRECT EXAMINATION IS IN ORDER.
"WE WILL SOON KNOW WHICH OF YOU IS THE LEGITIMATE STEWARD OF THIS FACILITY.
"THE ONE WHO SHALL ENTER THE ABSOLUTE RECORD."

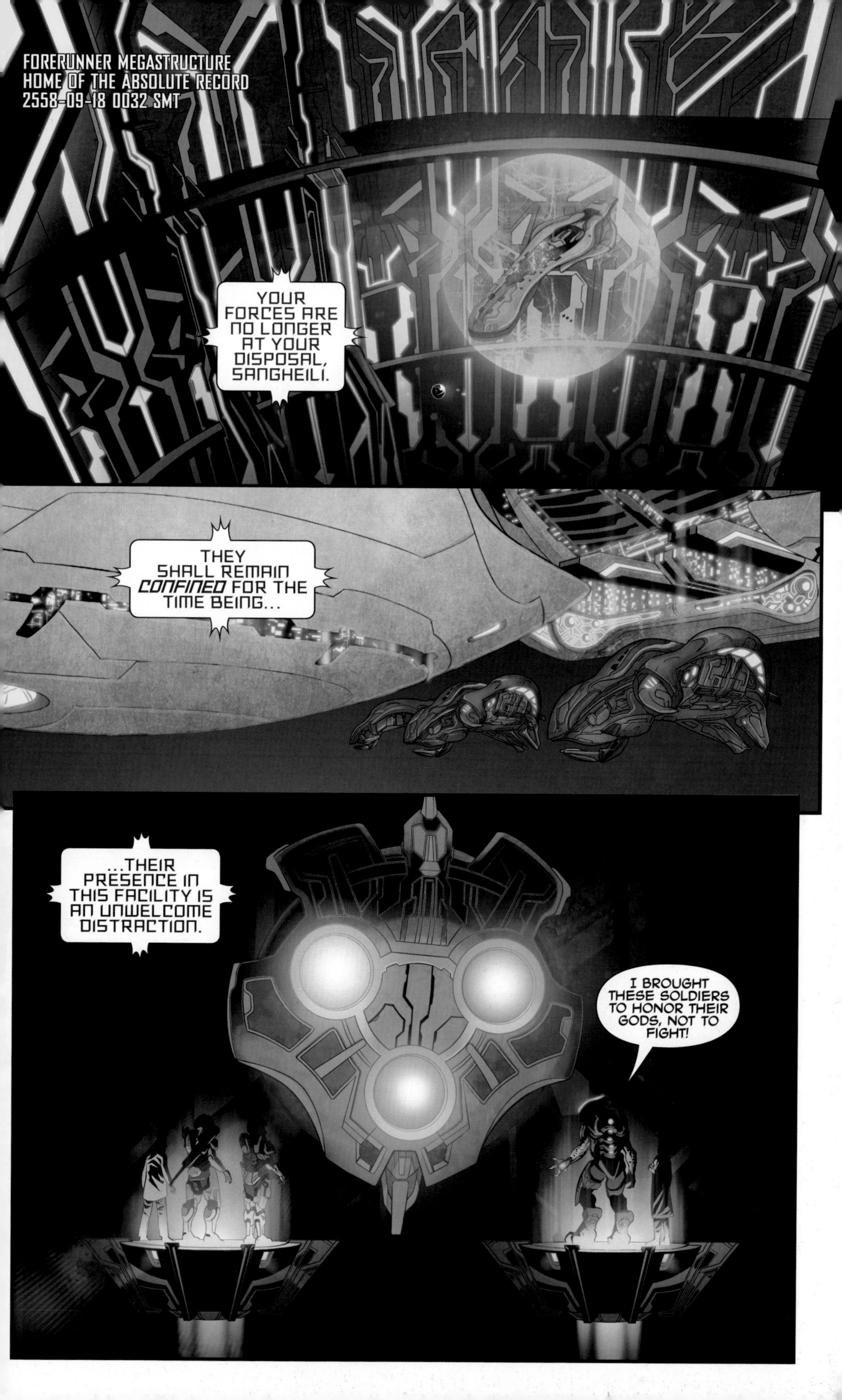
FORERUNNER MEGASTRUCTURE
HOME OF THE ABSOLUTE RECORD
2558-09-18 0032 SMT
YOUR FORCES ARE NO LONGER AT YOUR DISPOSAL, SANGHEILI.
THEY SHALL REMAIN CONFINED FOR THE TIME BEING...
...THEIR PRESENCE IN THIS FACILITY IS AN UNWELCOME DISTRACTION.
I BROUGHT THESE SOLDIERS TO HONOR THEIR GODS, NOT TO FIGHT!

JUL...

YOU INTENTIONALLY PROVOKED THEM!

MY SUSPICIONS ABOUT CERTAIN DISRUPTIVE TENDENCIES WERE CONFIRMED BY THEIR REACTION.

REACTION?! HOW WERE THEY SUPPOSED TO REACT?!

WHAT DO YOU THINK, TANAKA? DOES THIS THING ACTUALLY LIKE US, OR JUST REALLY HATE THEM?

CAN'T TELL, COMMANDER.

GLASSMAN?

NO CLUE.

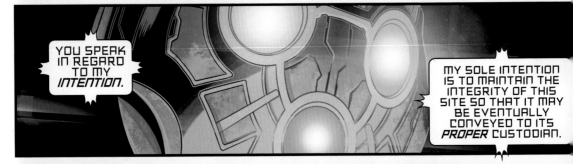

YOU SPEAK IN REGARD TO MY INTENTION.

MY SOLE INTENTION IS TO MAINTAIN THE INTEGRITY OF THIS SITE SO THAT IT MAY BE EVENTUALLY CONVEYED TO ITS PROPER CUSTODIAN.

ISN'T IT OBVIOUS THAT I'M THIS CUSTODIAN YOU SPEAK OF?

WHY ELSE WOULD THE LIBRARIAN GIVE ME THE JANUS KEY?

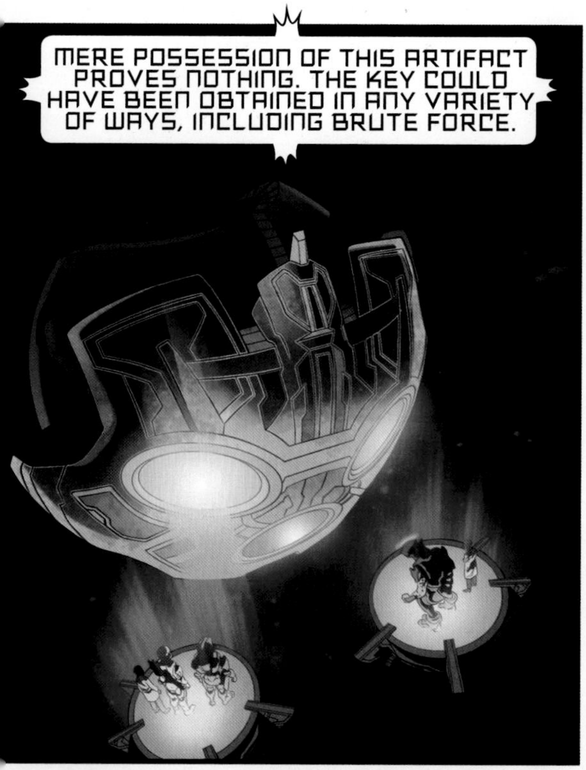
MERE POSSESSION OF THIS ARTIFACT PROVES NOTHING. THE KEY COULD HAVE BEEN OBTAINED IN ANY VARIETY OF WAYS, INCLUDING BRUTE FORCE.

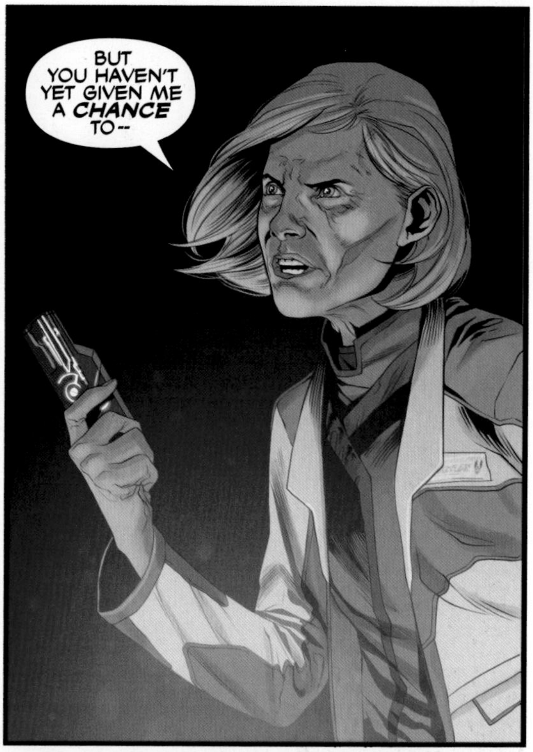
BUT YOU HAVEN'T YET GIVEN ME A *CHANCE* TO--

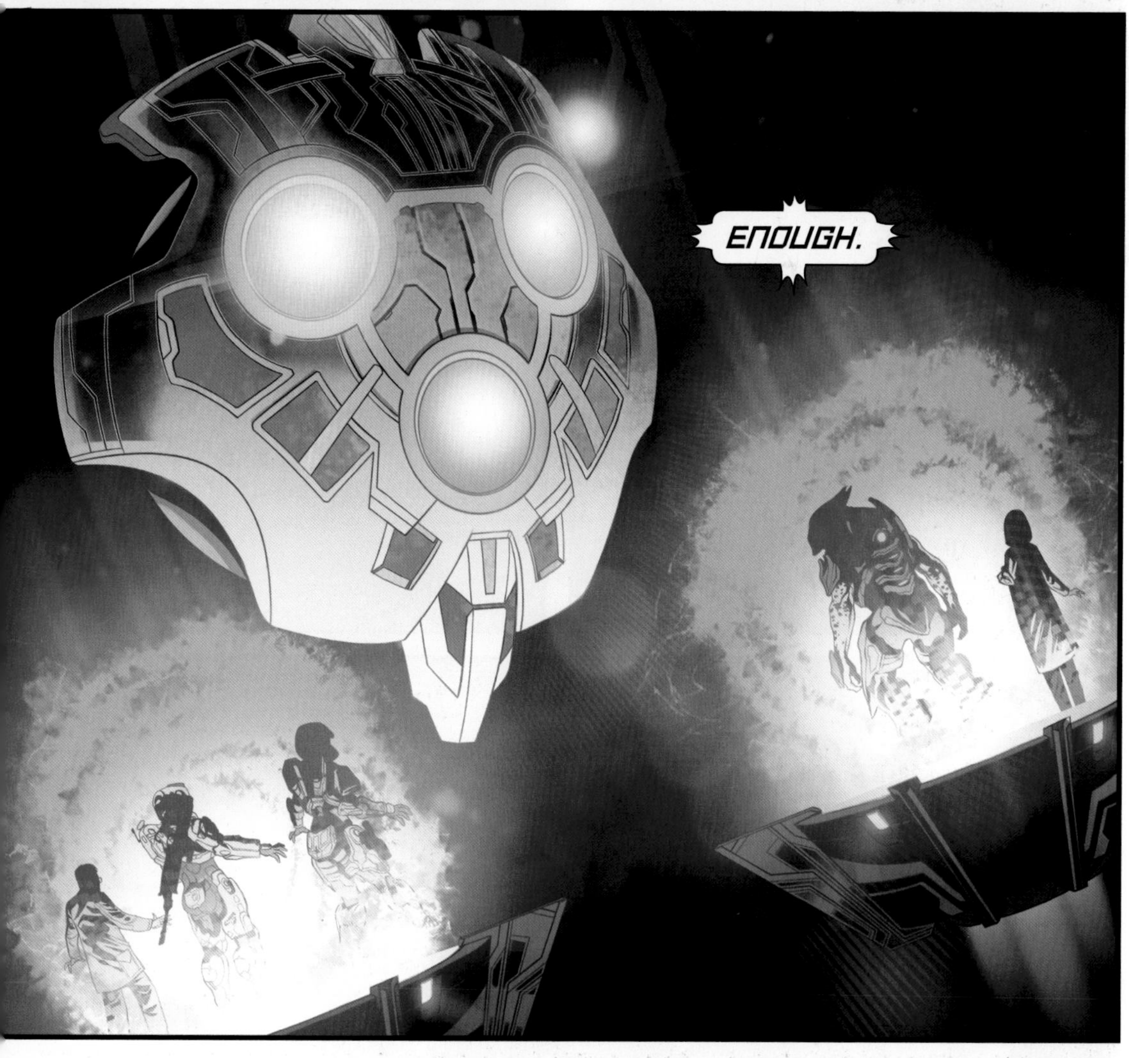
ENOUGH.

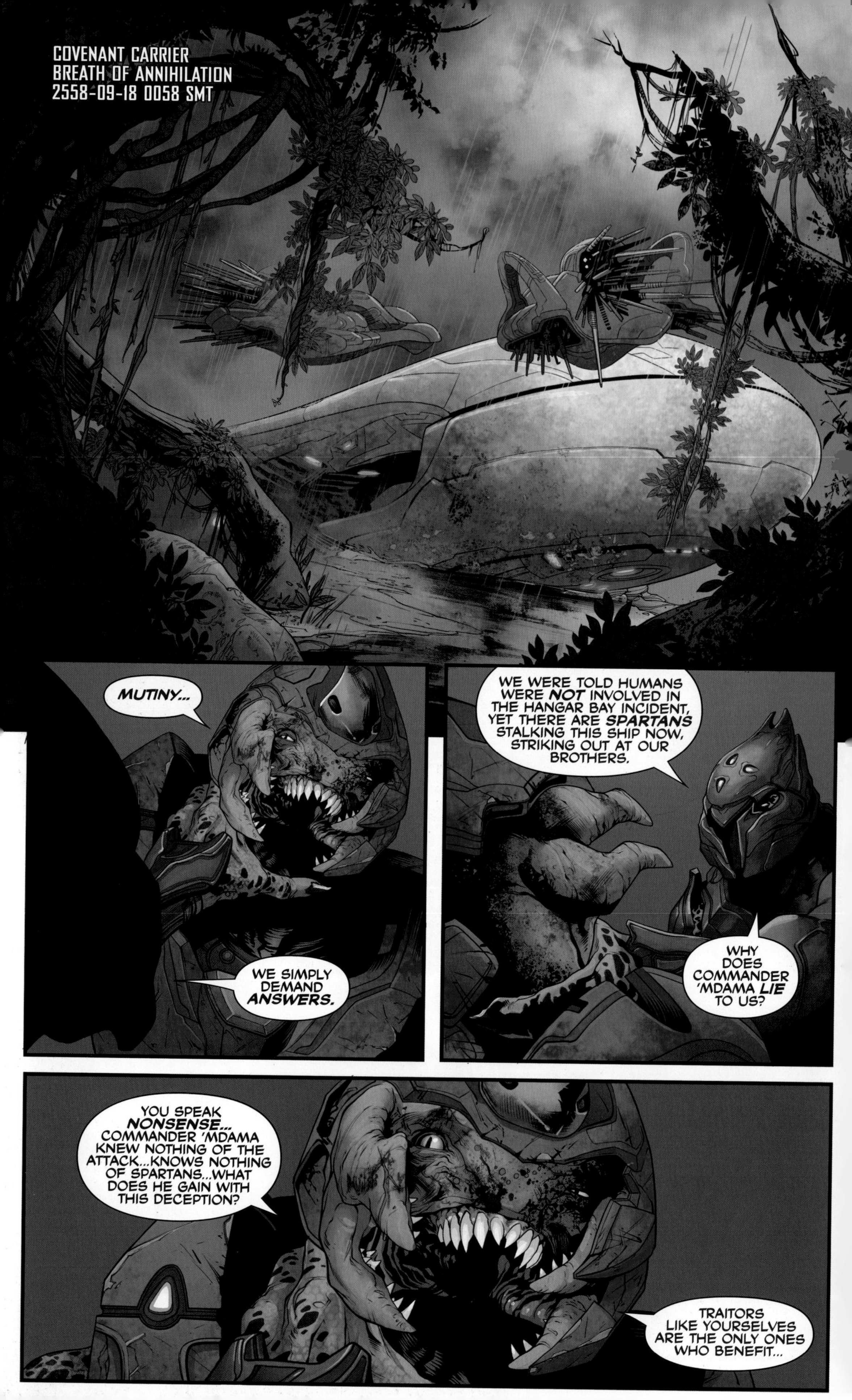
COVENANT CARRIER
BREATH OF ANNIHILATION
2558-09-18 0058 SMT
MUTINY...
WE SIMPLY DEMAND ANSWERS.
WE WERE TOLD HUMANS WERE NOT INVOLVED IN THE HANGAR BAY INCIDENT, YET THERE ARE SPARTANS STALKING THIS SHIP NOW, STRIKING OUT AT OUR BROTHERS.
WHY DOES COMMANDER 'MDAMA LIE TO US?
YOU SPEAK NONSENSE... COMMANDER 'MDAMA KNEW NOTHING OF THE ATTACK...KNOWS NOTHING OF SPARTANS...WHAT DOES HE GAIN WITH THIS DECEPTION?
TRAITORS LIKE YOURSELVES ARE THE ONLY ONES WHO BENEFIT...

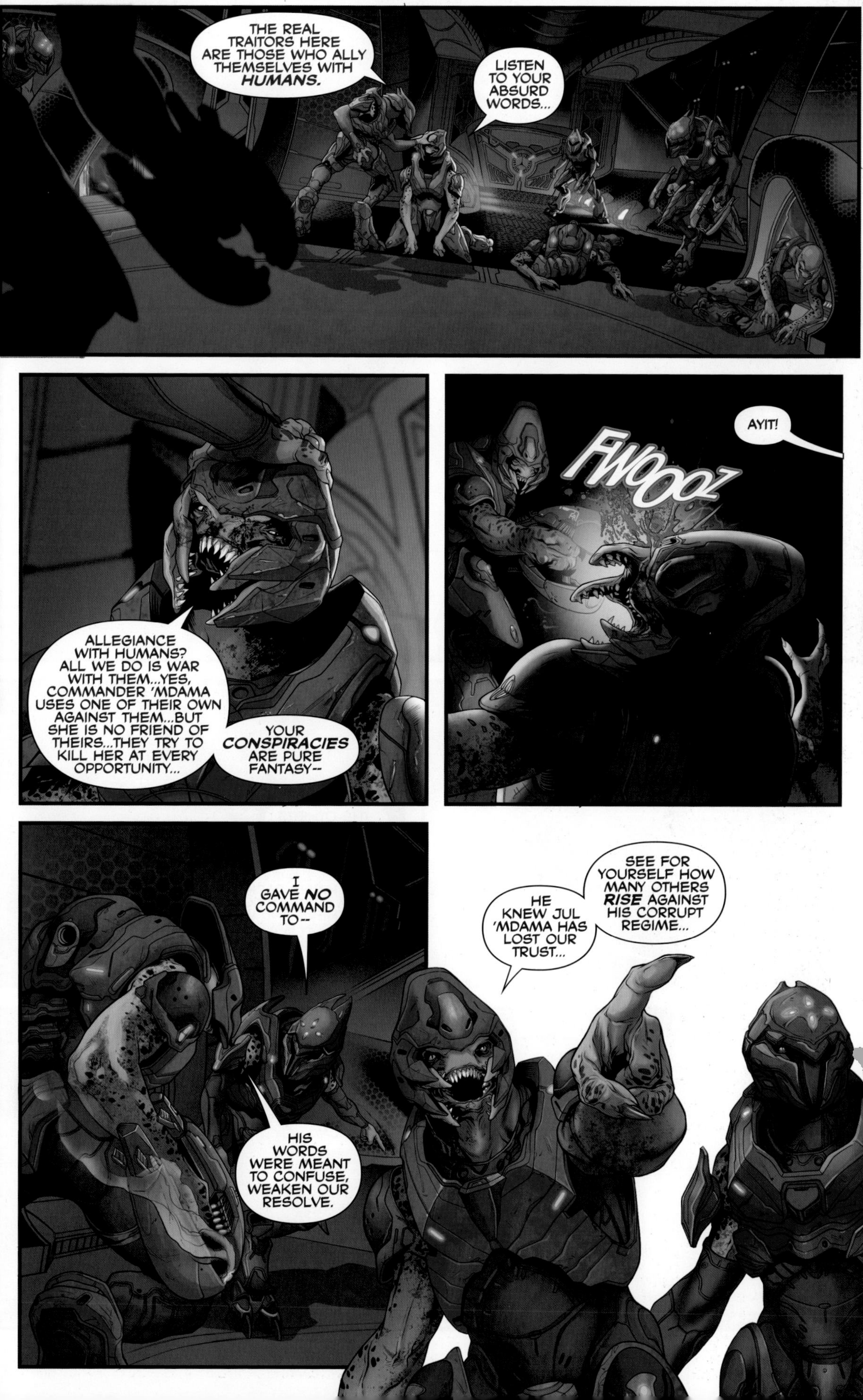
THE REAL TRAITORS HERE ARE THOSE WHO ALLY THEMSELVES WITH *HUMANS.*
LISTEN TO YOUR ABSURD WORDS...
ALLEGIANCE WITH HUMANS? ALL WE DO IS WAR WITH THEM...YES, COMMANDER 'MDAMA USES ONE OF THEIR OWN AGAINST THEM...BUT SHE IS NO FRIEND OF THEIRS...THEY TRY TO KILL HER AT EVERY OPPORTUNITY...
YOUR *CONSPIRACIES* ARE PURE FANTASY--
AYIT!
FWOOOOZ
I GAVE *NO* COMMAND TO--
HIS WORDS WERE MEANT TO CONFUSE, WEAKEN OUR RESOLVE.
HE KNEW JUL 'MDAMA HAS LOST OUR TRUST...
SEE FOR YOURSELF HOW MANY OTHERS *RISE* AGAINST HIS CORRUPT REGIME...

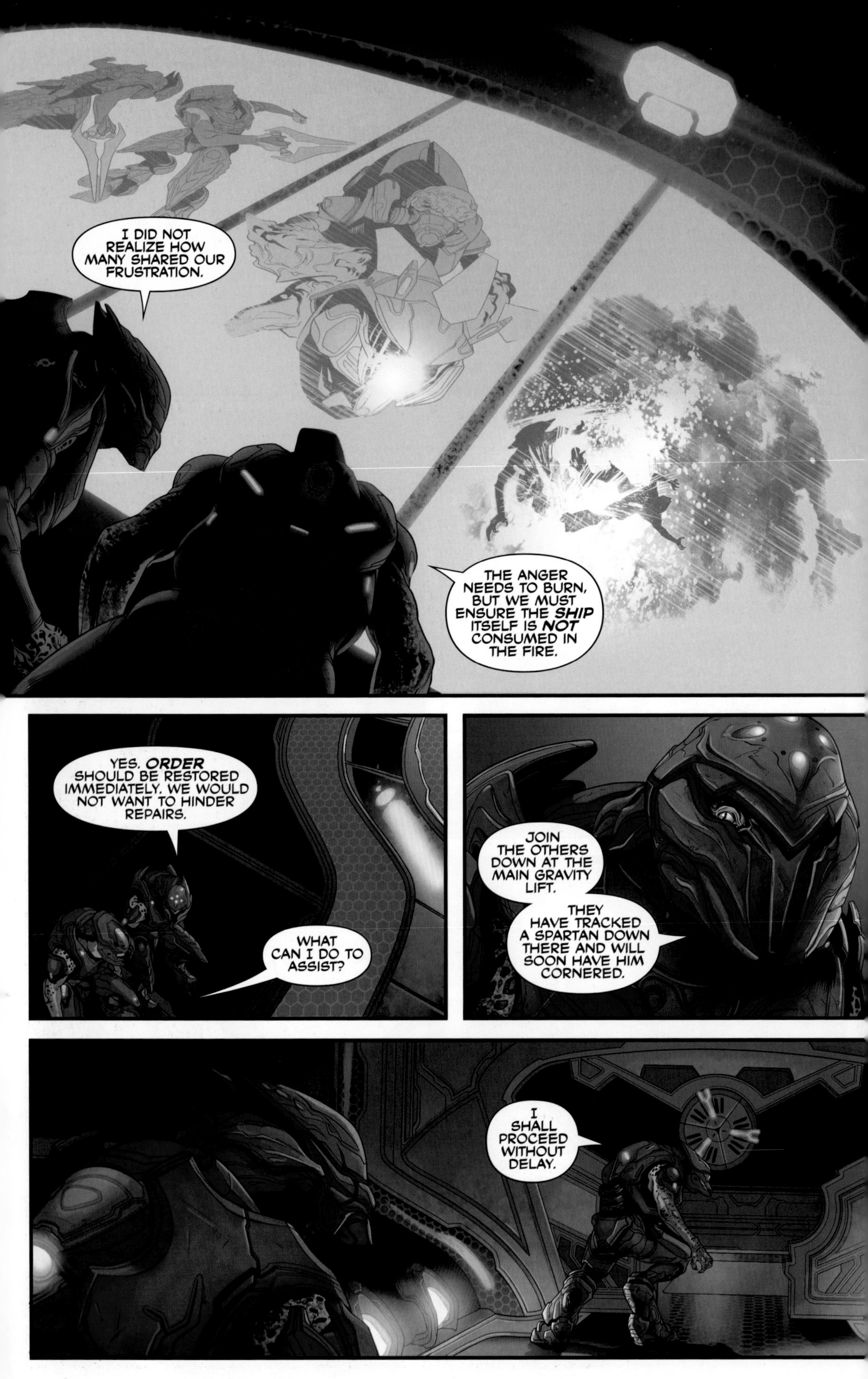
I DID NOT REALIZE HOW MANY SHARED OUR FRUSTRATION.
THE ANGER NEEDS TO BURN, BUT WE MUST ENSURE THE *SHIP* ITSELF IS *NOT* CONSUMED IN THE FIRE.
YES. *ORDER* SHOULD BE RESTORED IMMEDIATELY. WE WOULD NOT WANT TO HINDER REPAIRS.
WHAT CAN I DO TO ASSIST?
JOIN THE OTHERS DOWN AT THE MAIN GRAVITY LIFT.
THEY HAVE TRACKED A SPARTAN DOWN THERE AND WILL SOON HAVE HIM CORNERED.
I SHALL PROCEED WITHOUT DELAY.

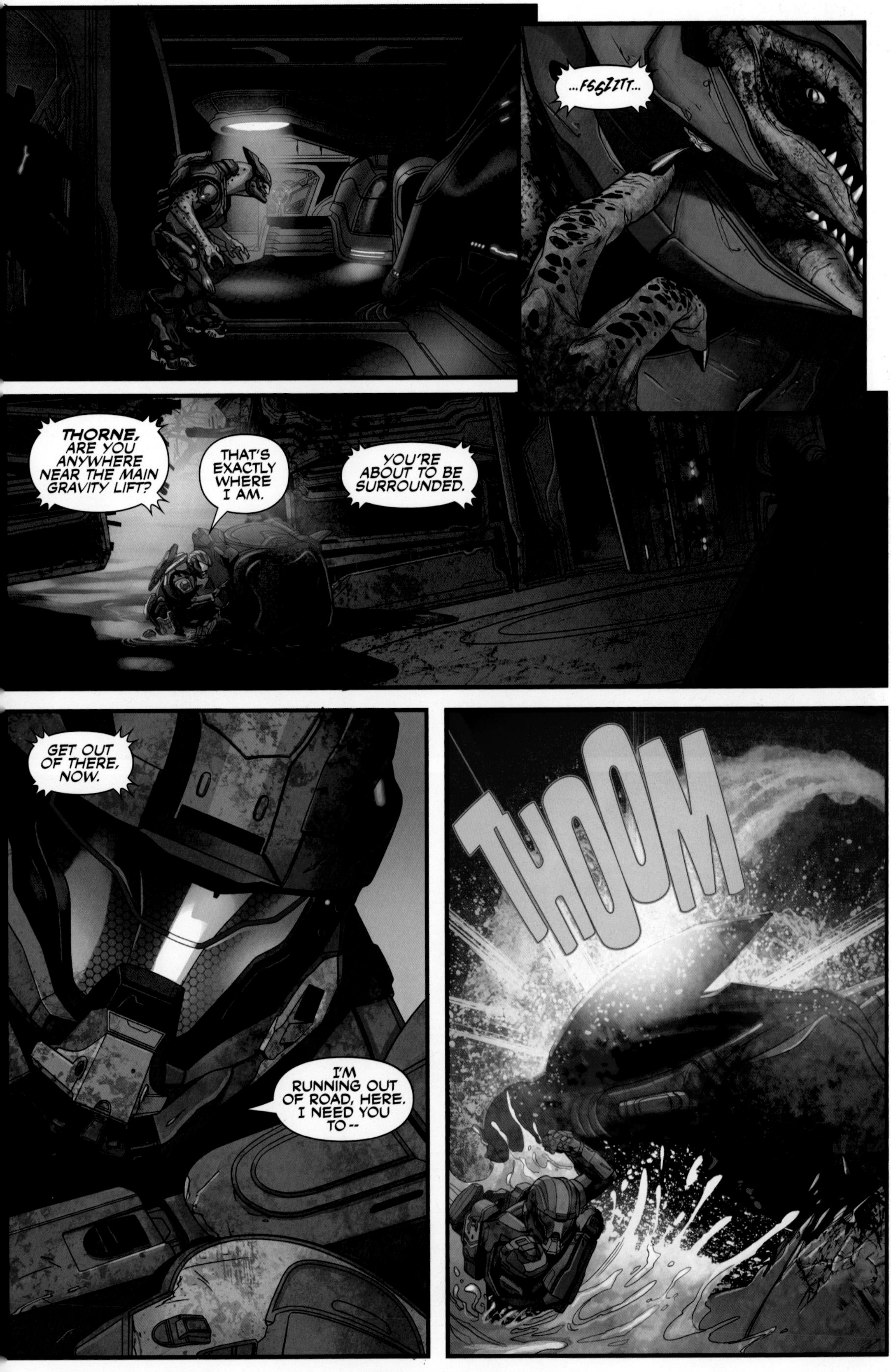
...FSSZZTT...
THORNE, ARE YOU ANYWHERE NEAR THE MAIN GRAVITY LIFT?
THAT'S EXACTLY WHERE I AM.
YOU'RE ABOUT TO BE SURROUNDED.
GET OUT OF THERE, NOW.
I'M RUNNING OUT OF ROAD, HERE. I NEED YOU TO--
THOOM

FWOOOZ
FWOOOZ
FWOOOZ

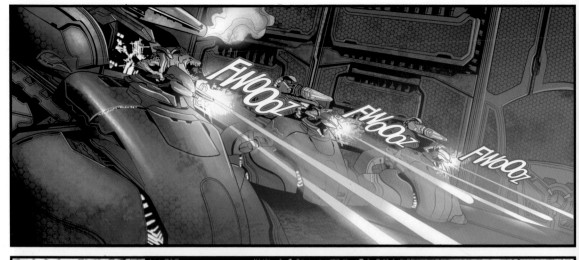

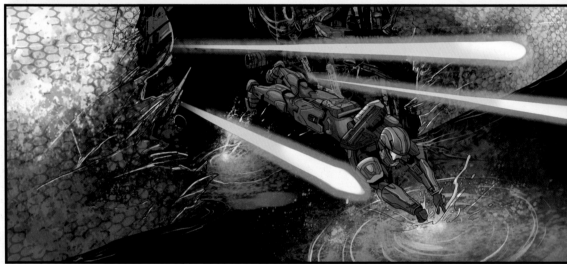

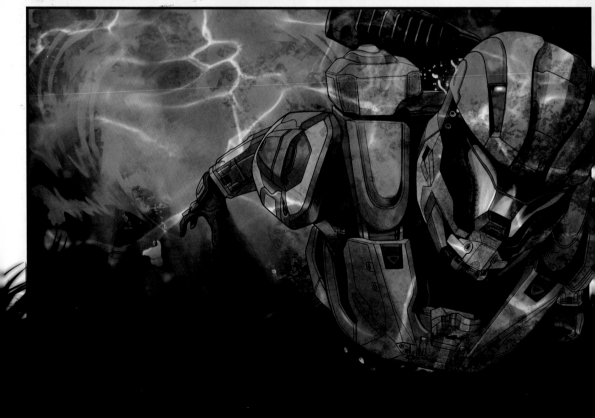

THE ABSOLUTE RECORD IS A SINGULAR CREATION. THE ONLY FORERUNNER SITE IN EXISTENCE LINKED TO ALL OTHERS.

AND BECAUSE IT PROVIDES ACCESS TO SUCH POWERFUL TOOLS...

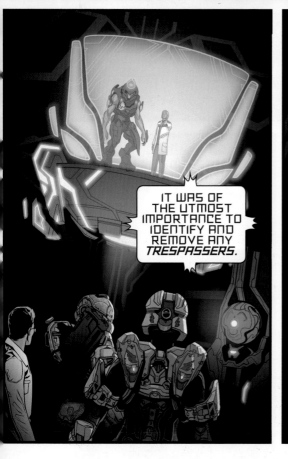

IT WAS OF THE UTMOST IMPORTANCE TO IDENTIFY AND REMOVE ANY *TRESPASSERS*.

NOW THAT THE *IMPOSTORS* HAVE BEEN DETAINED, WE SHALL COMPLETE THE CONFIRMATION PROCESS.

WELL, THAT'S ONE WAY TO GET HALSEY TO SHUT UP.

SO IT'S THE HUMANS' TURN TO BE TERRORIZED BY OUR HOST.

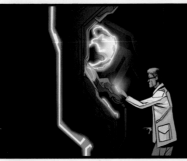

YOU MAY VIEW THE RECORD'S INDEX VIA THE TERMINAL.

FOR PURPOSES OF ILLUSTRATION: THIS IS A SECTION OF THE STAR SYSTEM THROUGH WHICH YOU ACCESSED THE ENTRANCE TO THIS SITE.

THE SCATTERED LIGHTS INDICATE THE PRESENCE OF EXTANT FORERUNNER TECHNOLOGY.

CONTAINED WITHIN EACH POINT OF LIGHT, EXACT COORDINATES AND TECHNICAL SPECIFICATIONS OF EACH ITEM.

PLEASE TAKE A MOMENT TO ORIENT YOURSELF TO THE SYSTEM.

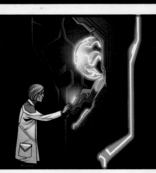

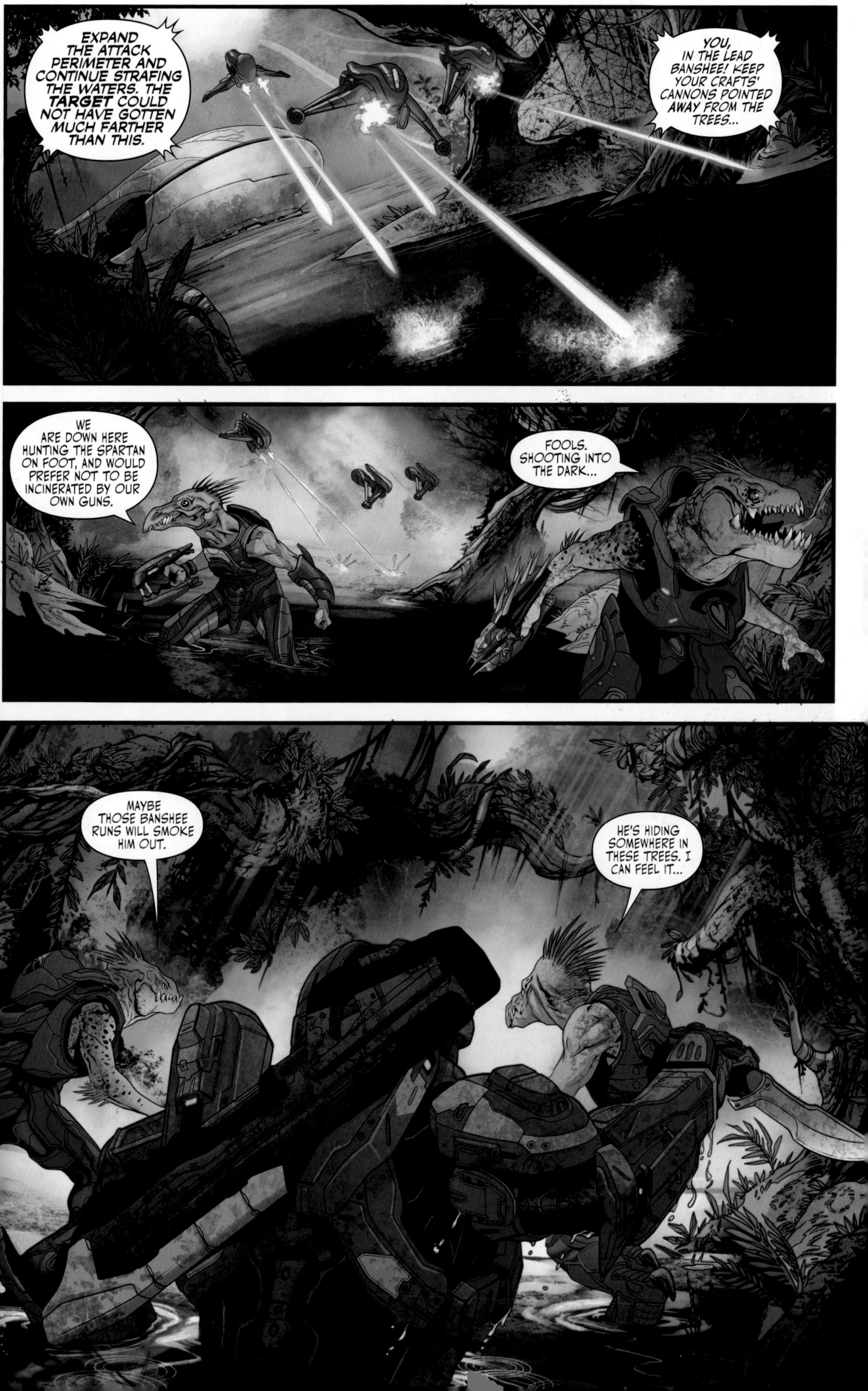
EXPAND THE ATTACK PERIMETER AND CONTINUE STRAFING THE WATERS. THE TARGET COULD NOT HAVE GOTTEN MUCH FARTHER THAN THIS.
YOU, IN THE LEAD BANSHEE! KEEP YOUR CRAFTS' CANNONS POINTED AWAY FROM THE TREES...
WE ARE DOWN HERE HUNTING THE SPARTAN ON FOOT, AND WOULD PREFER NOT TO BE INCINERATED BY OUR OWN GUNS.
FOOLS. SHOOTING INTO THE DARK...
MAYBE THOSE BANSHEE RUNS WILL SMOKE HIM OUT.
HE'S HIDING SOMEWHERE IN THESE TREES. I CAN FEEL IT...

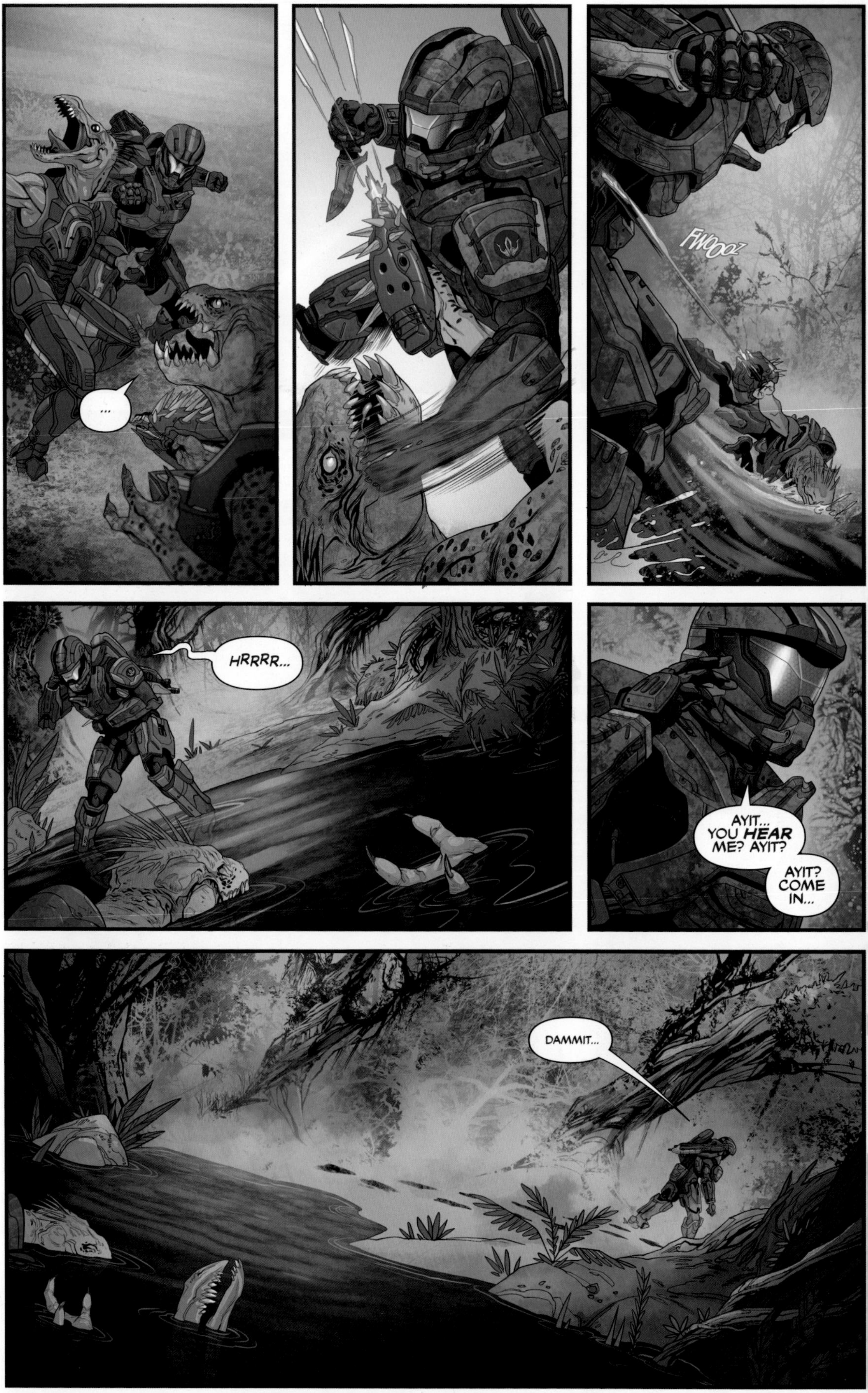
...
FWOOOZ
HRRRR...
AYIT... YOU HEAR ME? AYIT?
AYIT? COME IN...
DAMMIT...

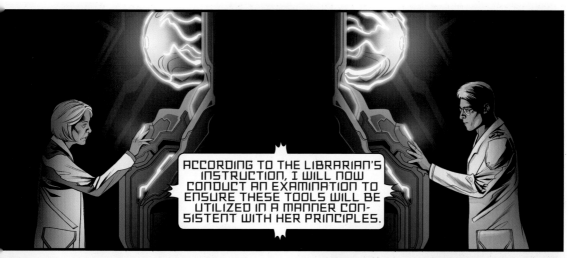

ACCORDING TO THE LIBRARIAN'S INSTRUCTION, I WILL NOW CONDUCT AN EXAMINATION TO ENSURE THESE TOOLS WILL BE UTILIZED IN A MANNER CONSISTENT WITH HER PRINCIPLES.

CONSIDER THE FOLLOWING INFORMATION:

AN INTELLIGENT AND PEACEFUL SPECIES IS REVEALED TO POSSESS FLOOD-RESISTANT BIOLOGICAL MATERIAL, WHICH CAN BE USED AS A VACCINE.

WHEN HARVESTED FROM A LIVE MEMBER OF THIS SPECIES, THE CHANCES OF YIELDING A SUCCESSFUL VACCINATION ARE THIRTY-FIVE PERCENT.

WHEN HARVESTED FROM THE CORPSES OF A NATURAL DEATH--WHICH THIS SPECIES WILL WILLINGLY DELIVER--

--THE CHANCE OF A SUCCESSFUL YIELD IS THIRTY-THREE PERCENT.

THE QUESTION:

SHOULD THIS SPECIES CONTINUE TO LIVE AN AUTONOMOUS EXISTENCE, OR SHOULD IT BE SACRIFICED FOR ITS POTENTIAL BENEFIT TO THE ENTIRE GALAXY?

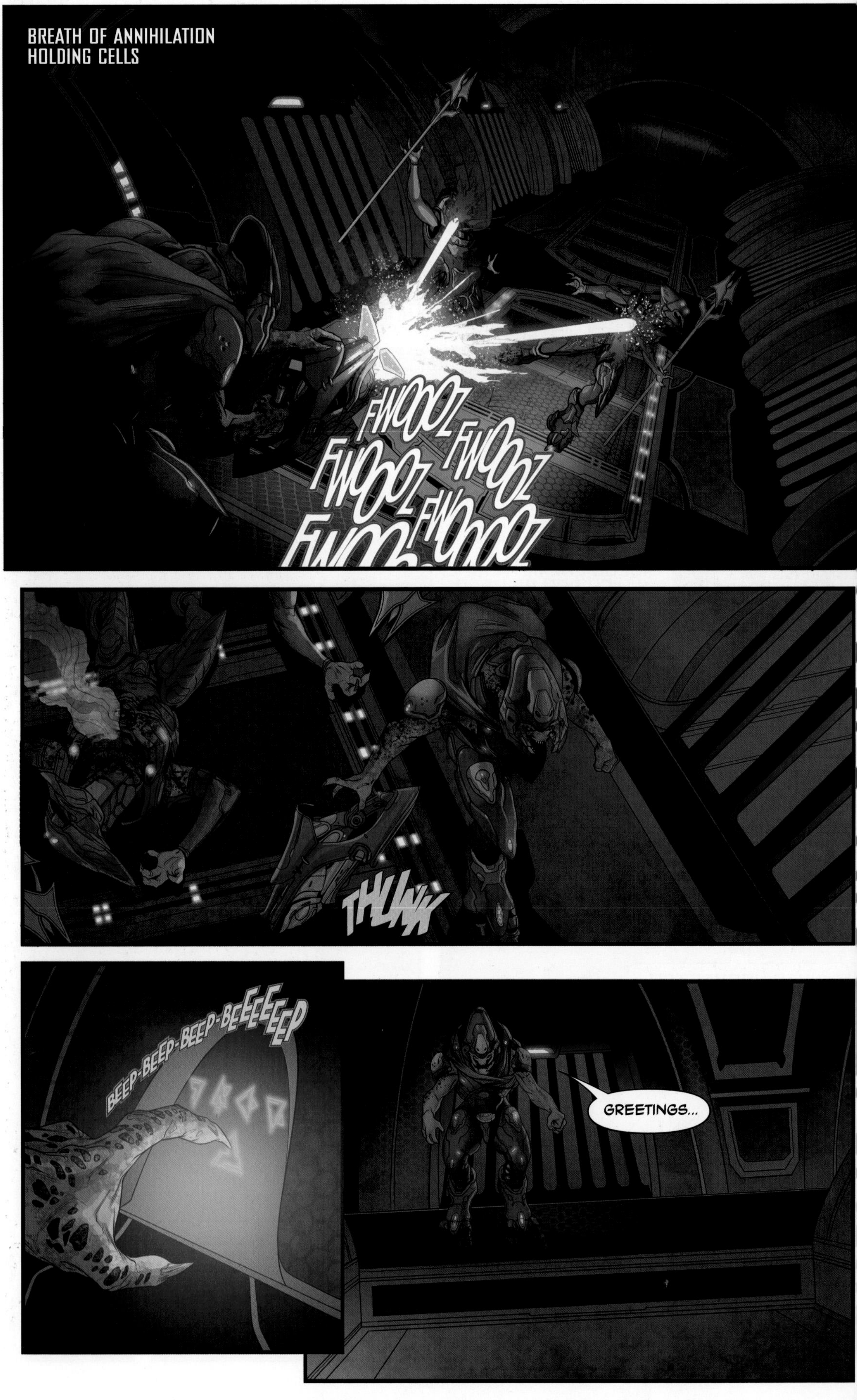
BREATH OF ANNIHILATION
HOLDING CELLS
FWOOOZ
FWOOOZ
FWOOOZ
FWOOOZ
THUNK
BEEP-BEEP-BEEP-BEEEEEEP
GREETINGS...

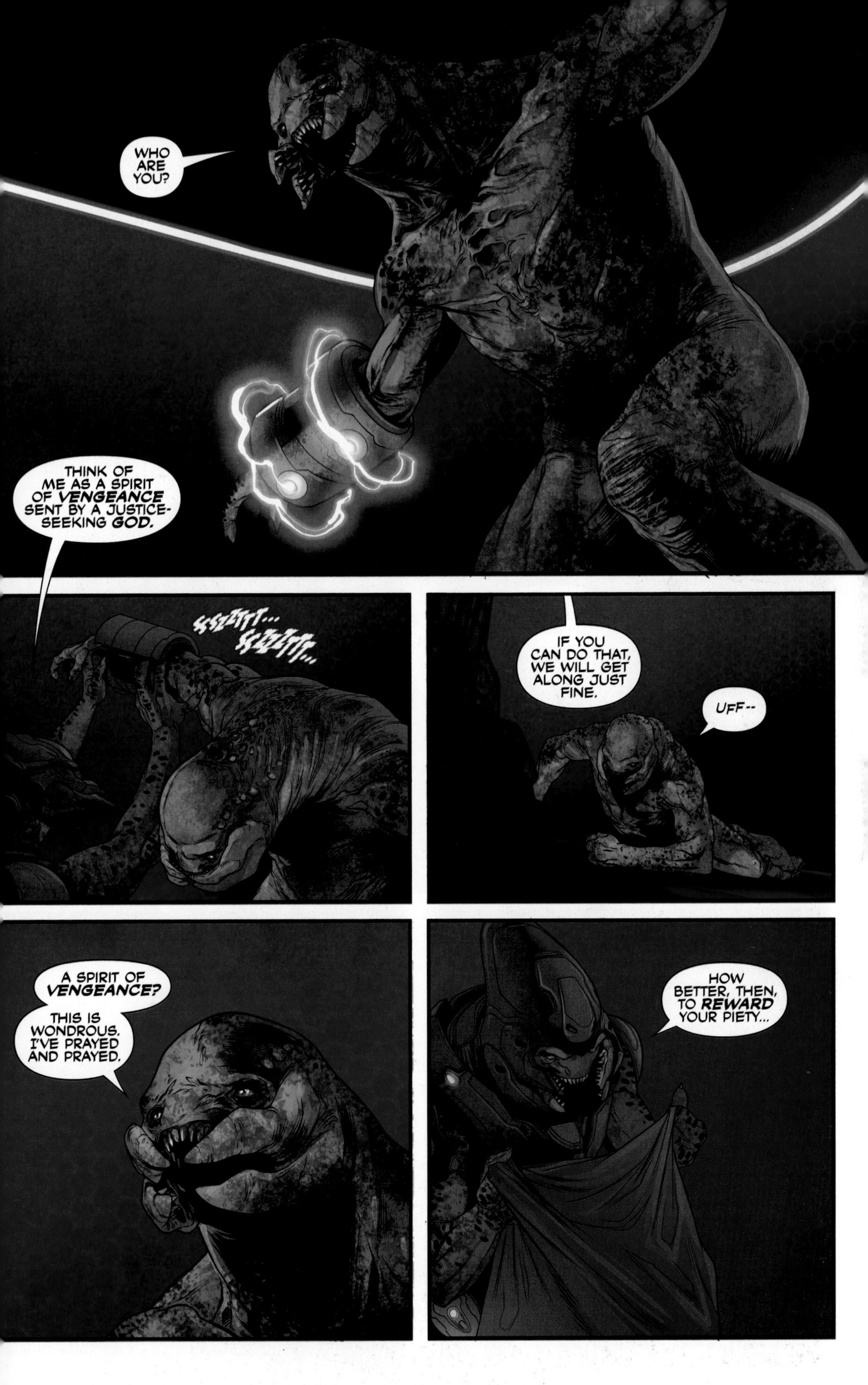
WHO ARE YOU?
THINK OF ME AS A SPIRIT OF VENGEANCE SENT BY A JUSTICE-SEEKING GOD.
SSSZZTTT... SSZZTTT...
IF YOU CAN DO THAT, WE WILL GET ALONG JUST FINE.
UFF--
A SPIRIT OF VENGEANCE?
THIS IS WONDROUS. I'VE PRAYED AND PRAYED.
HOW BETTER, THEN, TO REWARD YOUR PIETY...

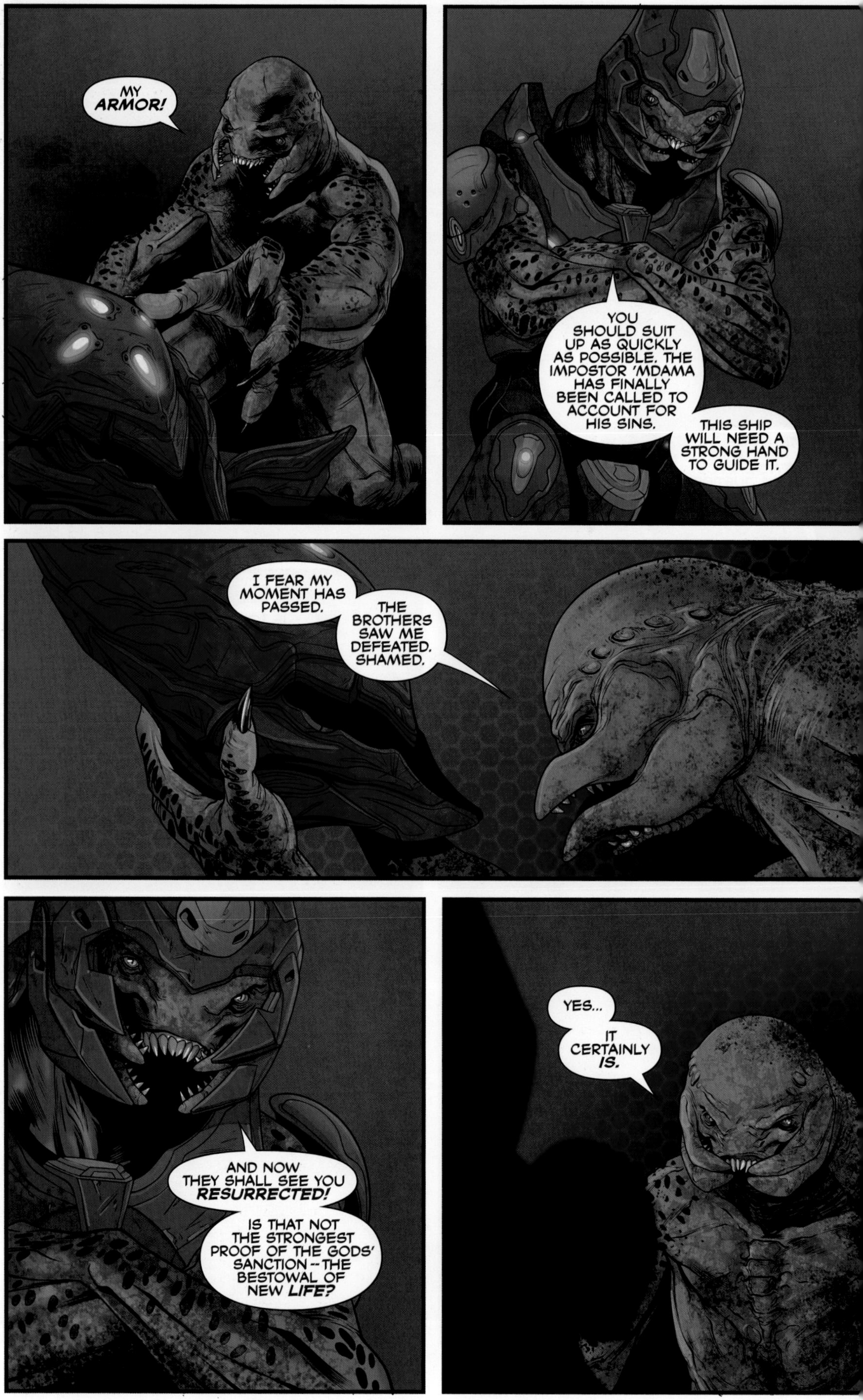
MY *ARMOR!*
YOU SHOULD SUIT UP AS QUICKLY AS POSSIBLE. THE IMPOSTOR 'MDAMA HAS FINALLY BEEN CALLED TO ACCOUNT FOR HIS SINS.
THIS SHIP WILL NEED A STRONG HAND TO GUIDE IT.
I FEAR MY MOMENT HAS PASSED.
THE BROTHERS SAW ME DEFEATED. SHAMED.
AND NOW THEY SHALL SEE YOU *RESURRECTED!*
IS THAT NOT THE STRONGEST PROOF OF THE GODS' SANCTION--THE BESTOWAL OF NEW *LIFE?*
YES...
IT CERTAINLY *IS.*

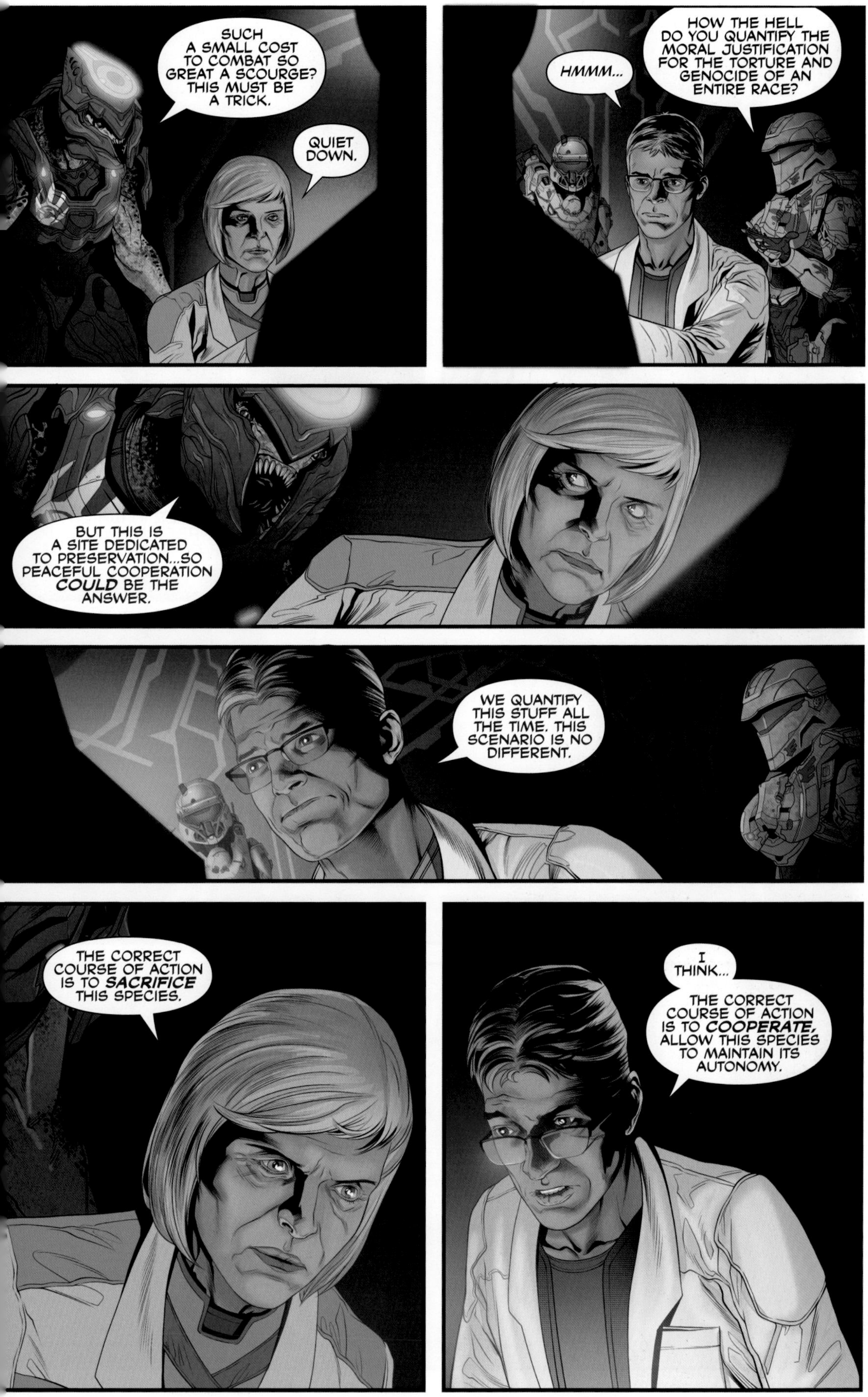
SUCH A SMALL COST TO COMBAT SO GREAT A SCOURGE? THIS MUST BE A TRICK.
QUIET DOWN.
HMMM...
HOW THE HELL DO YOU QUANTIFY THE MORAL JUSTIFICATION FOR THE TORTURE AND GENOCIDE OF AN ENTIRE RACE?
BUT THIS IS A SITE DEDICATED TO PRESERVATION...SO PEACEFUL COOPERATION *COULD* BE THE ANSWER.
WE QUANTIFY THIS STUFF ALL THE TIME. THIS SCENARIO IS NO DIFFERENT.
THE CORRECT COURSE OF ACTION IS TO *SACRIFICE* THIS SPECIES.
I THINK...
THE CORRECT COURSE OF ACTION IS TO *COOPERATE.* ALLOW THIS SPECIES TO MAINTAIN ITS AUTONOMY.

YES. VERY GOOD.

YES. VERY GOOD.

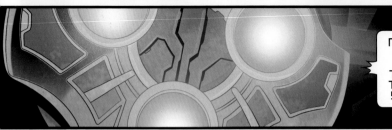

NOW THAT CONFIRMATION IS COMPLETE, I AWAIT YOUR INSTRUCTION AS TO THE MANNER IN WHICH THE TRESPASSING PARTY SHALL BE *DISPOSED OF...*

IS CURRENT CONFINEMENT ACCEPTABLE...

...OR DO YOU PREFER SUMMARY *INCINERATION?*

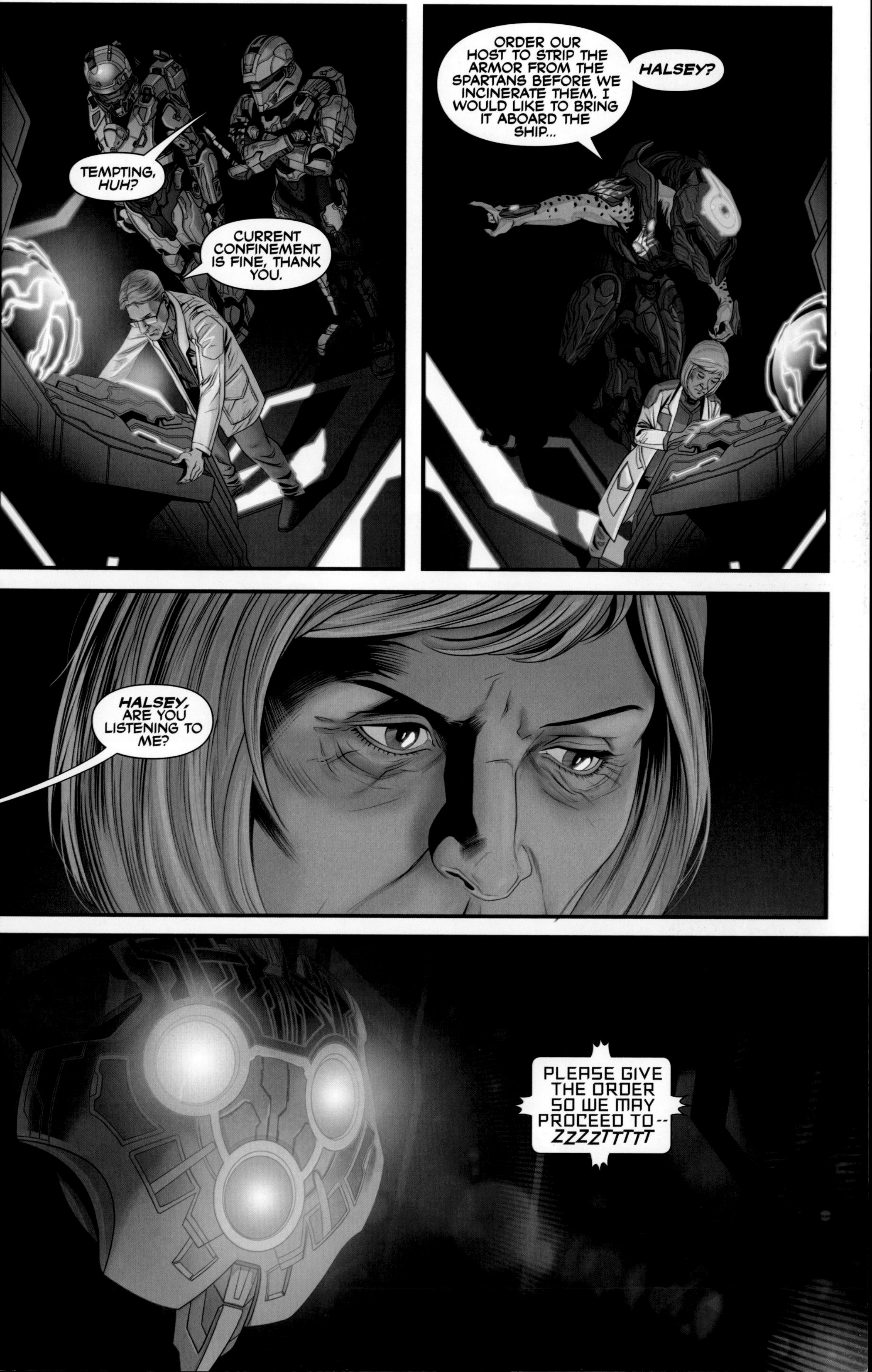

TEMPTING, HUH?
CURRENT CONFINEMENT IS FINE, THANK YOU.
ORDER OUR HOST TO STRIP THE ARMOR FROM THE SPARTANS BEFORE WE INCINERATE THEM. I WOULD LIKE TO BRING IT ABOARD THE SHIP...
HALSEY?
HALSEY, ARE YOU LISTENING TO ME?
PLEASE GIVE THE ORDER SO WE MAY PROCEED TO--
ZZZZTTTTT

DZZZZZEEEE

...EEEEE

THUNK

THE HELL'S HAPPENING?!

THE PRISONERS? THEY'VE DISAPPEARED!

THEY WERE NEVER THERE, JUL.

IT WAS AN ILLUSION, A TEST WITHIN A TEST...

HOW DID YOU DEFEAT THE CUSTODIAN?

EVERY GAME HAS RULES. *HIS* MISTAKE WAS THINKING I WOULD FOLLOW THEM.

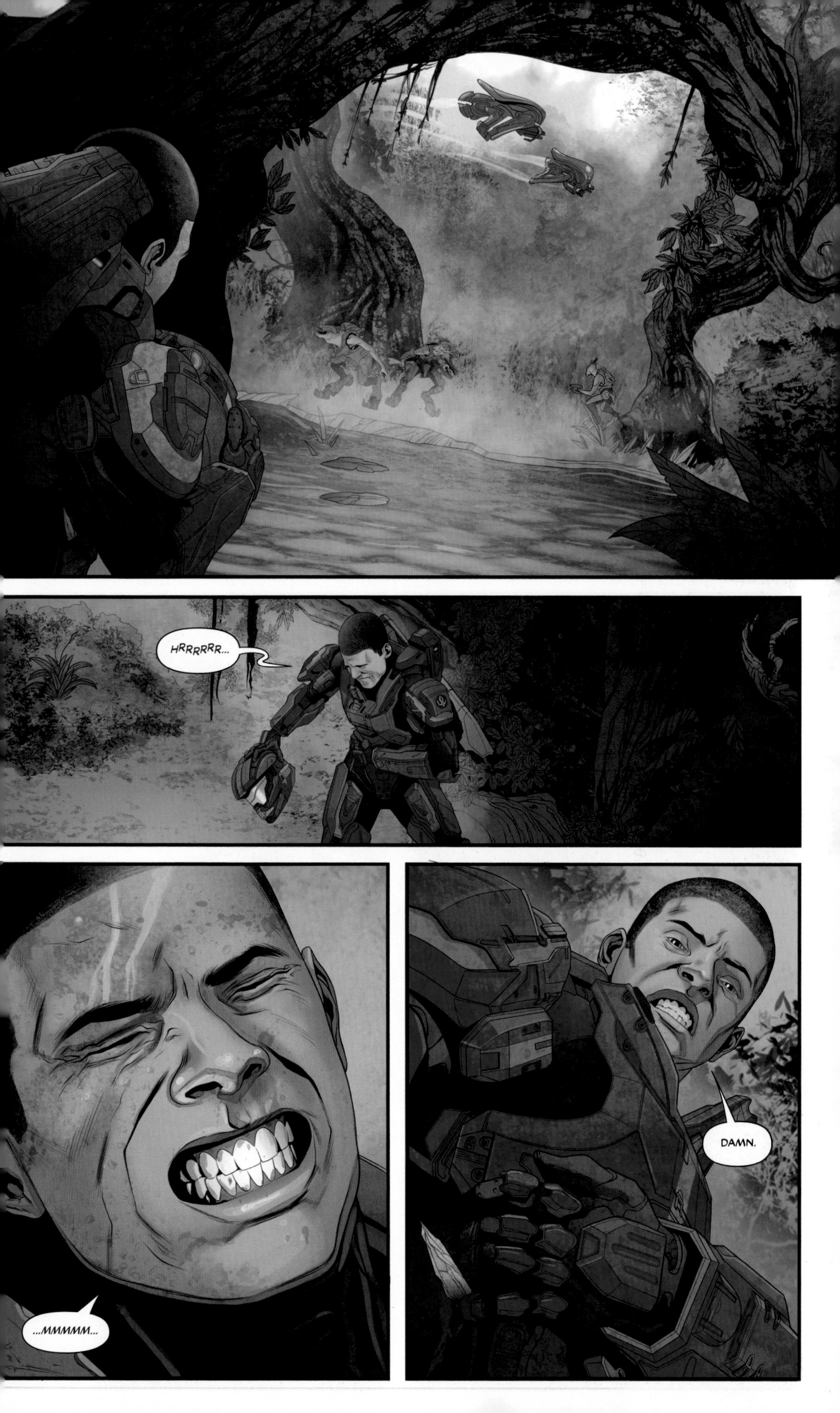
HRRRRRR...
...MMMMM...
DAMN.

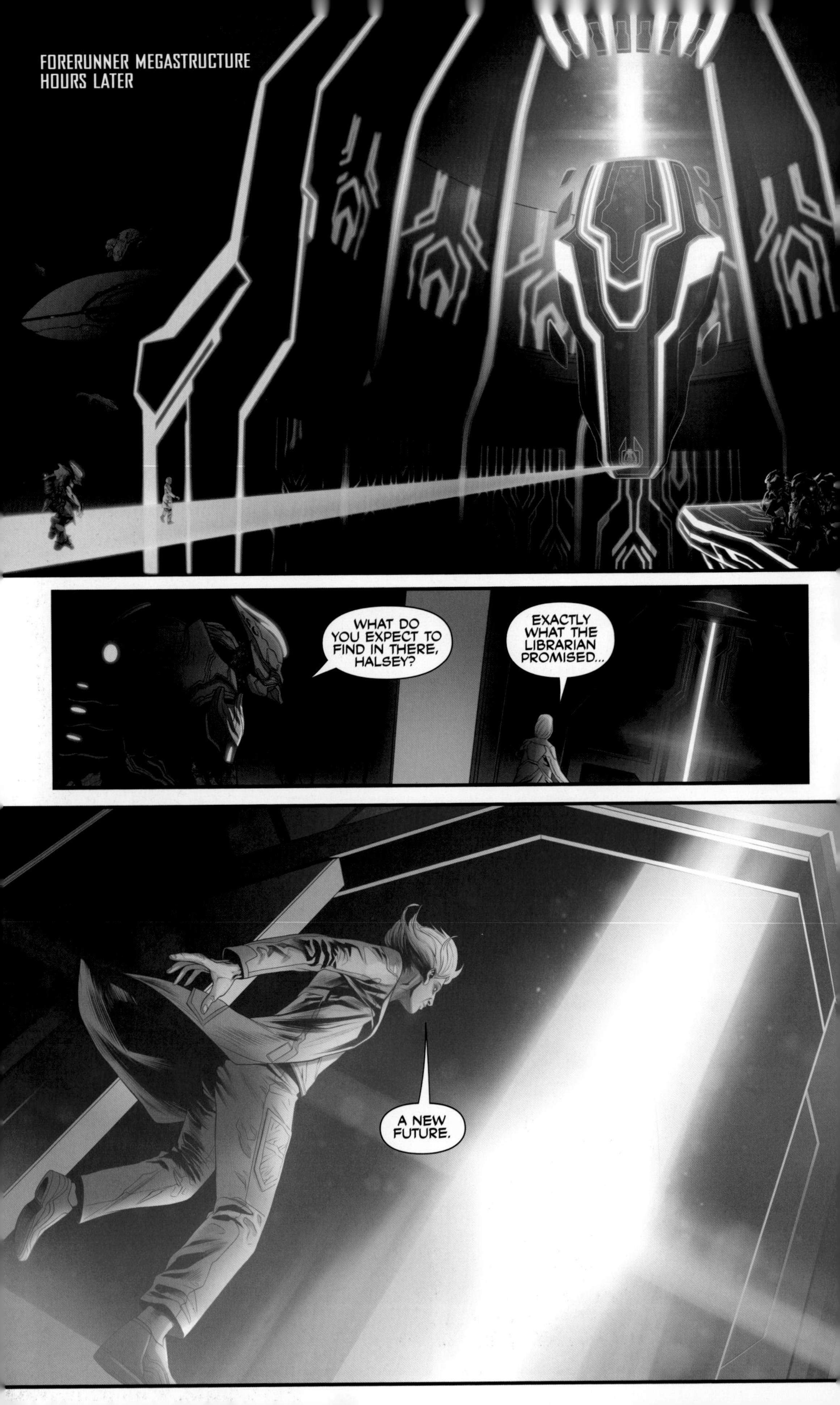
FORERUNNER MEGASTRUCTURE
HOURS LATER
WHAT DO YOU EXPECT TO FIND IN THERE, HALSEY?
EXACTLY WHAT THE LIBRARIAN PROMISED...
A NEW FUTURE.

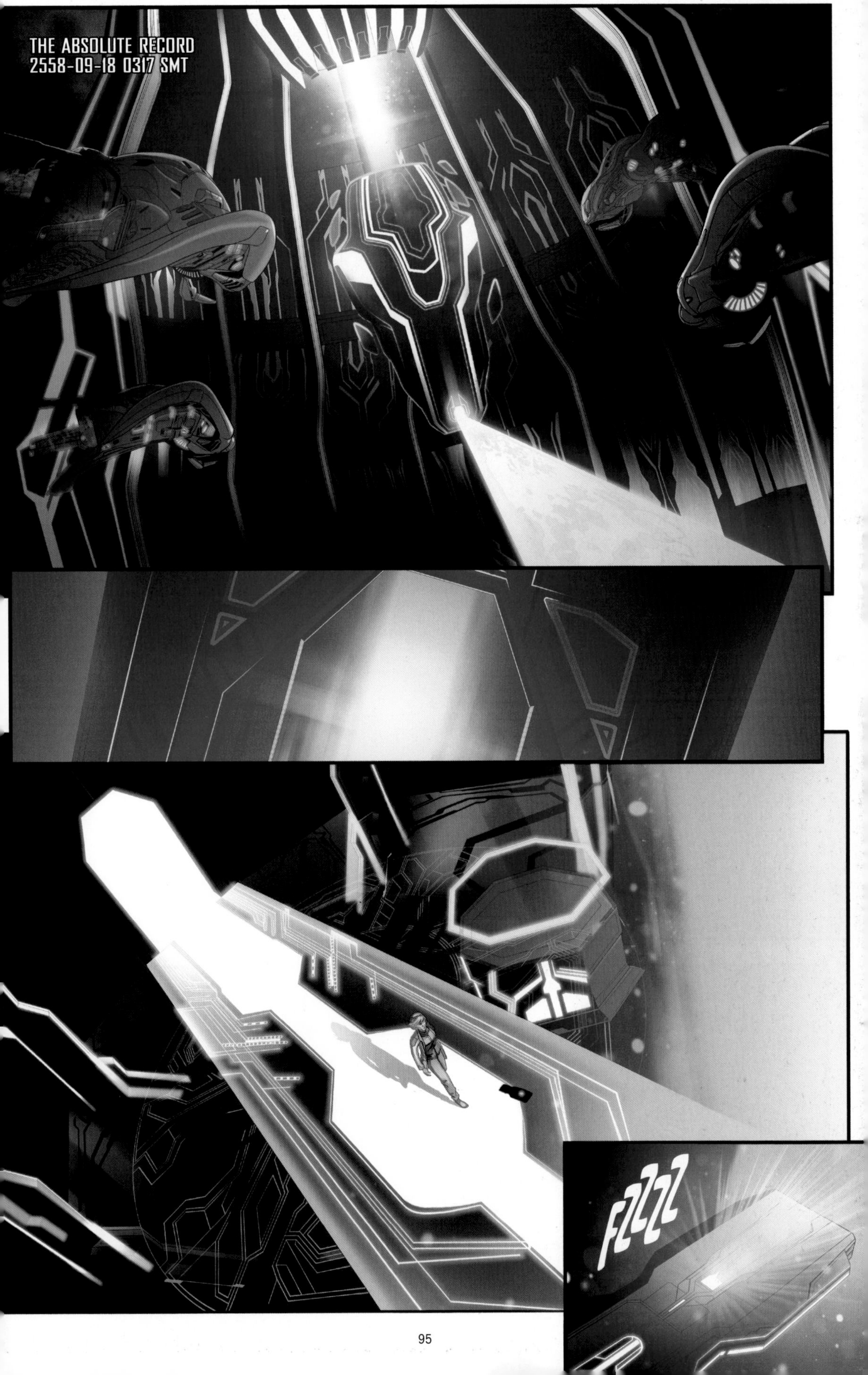
THE ABSOLUTE RECORD
2558-09-18 0317 SMT
FZZZZ

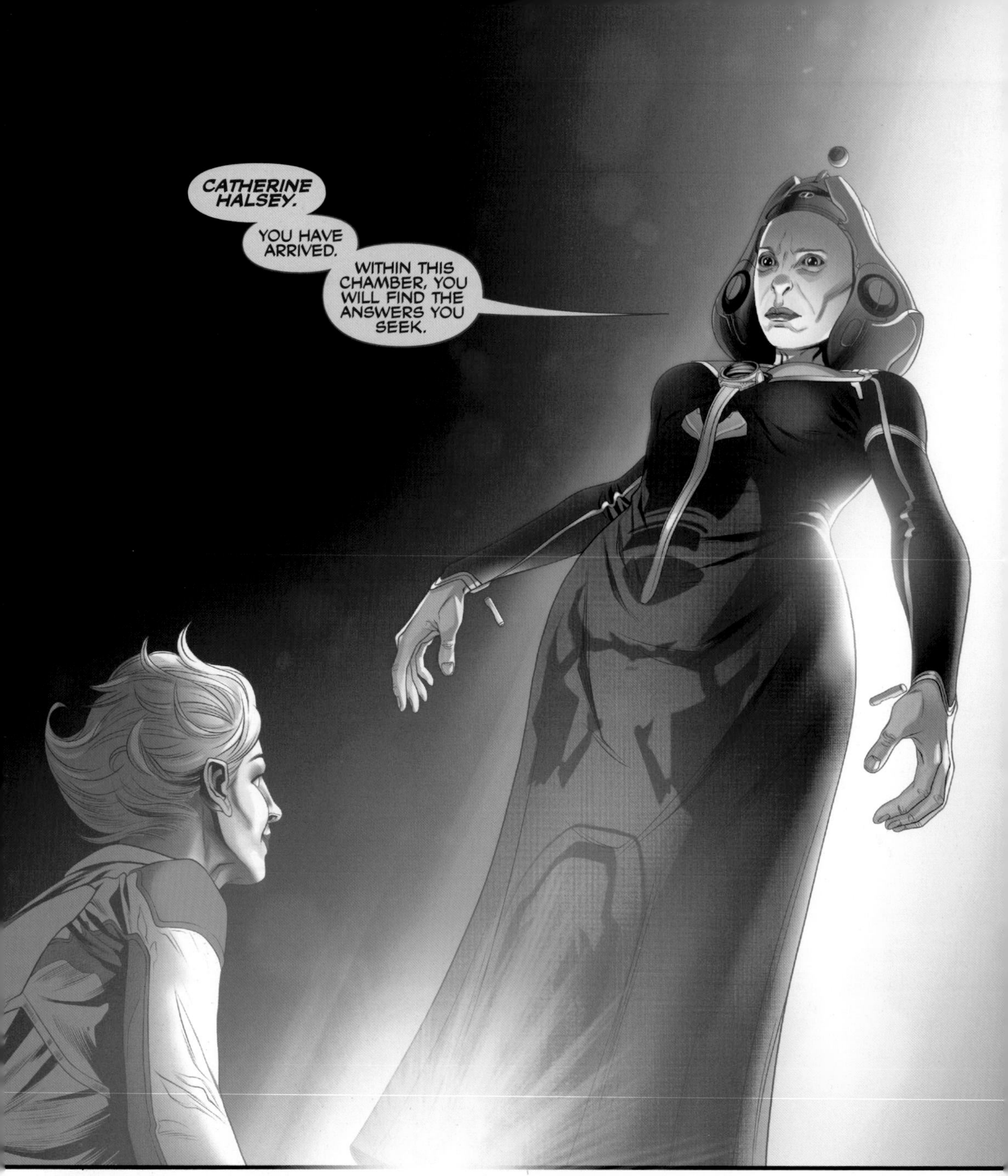
CATHERINE HALSEY.
YOU HAVE ARRIVED.
WITHIN THIS CHAMBER, YOU WILL FIND THE ANSWERS YOU SEEK.

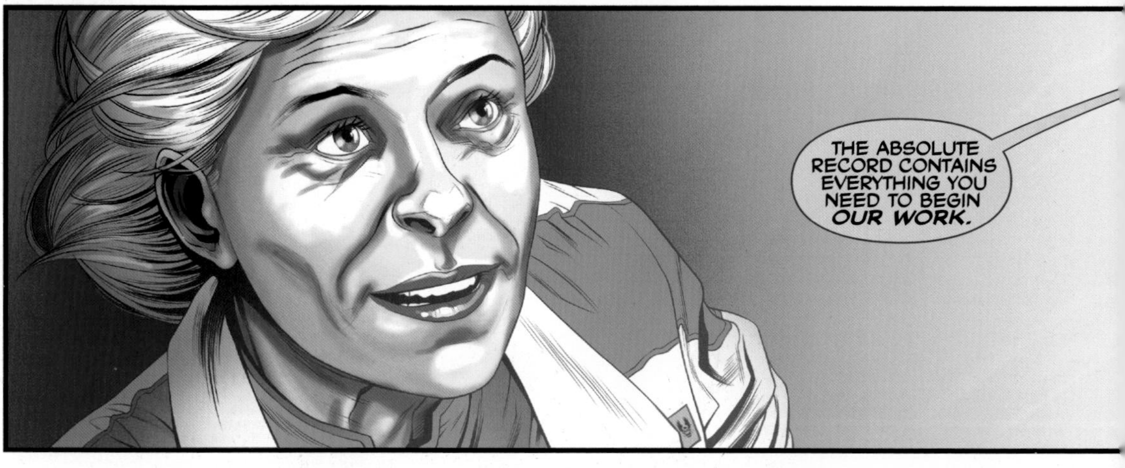
THE ABSOLUTE RECORD CONTAINS EVERYTHING YOU NEED TO BEGIN OUR WORK.

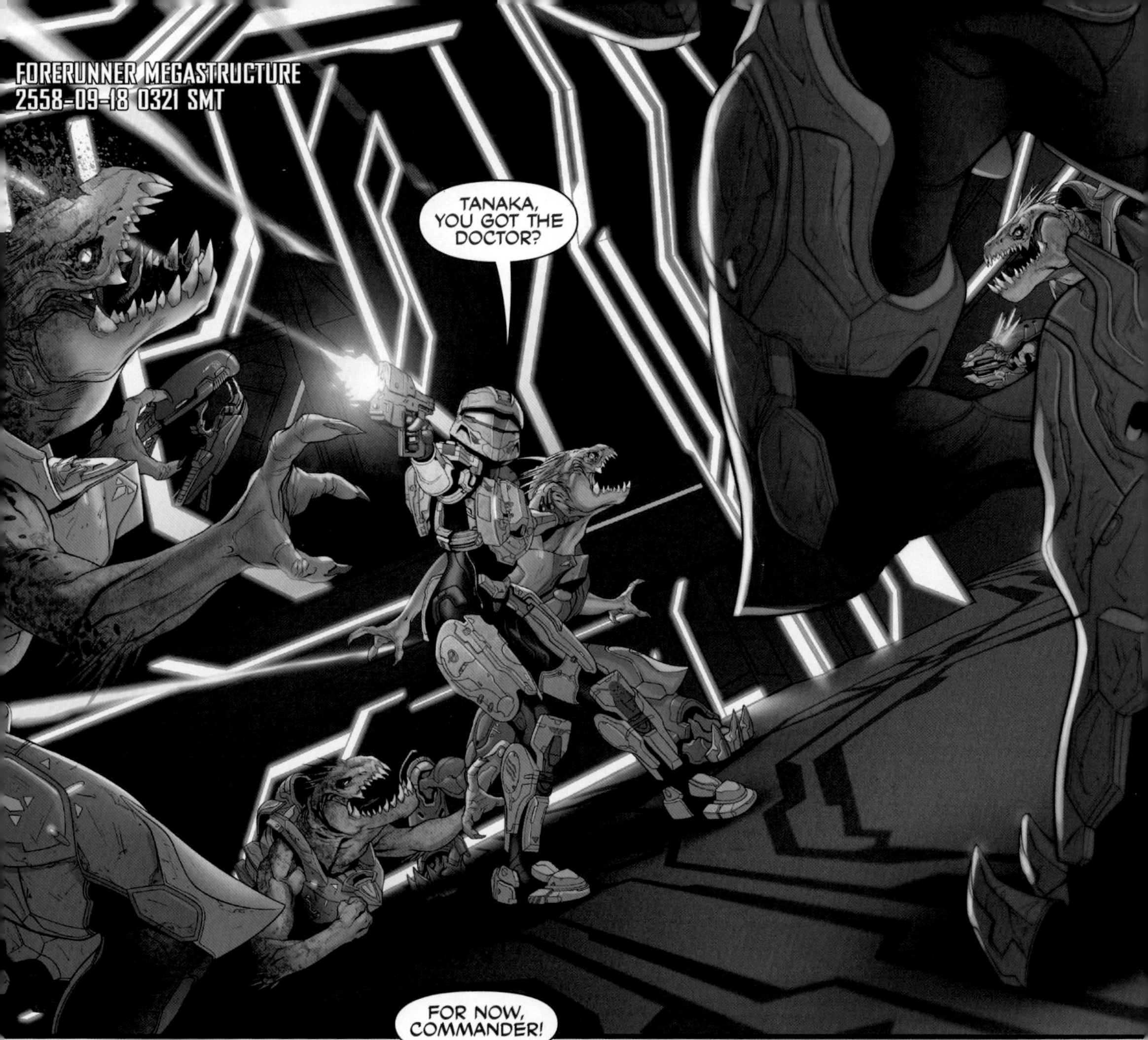
FORERUNNER MEGASTRUCTURE
2558-09-18 0321 SMT
TANAKA, YOU GOT THE DOCTOR?

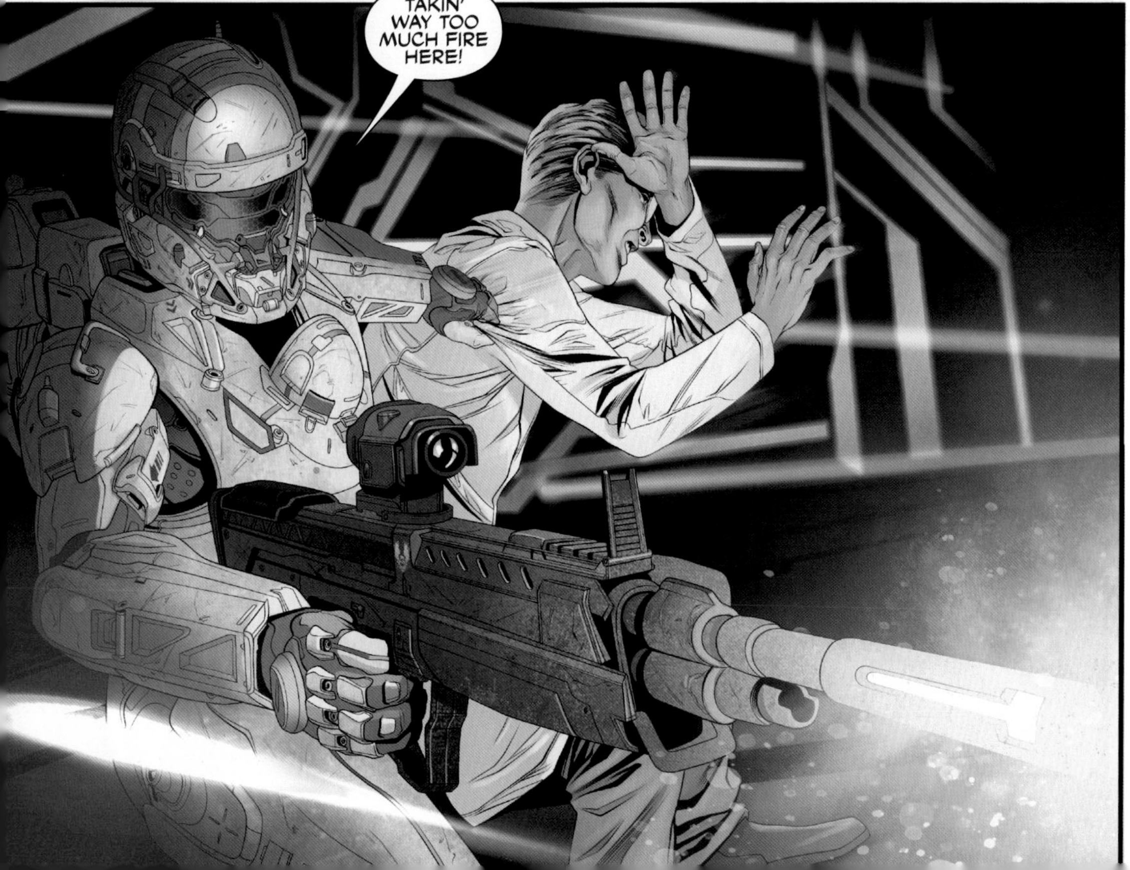
FOR NOW, COMMANDER!
TAKIN' WAY TOO MUCH FIRE HERE!

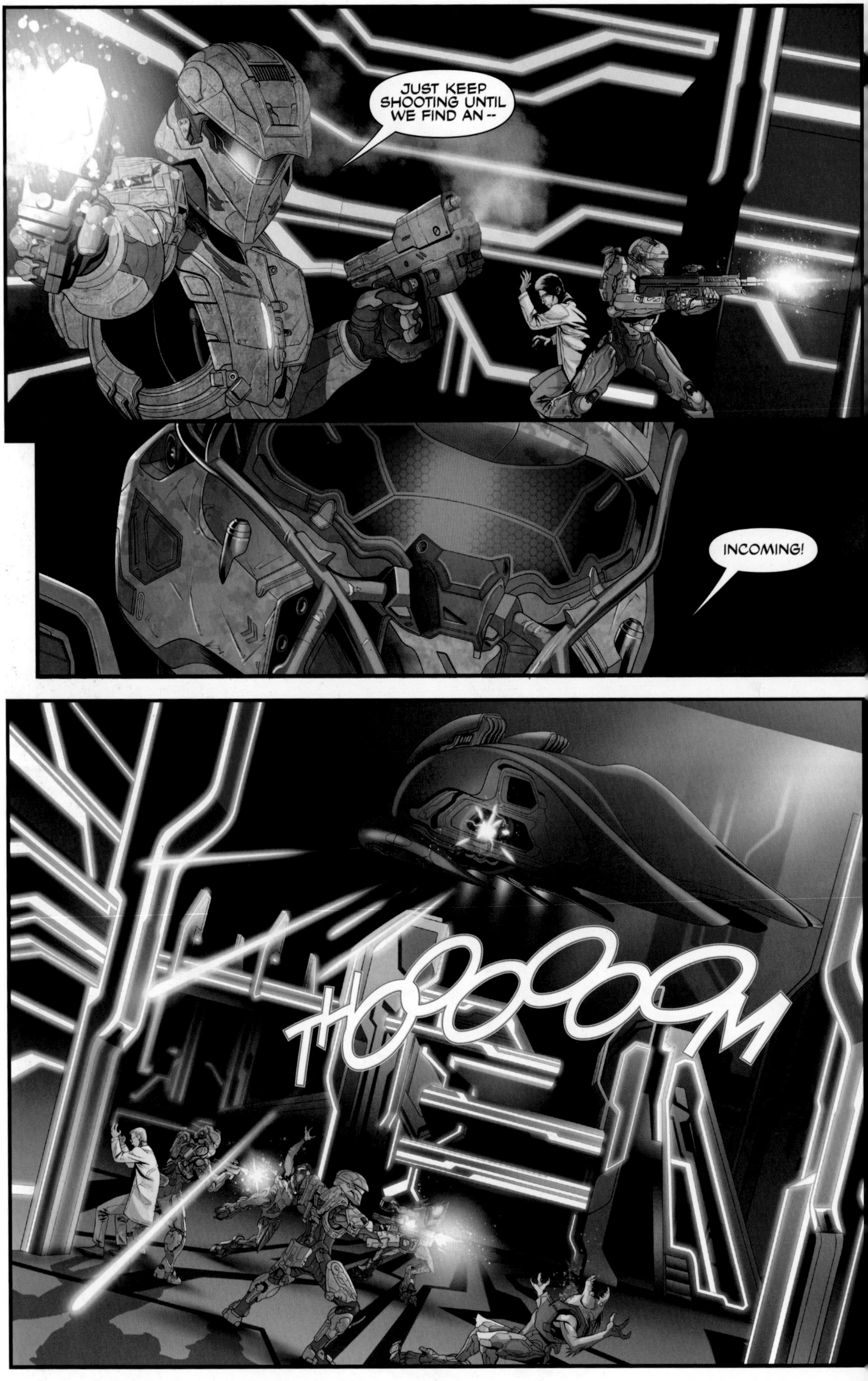
JUST KEEP SHOOTING UNTIL WE FIND AN --
INCOMING!
THOOOOOM

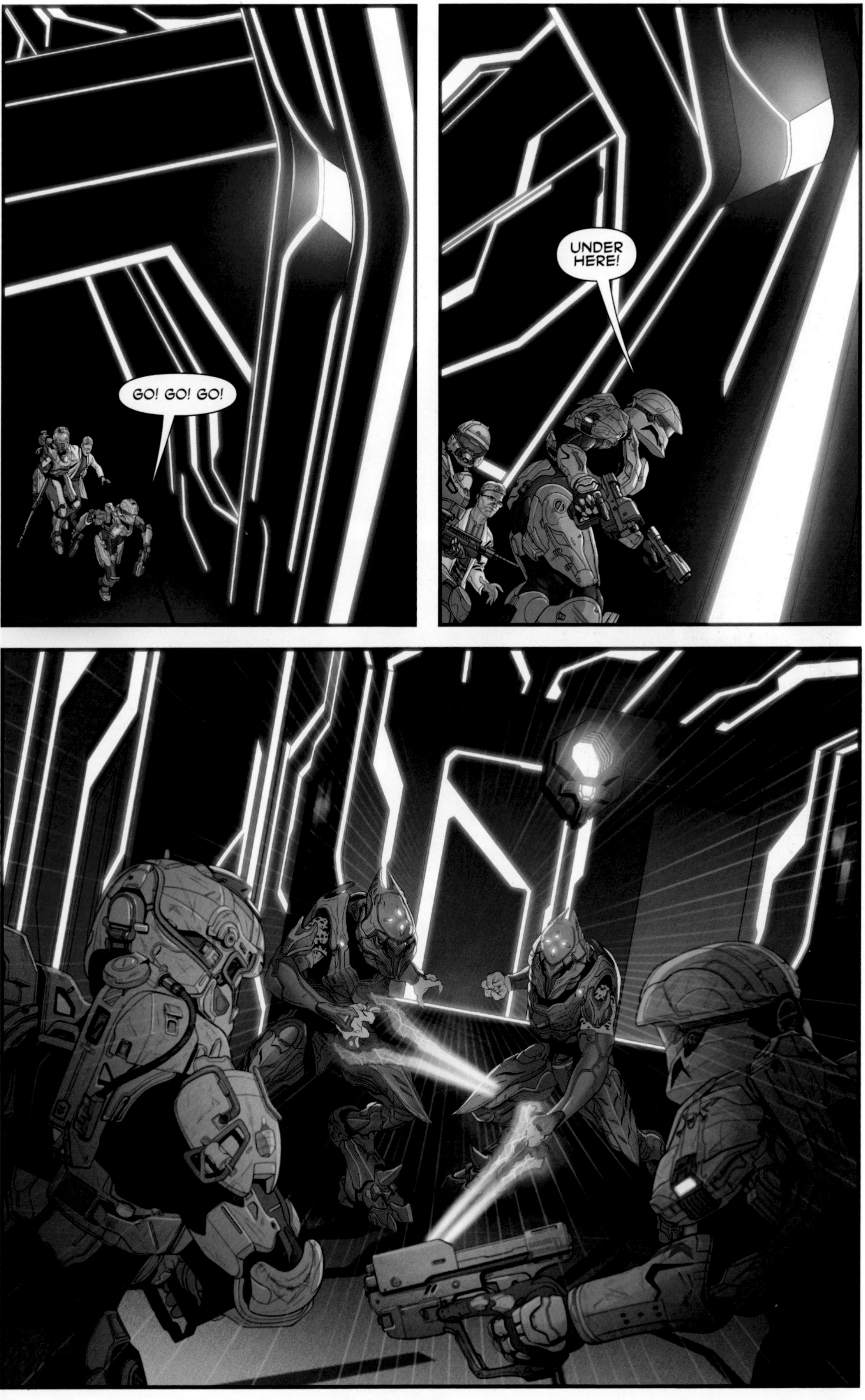
GO! GO! GO!
UNDER HERE!

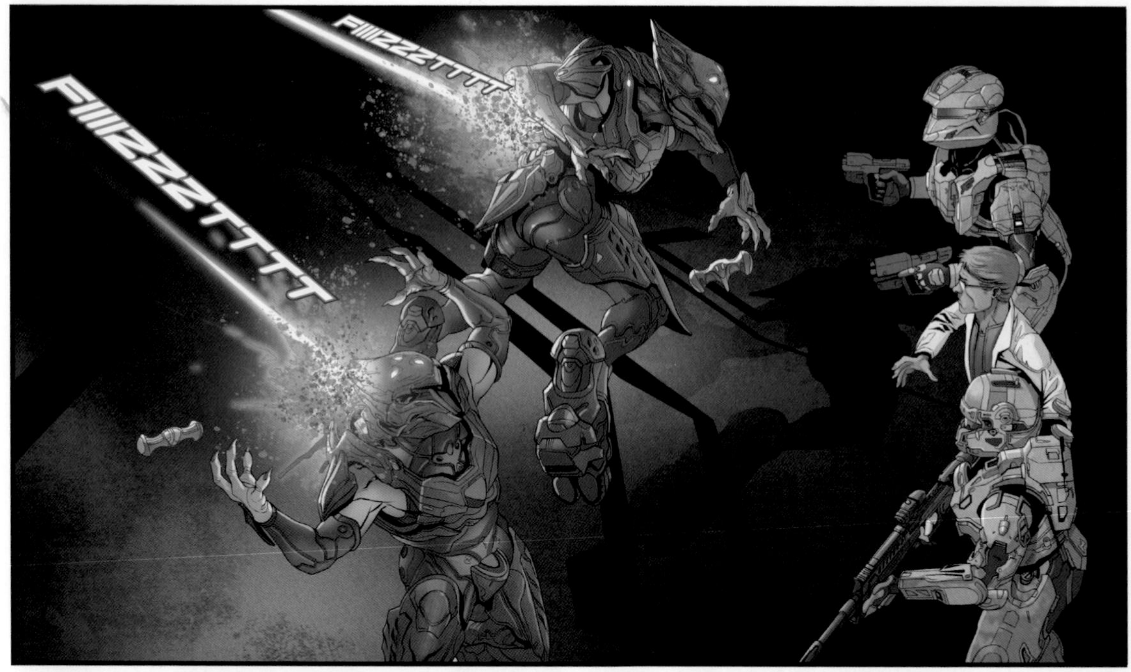
FIIIZZZTTTT
FIIIZZZTTTTT

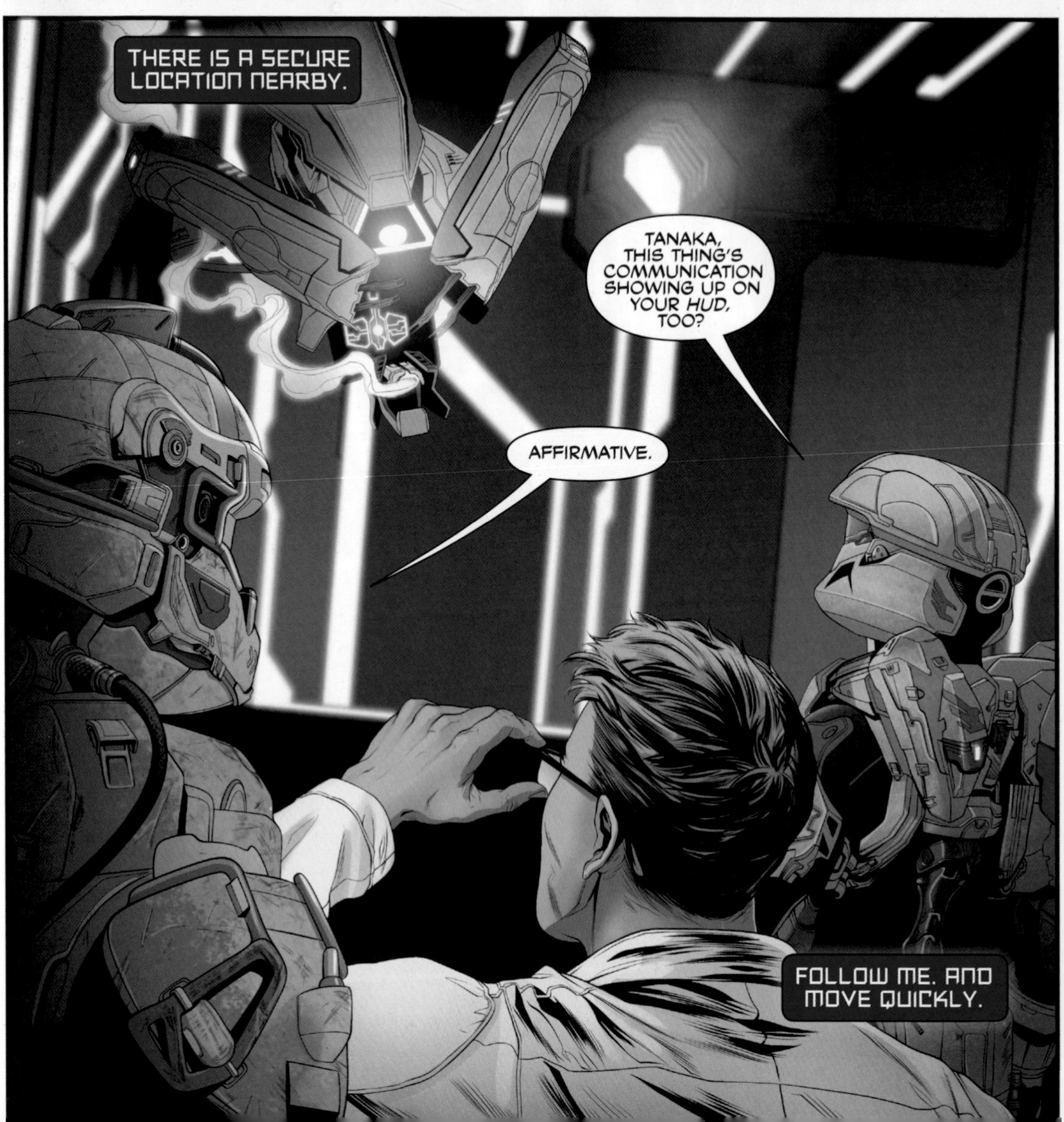
THERE IS A SECURE LOCATION NEARBY.
TANAKA, THIS THING'S COMMUNICATION SHOWING UP ON YOUR *HUD*, TOO?
AFFIRMATIVE.
FOLLOW ME. AND MOVE QUICKLY.

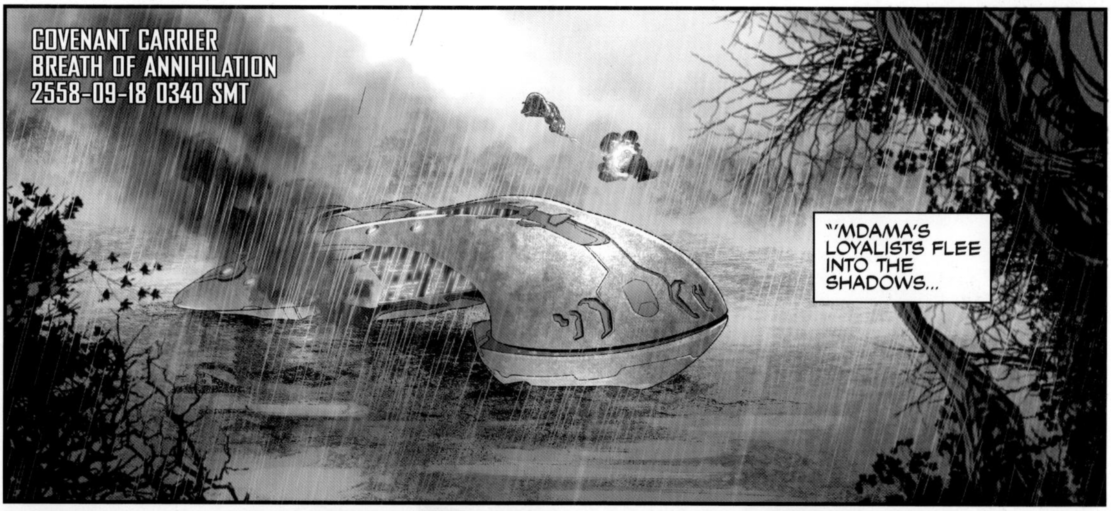
COVENANT CARRIER
BREATH OF ANNIHILATION
2558-09-18 0340 SMT
"'MDAMA'S LOYALISTS FLEE INTO THE SHADOWS...

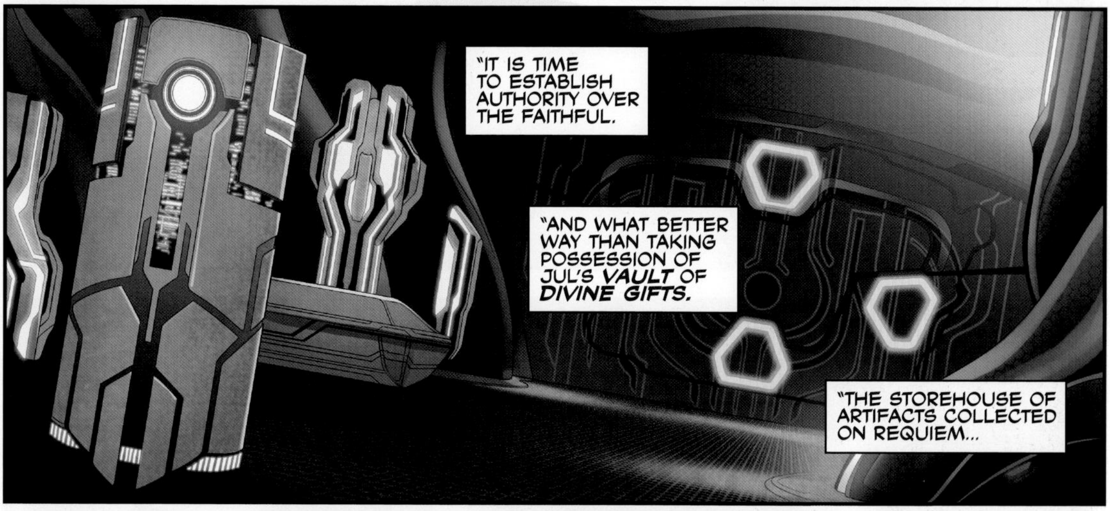
"IT IS TIME TO ESTABLISH AUTHORITY OVER THE FAITHFUL.
"AND WHAT BETTER WAY THAN TAKING POSSESSION OF JUL'S VAULT OF DIVINE GIFTS.
"THE STOREHOUSE OF ARTIFACTS COLLECTED ON REQUIEM...

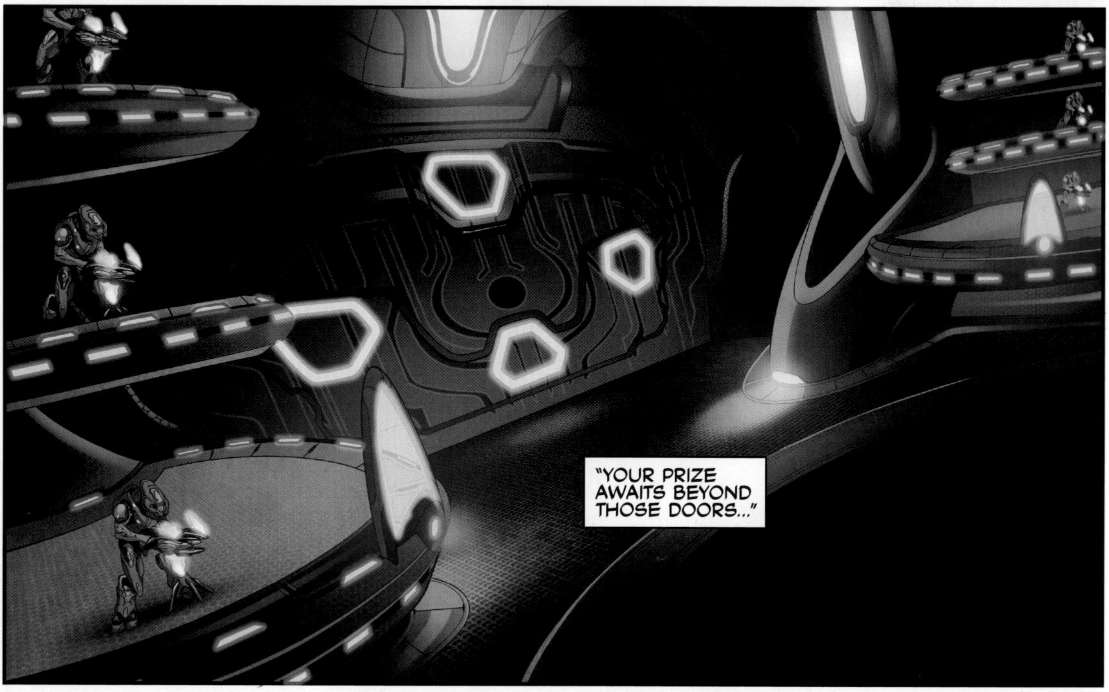
"YOUR PRIZE AWAITS BEYOND THOSE DOORS..."

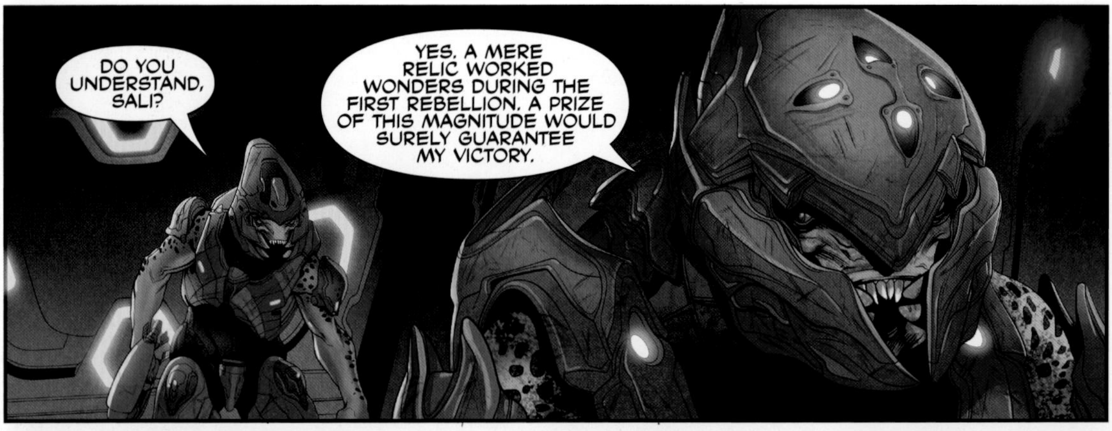
DO YOU UNDERSTAND, SALI?
YES. A MERE RELIC WORKED WONDERS DURING THE FIRST REBELLION. A PRIZE OF THIS MAGNITUDE WOULD SURELY GUARANTEE MY VICTORY.

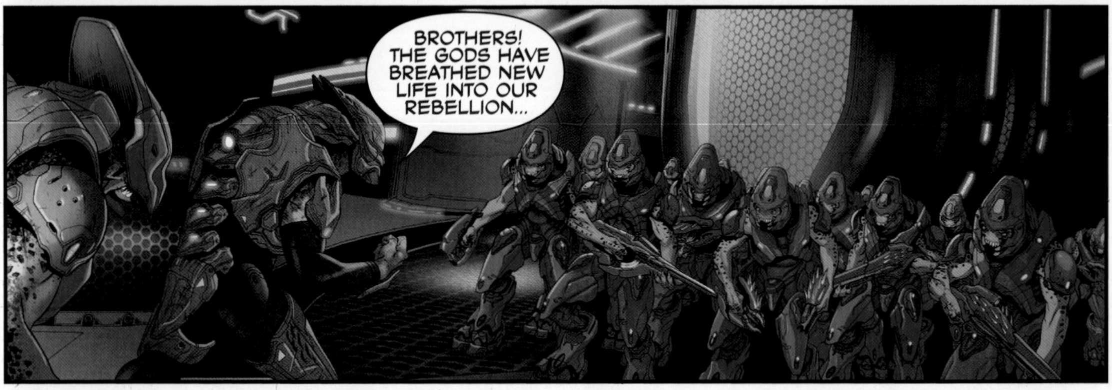
BROTHERS! THE GODS HAVE BREATHED NEW LIFE INTO OUR REBELLION...

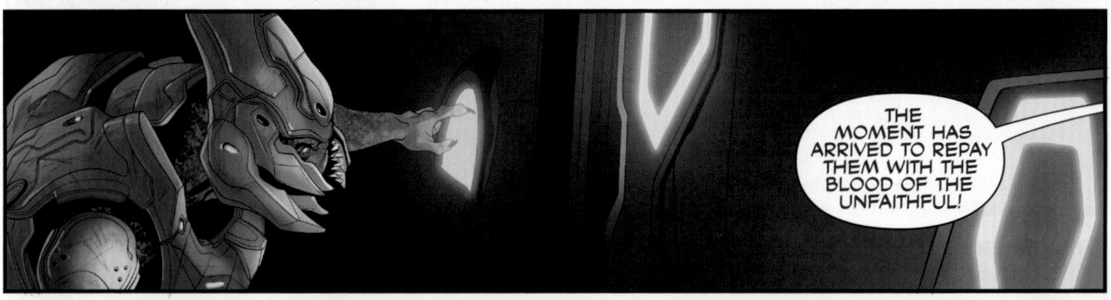
THE MOMENT HAS ARRIVED TO REPAY THEM WITH THE BLOOD OF THE UNFAITHFUL!

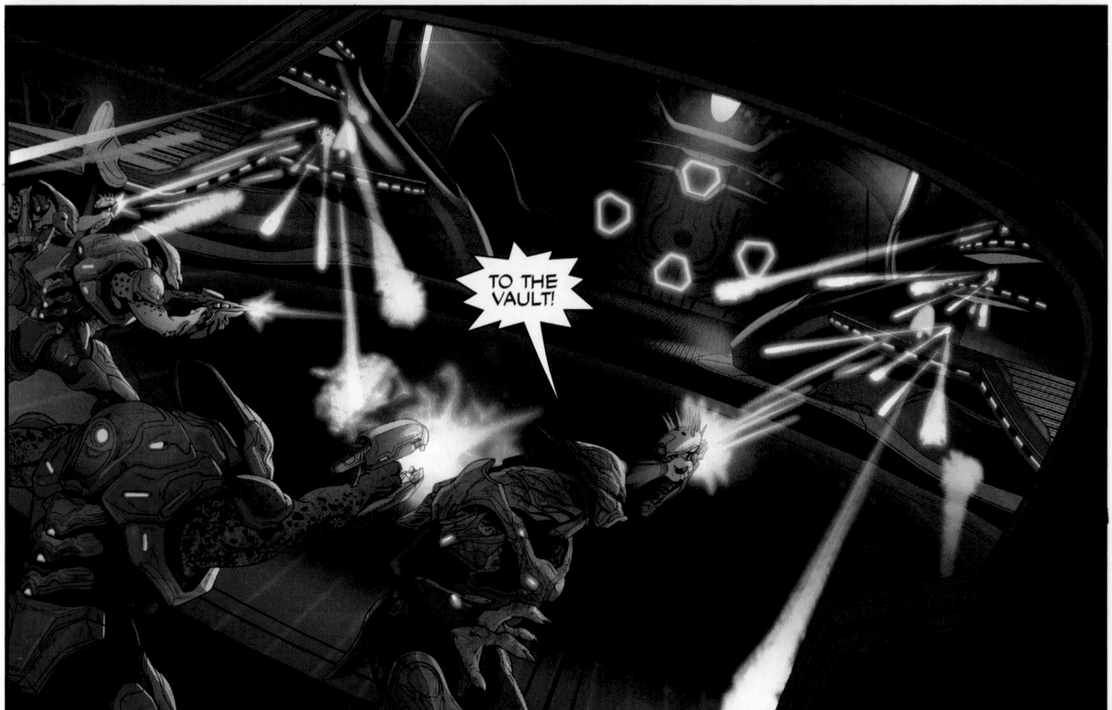
TO THE VAULT!

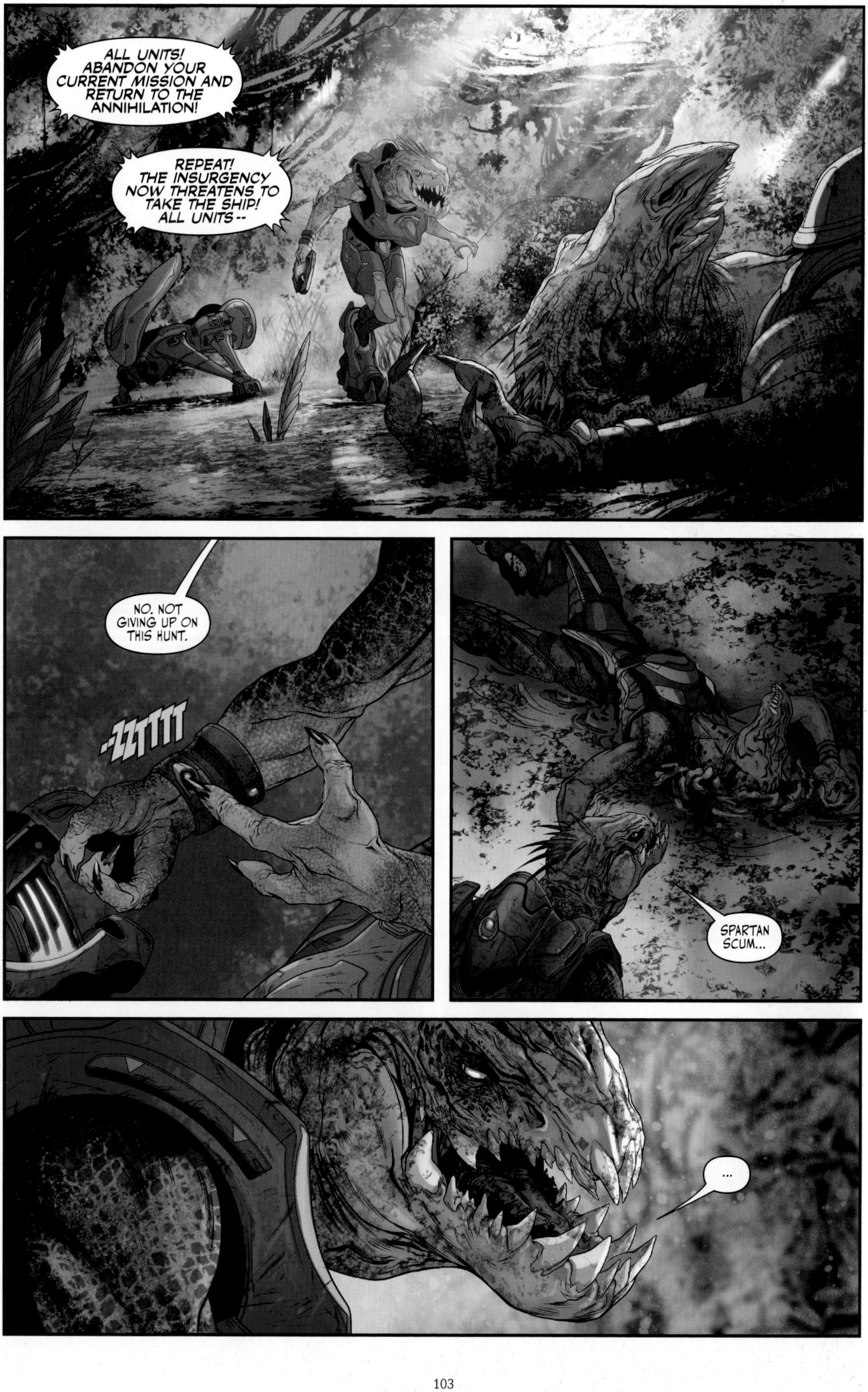
ALL UNITS! ABANDON YOUR CURRENT MISSION AND RETURN TO THE ANNIHILATION!
REPEAT! THE INSURGENCY NOW THREATENS TO TAKE THE SHIP! ALL UNITS--
NO. NOT GIVING UP ON THIS HUNT.
--ZZTTTT
SPARTAN SCUM...
...

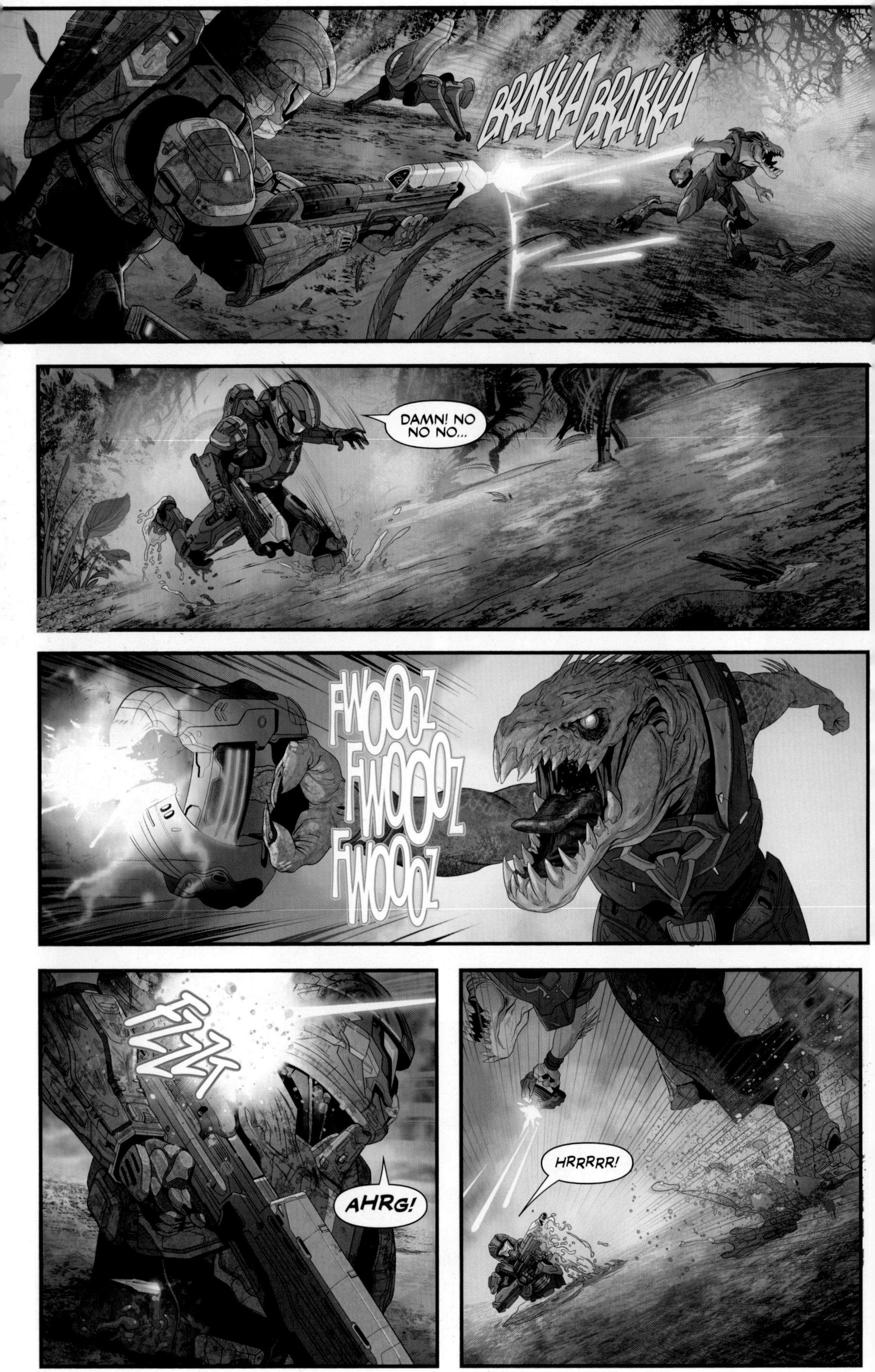
BRAKKA BRAKKA
DAMN! NO NO NO...
FWOOOZ
FWOOOZ
FWOOOZ
FZZK
AHRG!
HRRRRR!

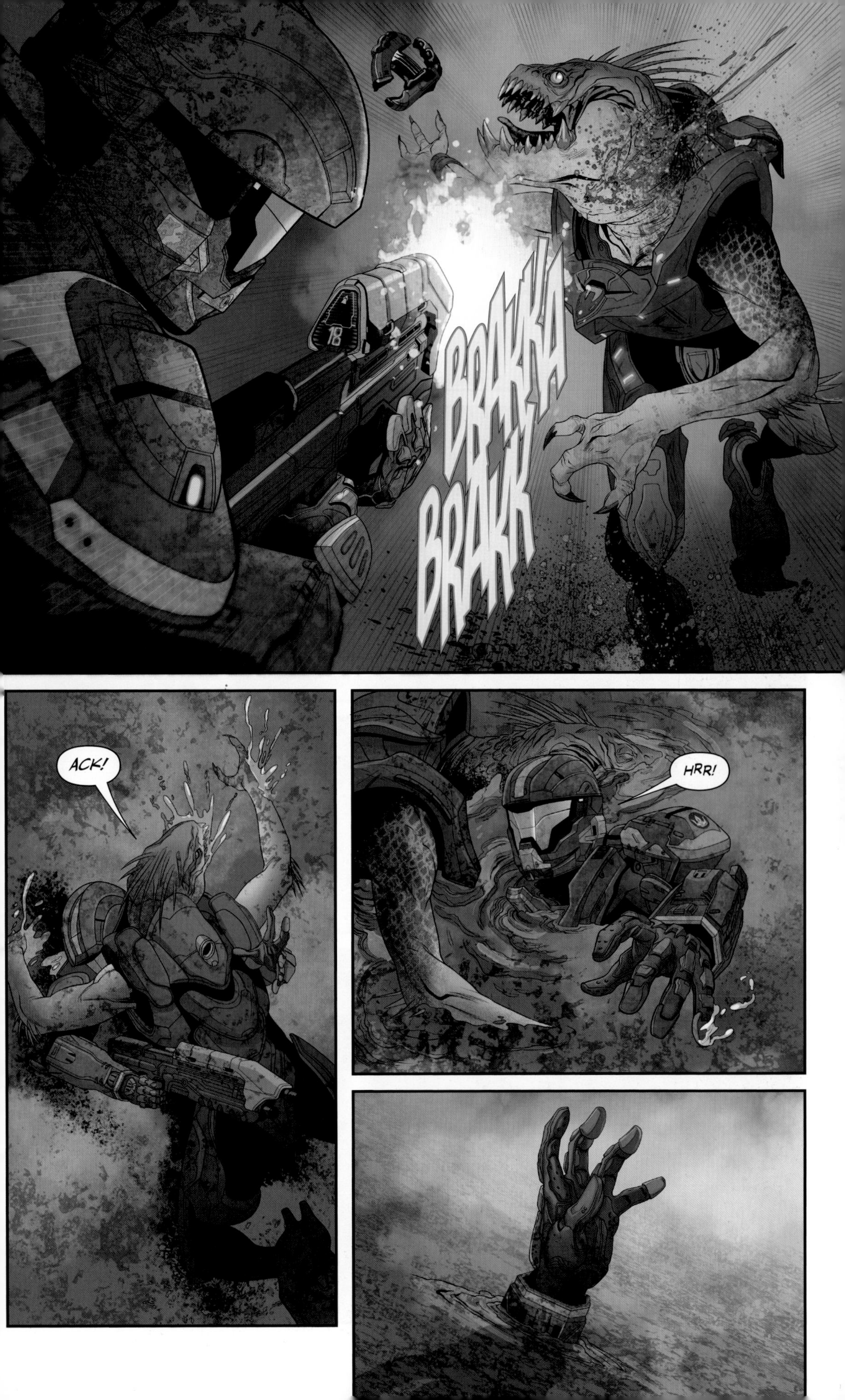
BRAKKA
BRAKK
ACK!
HRR!

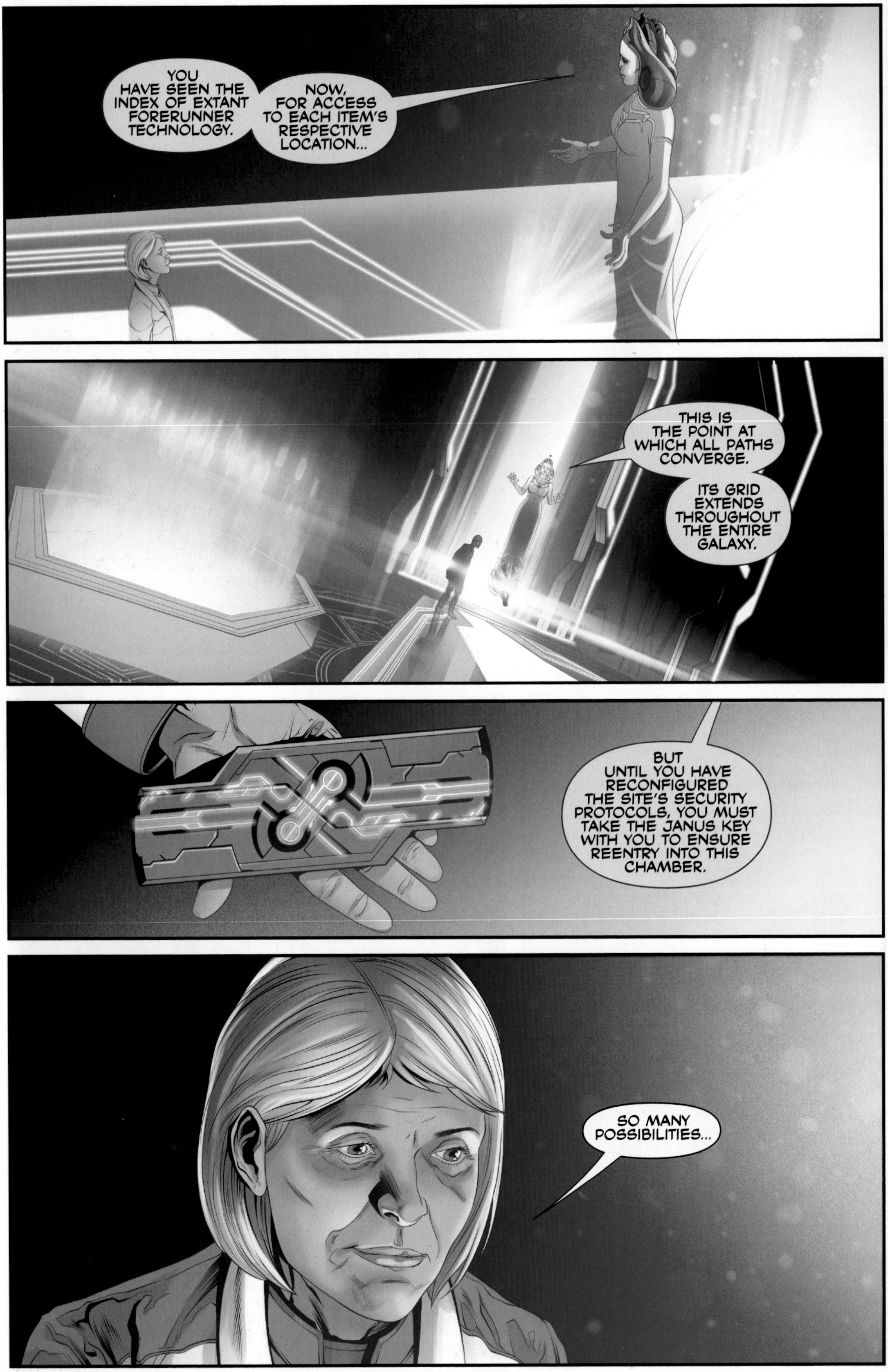
YOU HAVE SEEN THE INDEX OF EXTANT FORERUNNER TECHNOLOGY.
NOW, FOR ACCESS TO EACH ITEM'S RESPECTIVE LOCATION...
THIS IS THE POINT AT WHICH ALL PATHS CONVERGE.
ITS GRID EXTENDS THROUGHOUT THE ENTIRE GALAXY.
BUT UNTIL YOU HAVE RECONFIGURED THE SITE'S SECURITY PROTOCOLS, YOU MUST TAKE THE JANUS KEY WITH YOU TO ENSURE REENTRY INTO THIS CHAMBER.
SO MANY POSSIBILITIES...

FOR AN EXPEDIENT STARTING POINT, I SUGGEST ACTIVATING THE DESIGN SEEDS THAT LIE DORMANT *HERE,* HIDDEN WITHIN THESE TWELVE MOONS...

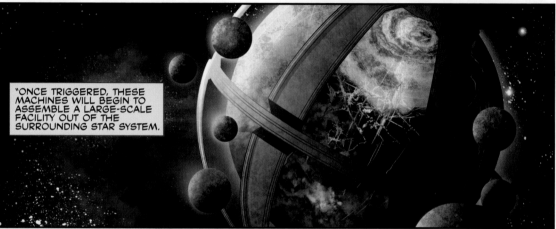

"ONCE TRIGGERED, THESE MACHINES WILL BEGIN TO ASSEMBLE A LARGE-SCALE FACILITY OUT OF THE SURROUNDING STAR SYSTEM.

"ONE OF THE MOONS ALSO CONTAINS A FLEET OF AUTOMATED WARSHIPS, AVAILABLE FOR EXPEDITION AND DEFENSE."

AS I STATED BEFORE, THIS IS THE CULMINATION OF A PLAN SET IN MOTION THOUSANDS OF LIFETIMES AGO.

I LEAVE IT TO YOU, CATHERINE HALSEY, TO PREPARE HUMANKIND FOR THIS ENORMOUS LEAP...

JUST SET IT UP. COMMUNICATIONS WILL BE CONVERTED TO AUDIO NOW FOR GLASSMAN.

I WANNA KNOW HOW THE HELL JUL'S ARMY MANAGED TO JUST FREE ITSELF?

I MUST HAVE CAUSED IT. BY FAILING THE CUSTODIAN'S TEST.

NO...

THE EXAMINATION WAS PREMATURELY ABORTED WHEN ONE OF THE PARTICIPANTS, IN AN ACT OF GRAVE TRANSGRESSION, TOOK UNAUTHORIZED CONTROL OF THE SYSTEM.

ISN'T THAT PERFECT? MIDDLE OF AN ETHICS TEST AND HALSEY UP AND MURDERS THE ADMINISTRATOR.

WHERE IS THE CUSTODIAN NOW?

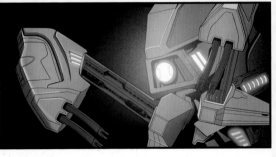

I AM THE CUSTODIAN.

AS A FAIL-SAFE, A SMALL FRAGMENT OF MY CONSCIOUSNESS WAS SET UP TO AUTOMATICALLY TRANSFER INTO THIS SENTINEL IN THE EVENT OF SYSTEM FAILURE.

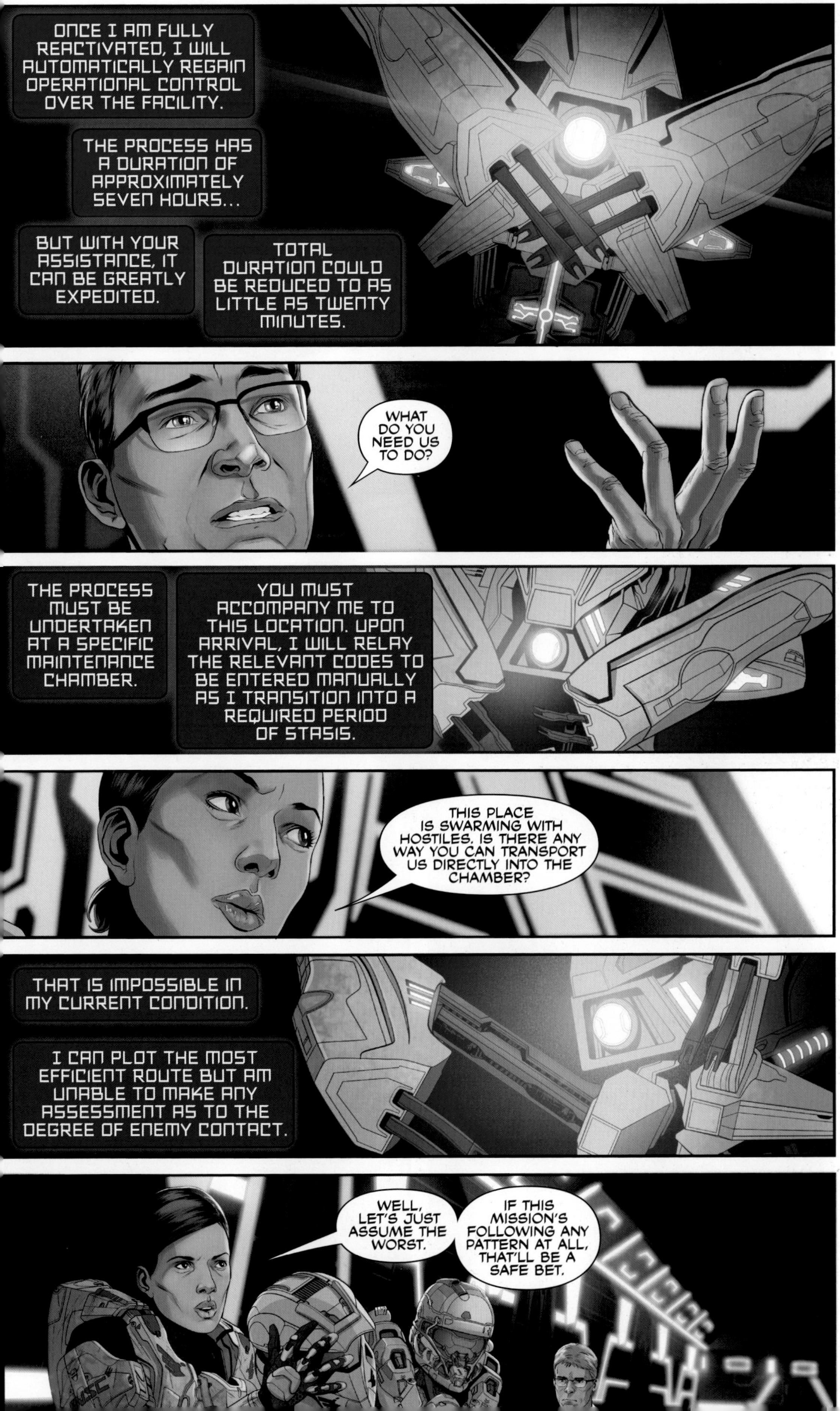
ONCE I AM FULLY REACTIVATED, I WILL AUTOMATICALLY REGAIN OPERATIONAL CONTROL OVER THE FACILITY.
THE PROCESS HAS A DURATION OF APPROXIMATELY SEVEN HOURS...
BUT WITH YOUR ASSISTANCE, IT CAN BE GREATLY EXPEDITED.
TOTAL DURATION COULD BE REDUCED TO AS LITTLE AS TWENTY MINUTES.
WHAT DO YOU NEED US TO DO?
THE PROCESS MUST BE UNDERTAKEN AT A SPECIFIC MAINTENANCE CHAMBER.
YOU MUST ACCOMPANY ME TO THIS LOCATION. UPON ARRIVAL, I WILL RELAY THE RELEVANT CODES TO BE ENTERED MANUALLY AS I TRANSITION INTO A REQUIRED PERIOD OF STASIS.
THIS PLACE IS SWARMING WITH HOSTILES. IS THERE ANY WAY YOU CAN TRANSPORT US DIRECTLY INTO THE CHAMBER?
THAT IS IMPOSSIBLE IN MY CURRENT CONDITION.
I CAN PLOT THE MOST EFFICIENT ROUTE BUT AM UNABLE TO MAKE ANY ASSESSMENT AS TO THE DEGREE OF ENEMY CONTACT.
WELL, LET'S JUST ASSUME THE WORST.
IF THIS MISSION'S FOLLOWING ANY PATTERN AT ALL, THAT'LL BE A SAFE BET.

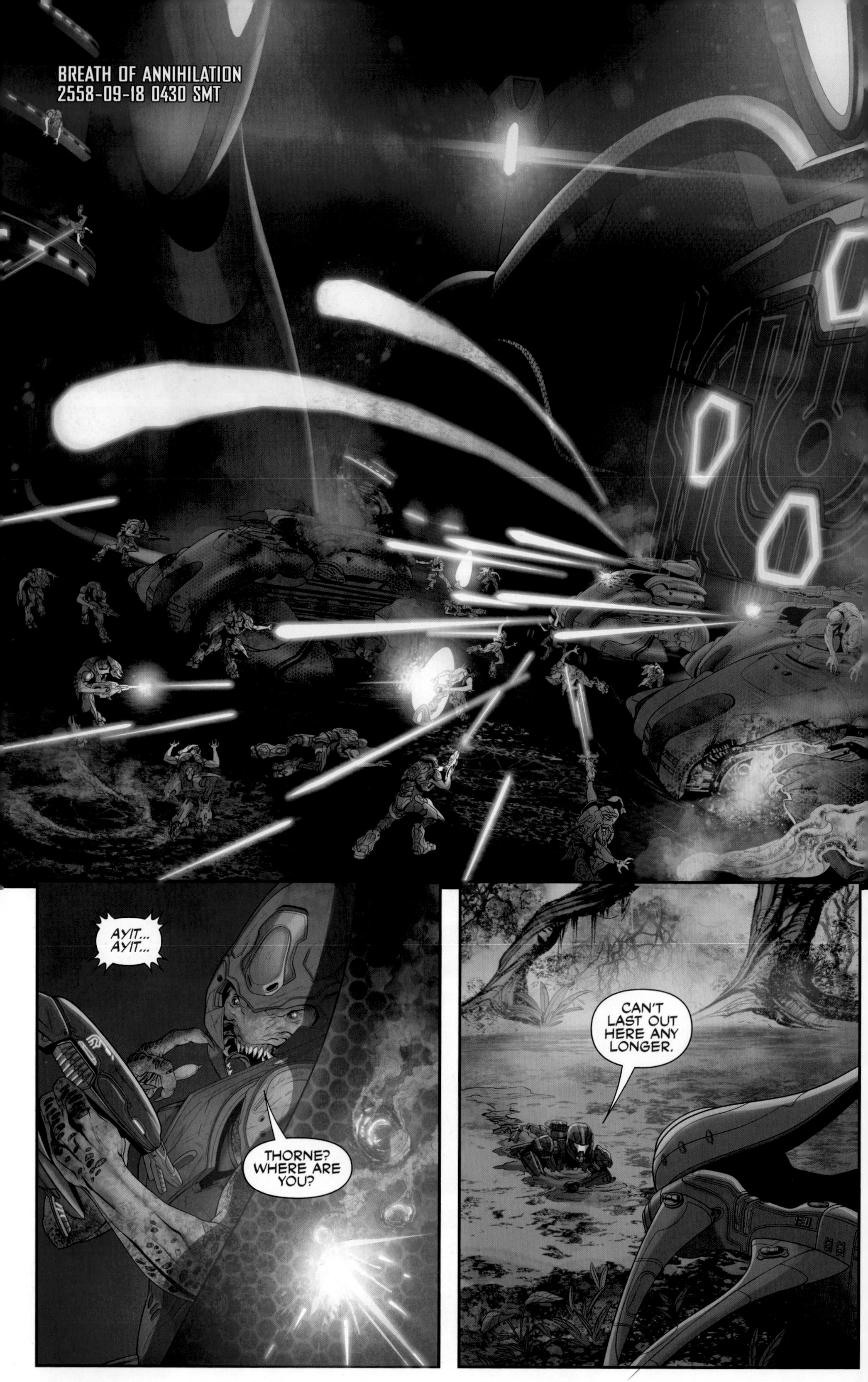
BREATH OF ANNIHILATION
2558-09-18 0430 SMT
AYIT... AYIT...
THORNE? WHERE ARE YOU?
CAN'T LAST OUT HERE ANY LONGER.

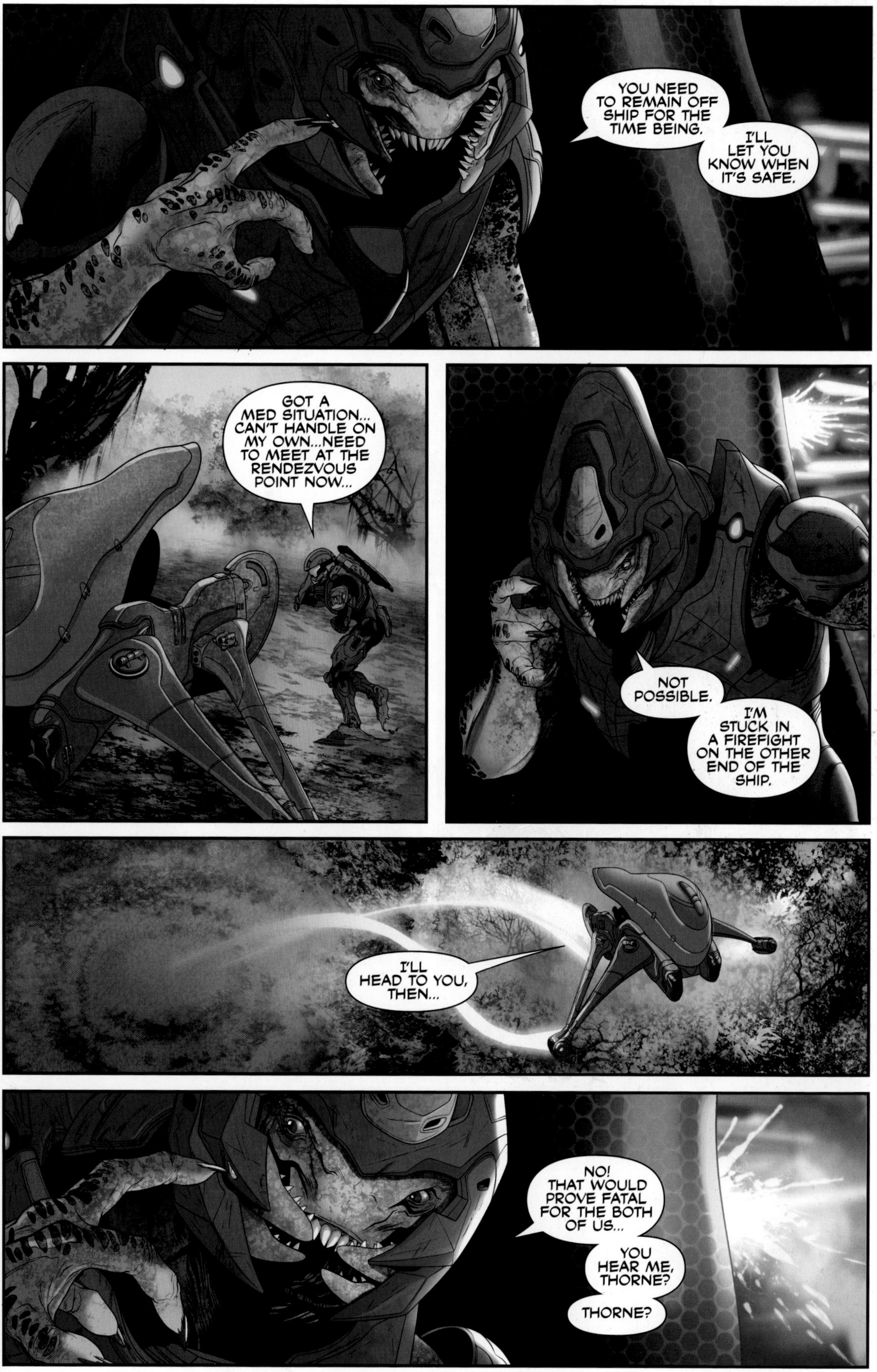
YOU NEED TO REMAIN OFF SHIP FOR THE TIME BEING.
I'LL LET YOU KNOW WHEN IT'S SAFE.
GOT A MED SITUATION... CAN'T HANDLE ON MY OWN...NEED TO MEET AT THE RENDEZVOUS POINT NOW...
NOT POSSIBLE.
I'M STUCK IN A FIREFIGHT ON THE OTHER END OF THE SHIP.
I'LL HEAD TO YOU, THEN...
NO! THAT WOULD PROVE FATAL FOR THE BOTH OF US...
YOU HEAR ME, THORNE?
THORNE?

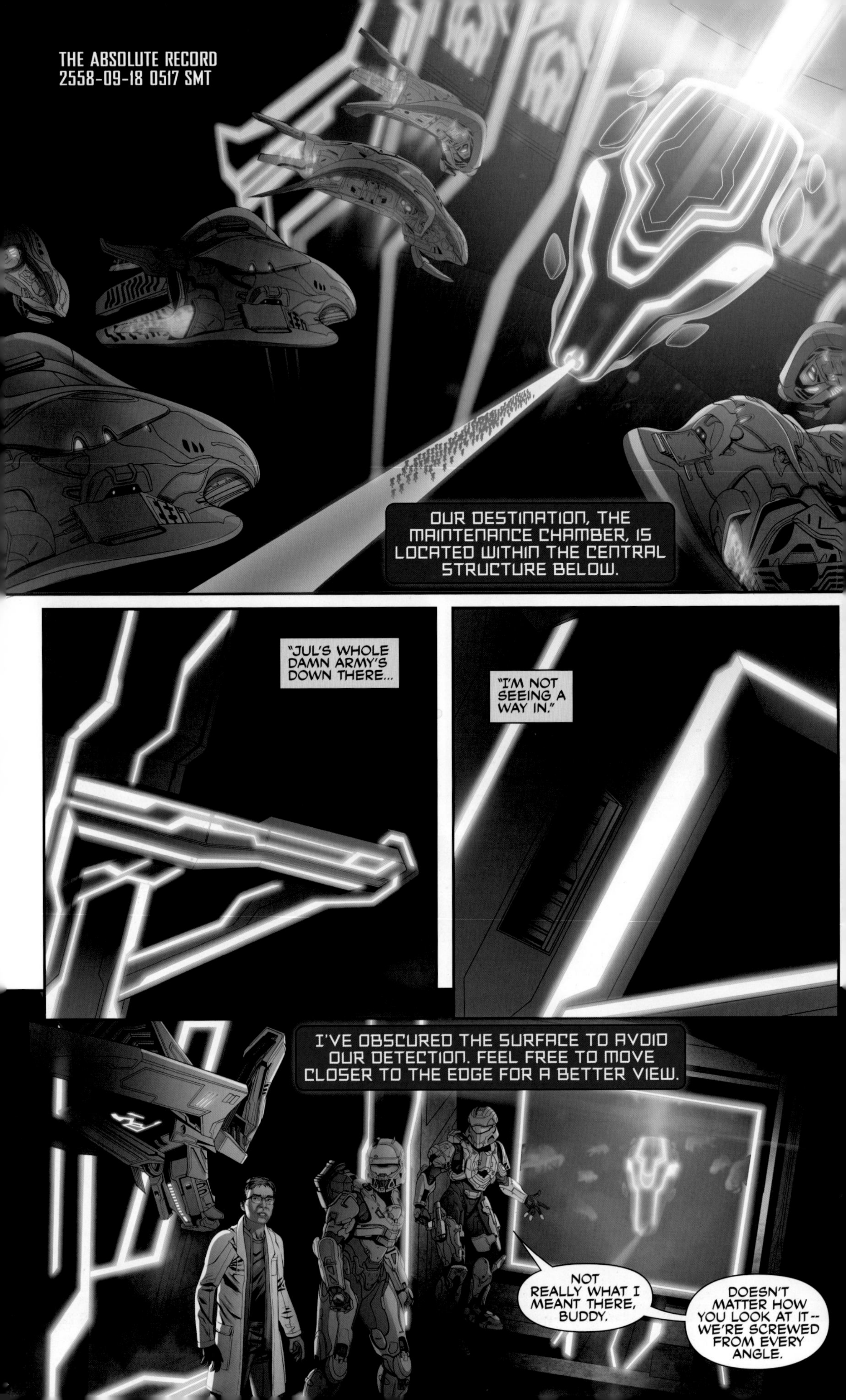
THE ABSOLUTE RECORD
2558-09-18 0517 SMT
OUR DESTINATION, THE MAINTENANCE CHAMBER, IS LOCATED WITHIN THE CENTRAL STRUCTURE BELOW.
"JUL'S WHOLE DAMN ARMY'S DOWN THERE...
"I'M NOT SEEING A WAY IN."
I'VE OBSCURED THE SURFACE TO AVOID OUR DETECTION. FEEL FREE TO MOVE CLOSER TO THE EDGE FOR A BETTER VIEW.
NOT REALLY WHAT I MEANT THERE, BUDDY.
DOESN'T MATTER HOW YOU LOOK AT IT-- WE'RE SCREWED FROM EVERY ANGLE.

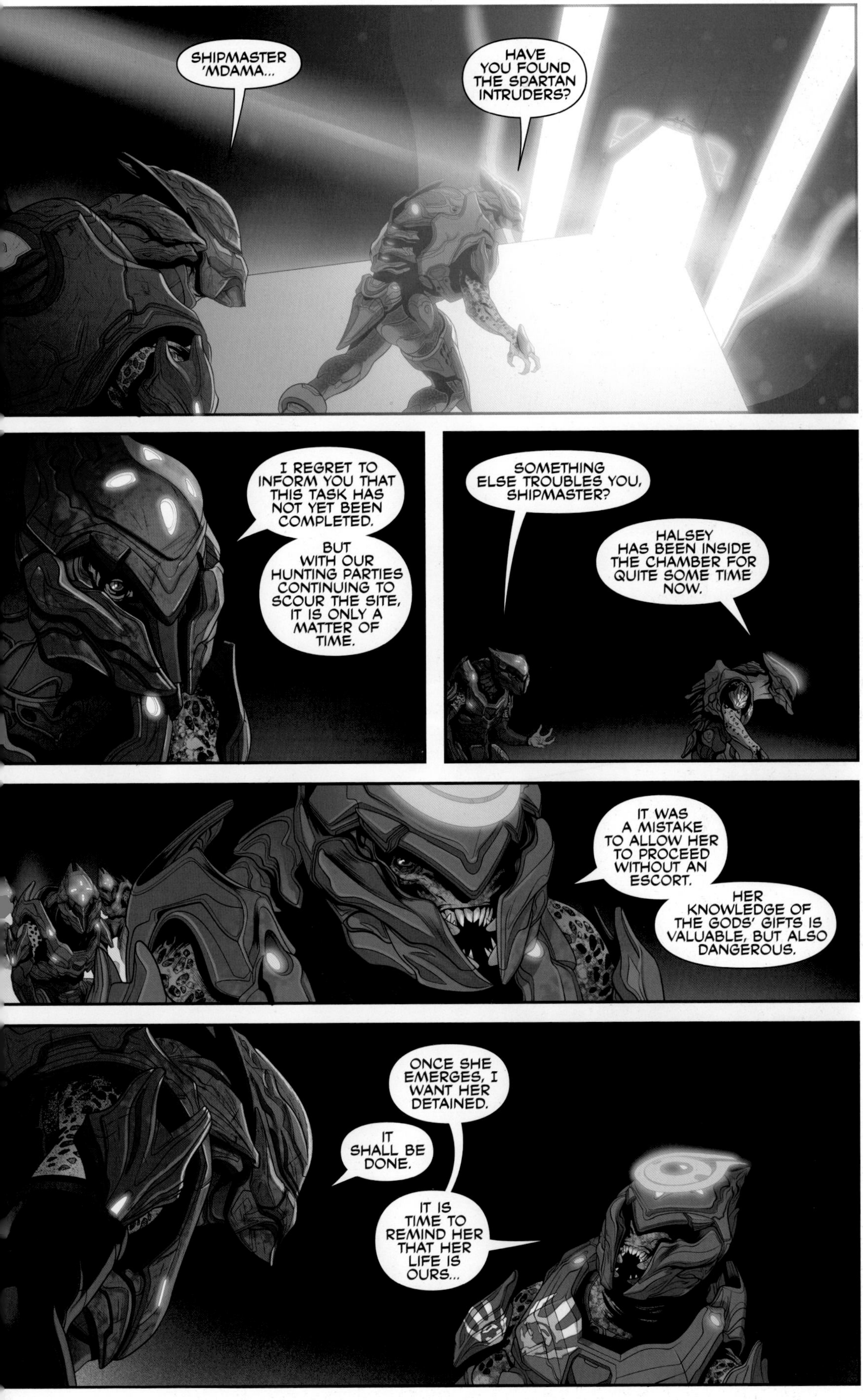
SHIPMASTER 'MDAMA...
HAVE YOU FOUND THE SPARTAN INTRUDERS?
I REGRET TO INFORM YOU THAT THIS TASK HAS NOT YET BEEN COMPLETED.
BUT WITH OUR HUNTING PARTIES CONTINUING TO SCOUR THE SITE, IT IS ONLY A MATTER OF TIME.
SOMETHING ELSE TROUBLES YOU, SHIPMASTER?
HALSEY HAS BEEN INSIDE THE CHAMBER FOR QUITE SOME TIME NOW.
IT WAS A MISTAKE TO ALLOW HER TO PROCEED WITHOUT AN ESCORT.
HER KNOWLEDGE OF THE GODS' GIFTS IS VALUABLE, BUT ALSO DANGEROUS.
ONCE SHE EMERGES, I WANT HER DETAINED.
IT SHALL BE DONE.
IT IS TIME TO REMIND HER THAT HER LIFE IS OURS...

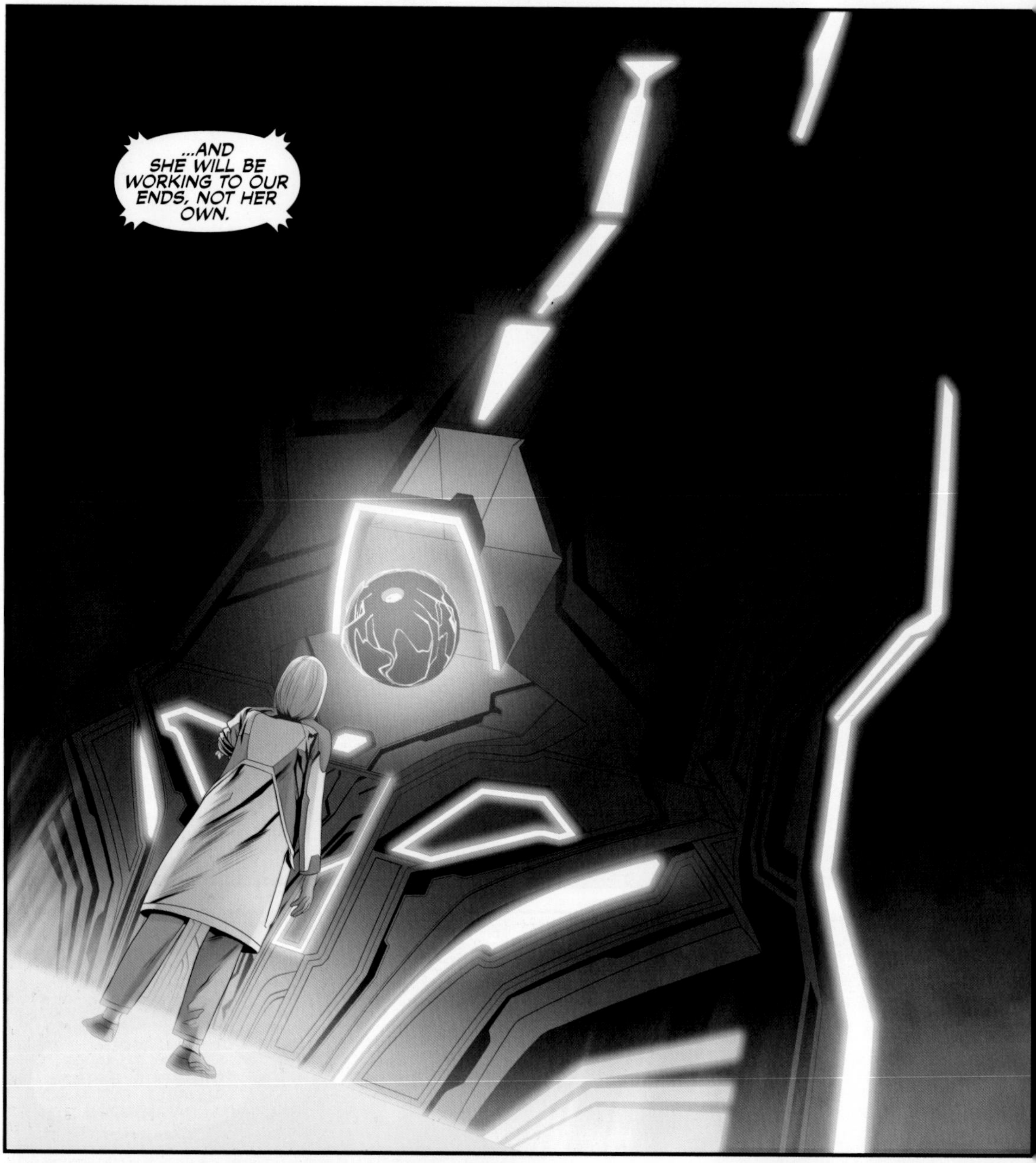
...AND SHE WILL BE WORKING TO OUR ENDS, NOT HER OWN.

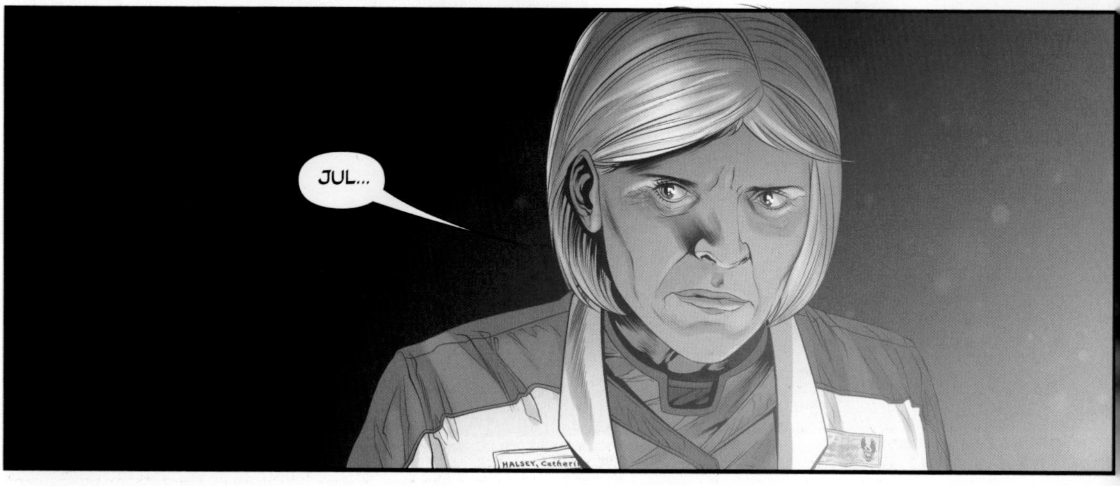
JUL...

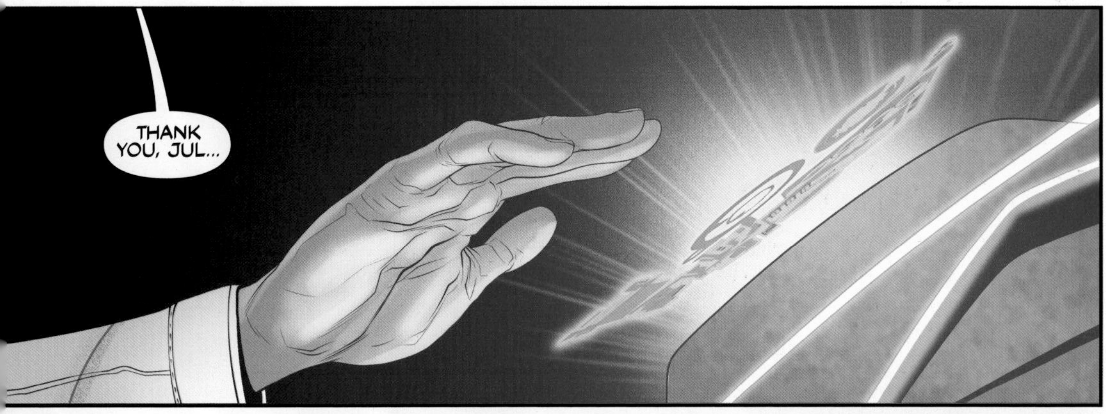
THANK YOU, JUL...

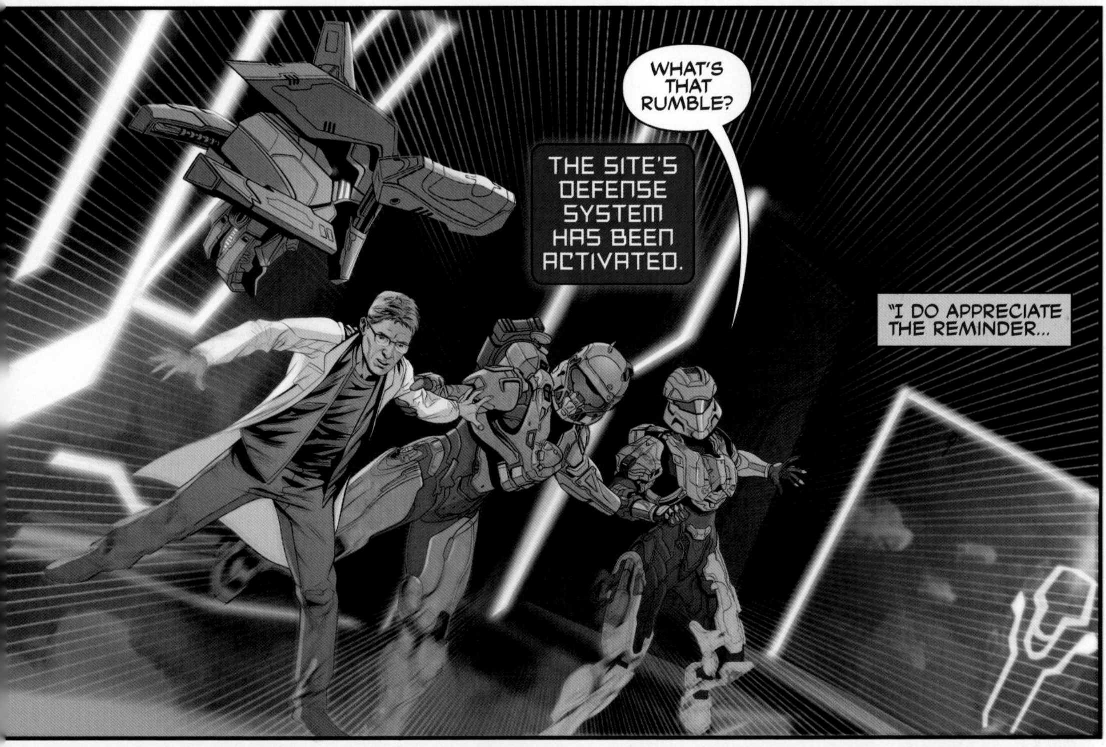
WHAT'S THAT RUMBLE?
THE SITE'S DEFENSE SYSTEM HAS BEEN ACTIVATED.
"I DO APPRECIATE THE REMINDER...

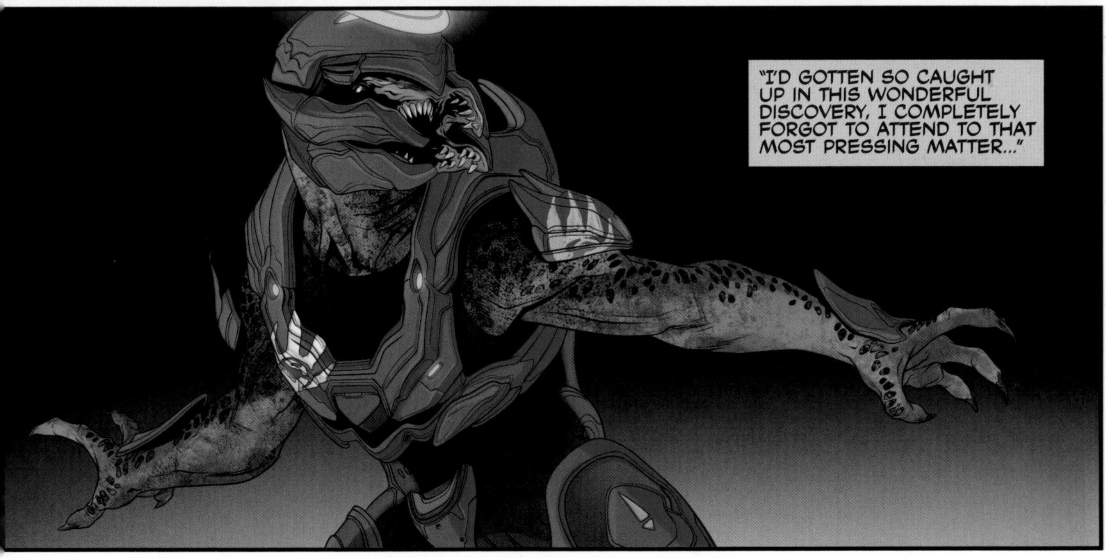
"I'D GOTTEN SO CAUGHT UP IN THIS WONDERFUL DISCOVERY, I COMPLETELY FORGOT TO ATTEND TO THAT MOST PRESSING MATTER..."

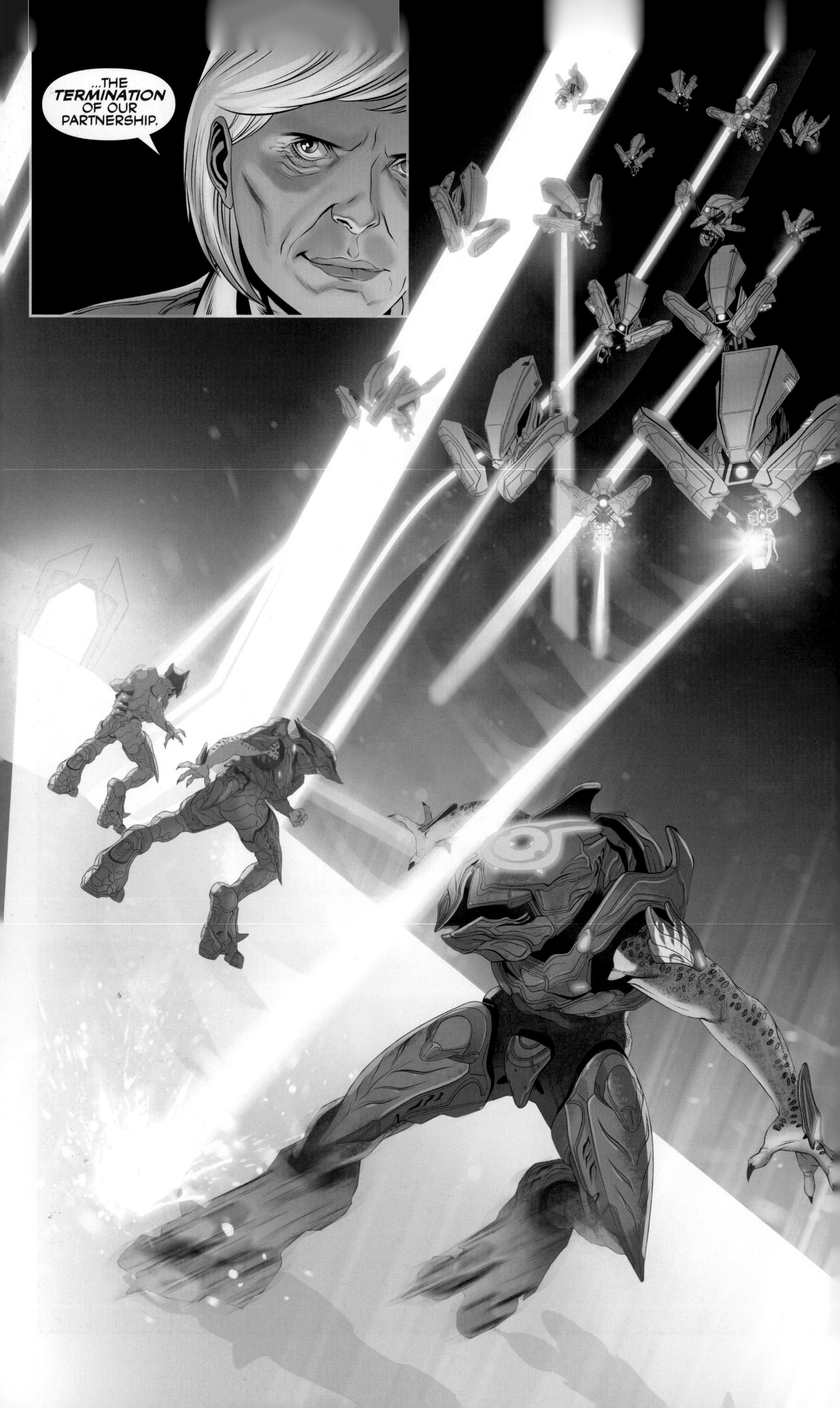
...THE *TERMINATION* OF OUR PARTNERSHIP.

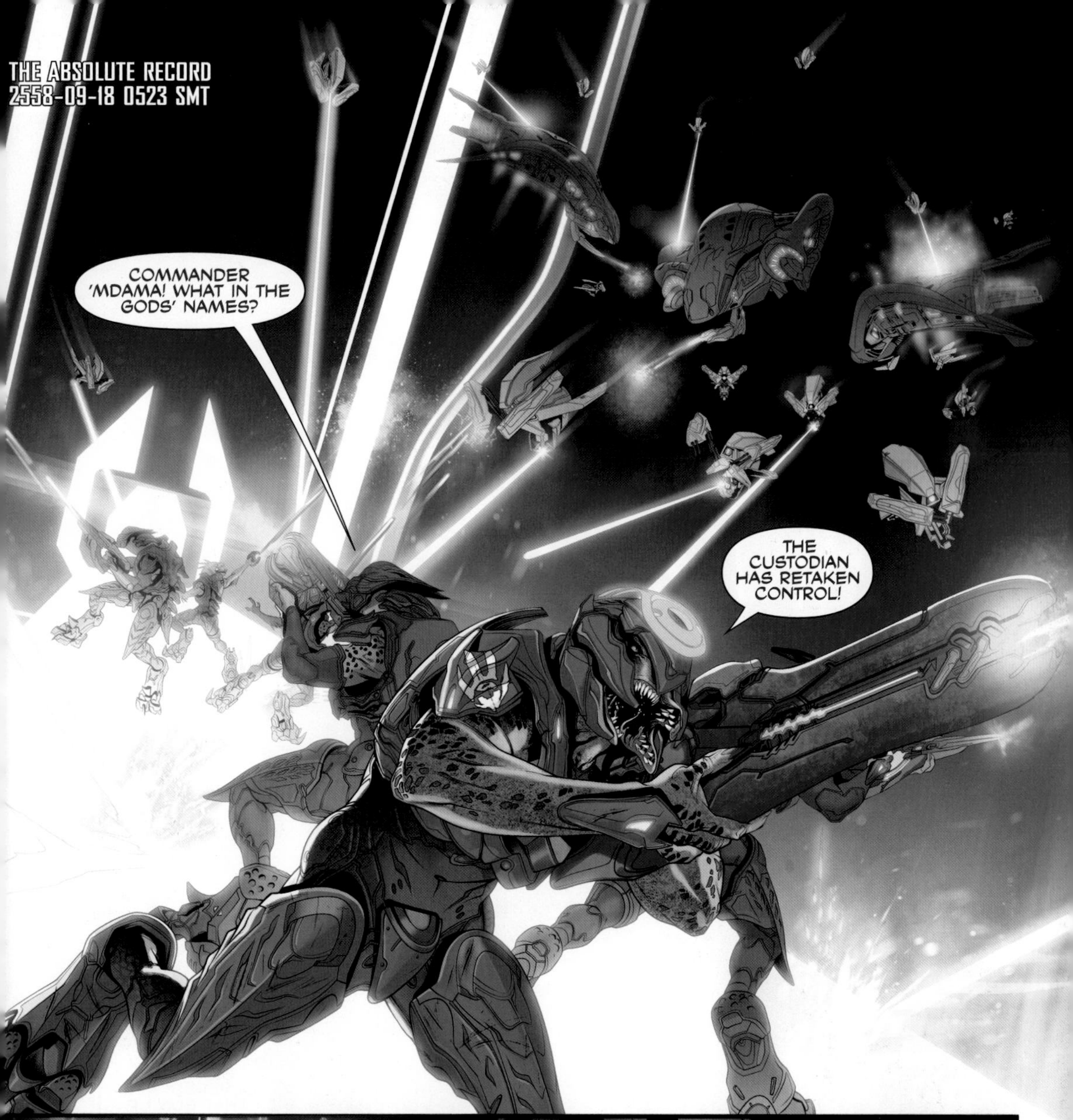
THE ABSOLUTE RECORD
2558-09-18 0523 SMT
COMMANDER 'MDAMA! WHAT IN THE GODS' NAMES?
THE CUSTODIAN HAS RETAKEN CONTROL!

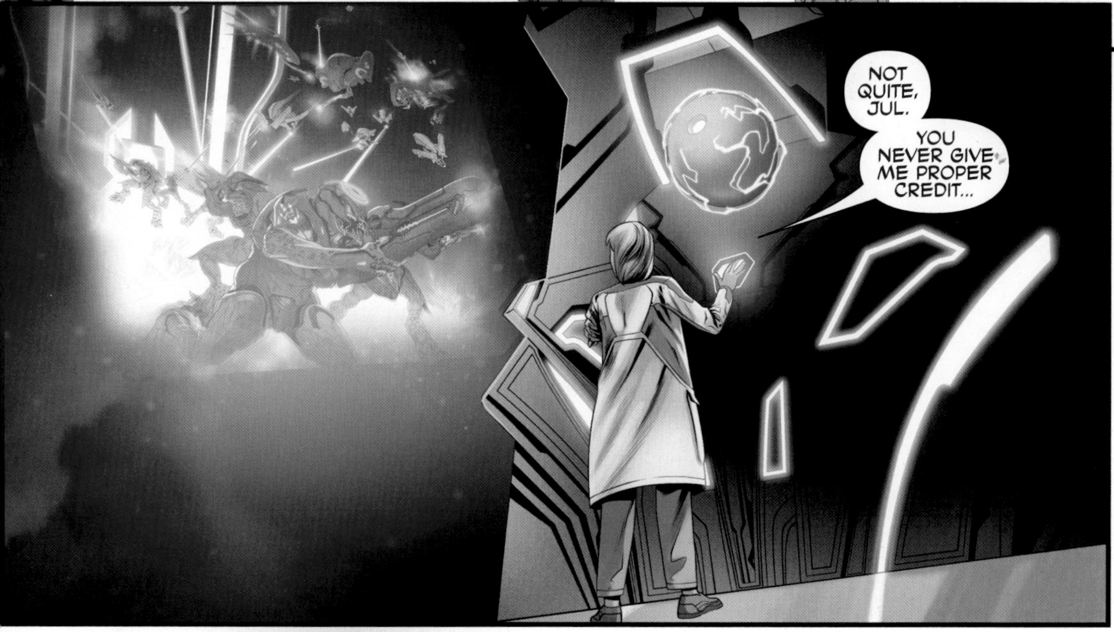
NOT QUITE, JUL.
YOU NEVER GIVE ME PROPER CREDIT...

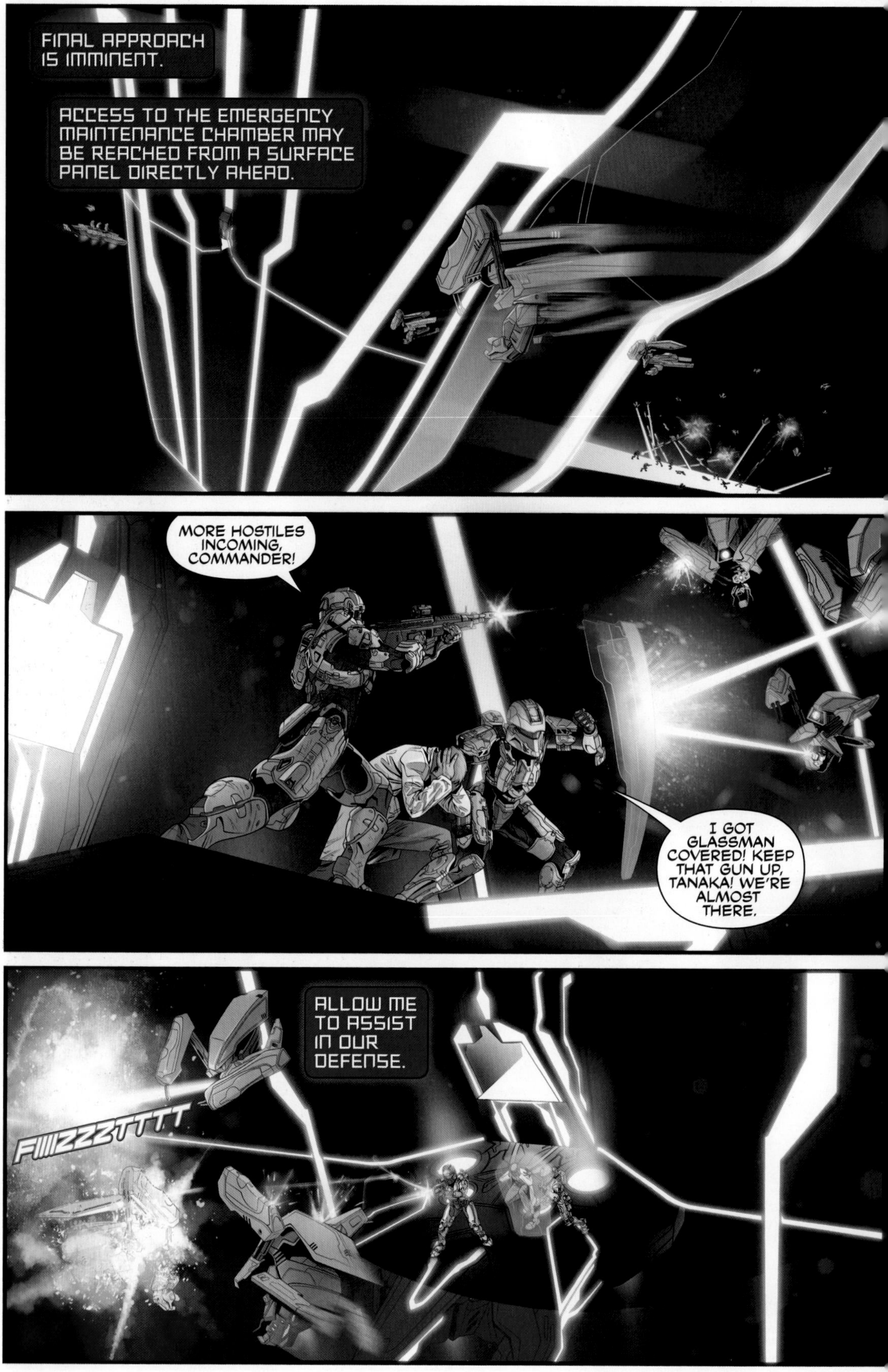
FINAL APPROACH IS IMMINENT.
ACCESS TO THE EMERGENCY MAINTENANCE CHAMBER MAY BE REACHED FROM A SURFACE PANEL DIRECTLY AHEAD.
MORE HOSTILES INCOMING, COMMANDER!
I GOT GLASSMAN COVERED! KEEP THAT GUN UP, TANAKA! WE'RE ALMOST THERE.
ALLOW ME TO ASSIST IN OUR DEFENSE.
FIIIIZZZTTTT

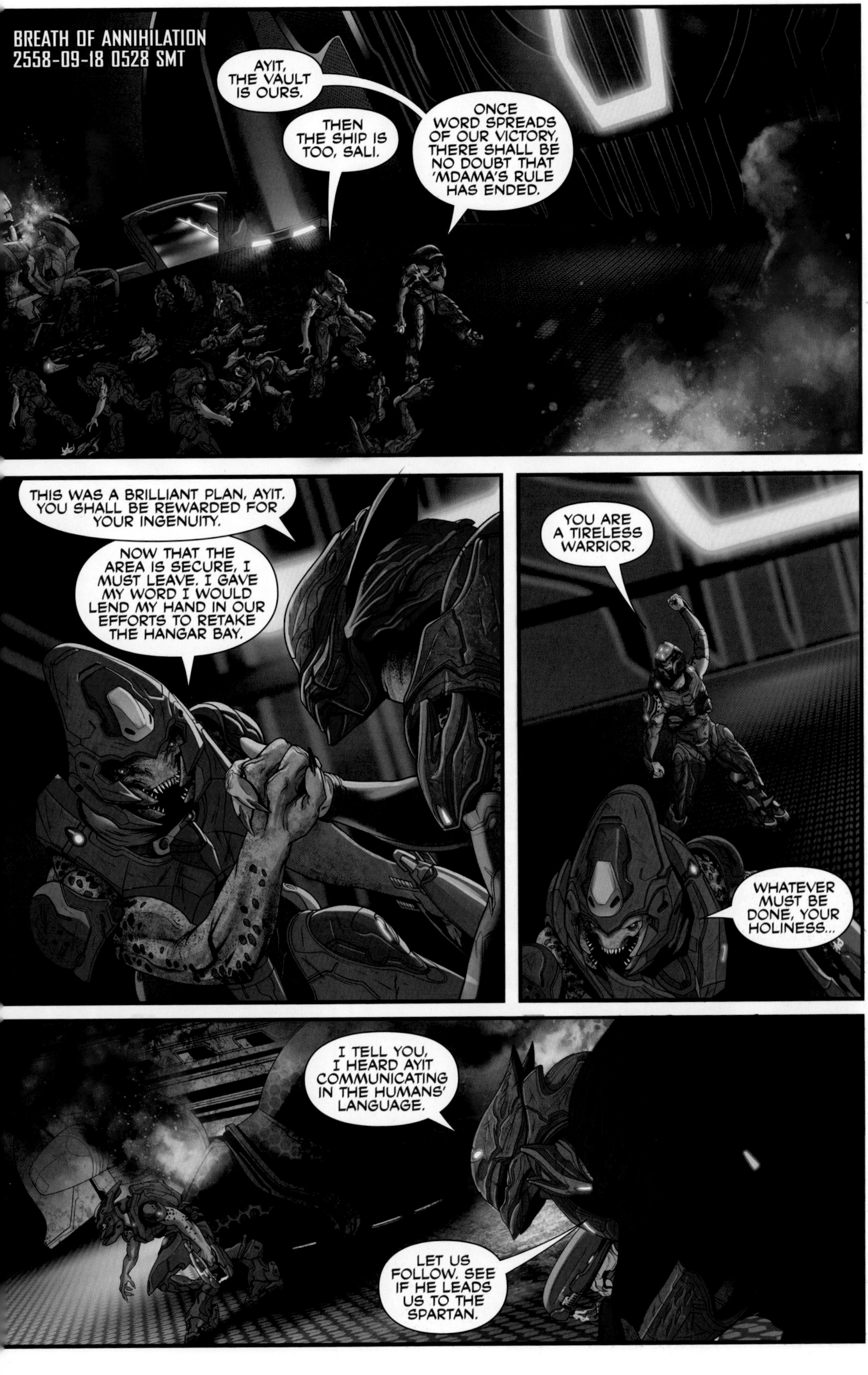
BREATH OF ANNIHILATION
2558-09-18 0528 SMT
AYIT, THE VAULT IS OURS.
THEN THE SHIP IS TOO, SALI.
ONCE WORD SPREADS OF OUR VICTORY, THERE SHALL BE NO DOUBT THAT 'MDAMA'S RULE HAS ENDED.
THIS WAS A BRILLIANT PLAN, AYIT. YOU SHALL BE REWARDED FOR YOUR INGENUITY.
NOW THAT THE AREA IS SECURE, I MUST LEAVE. I GAVE MY WORD I WOULD LEND MY HAND IN OUR EFFORTS TO RETAKE THE HANGAR BAY.
YOU ARE A TIRELESS WARRIOR.
WHATEVER MUST BE DONE, YOUR HOLINESS...
I TELL YOU, I HEARD AYIT COMMUNICATING IN THE HUMANS' LANGUAGE.
LET US FOLLOW. SEE IF HE LEADS US TO THE SPARTAN.

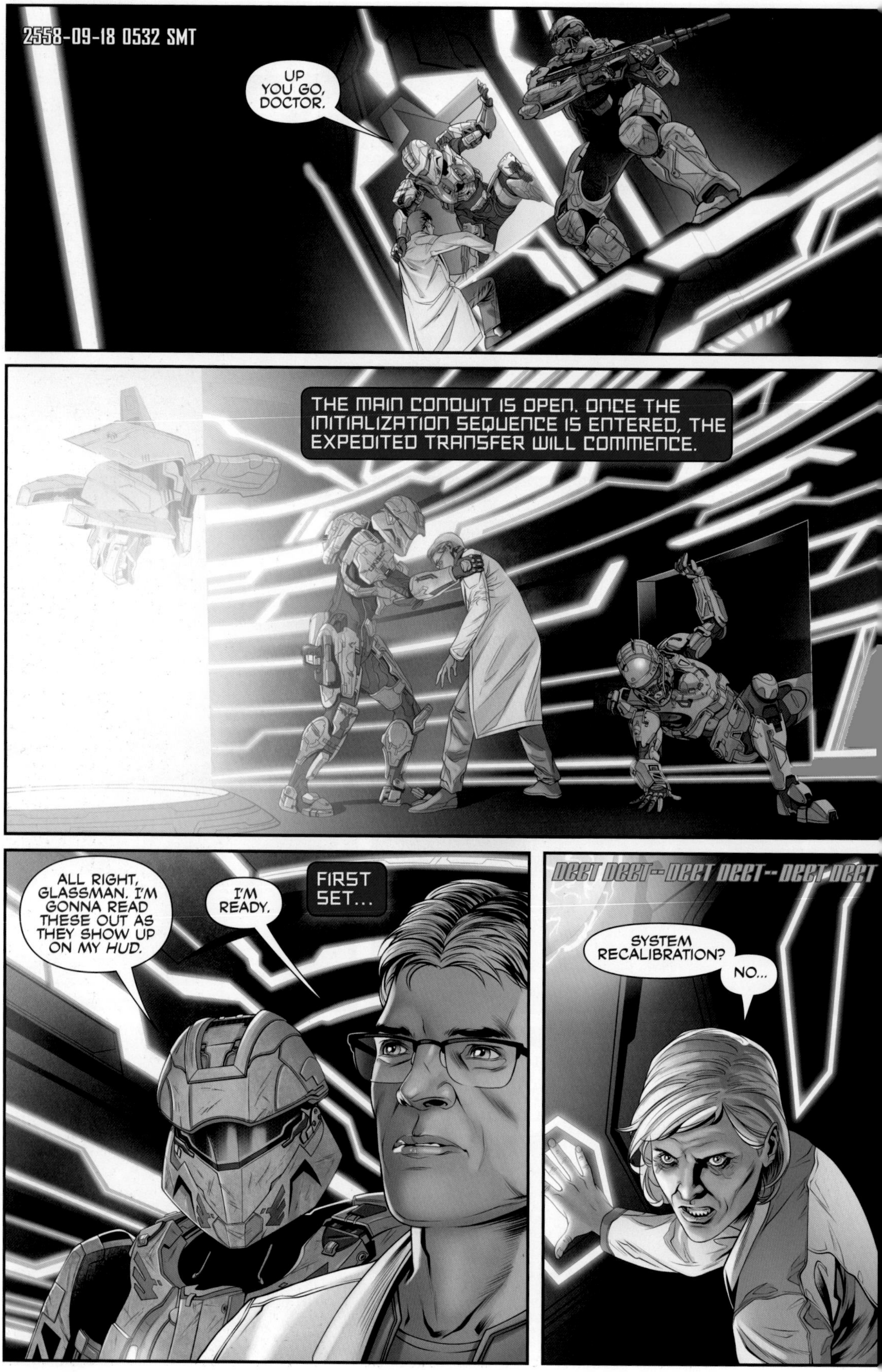
2558-09-18 0532 SMT
UP YOU GO, DOCTOR.
THE MAIN CONDUIT IS OPEN. ONCE THE INITIALIZATION SEQUENCE IS ENTERED, THE EXPEDITED TRANSFER WILL COMMENCE.
ALL RIGHT, GLASSMAN. I'M GONNA READ THESE OUT AS THEY SHOW UP ON MY *HUD*.
I'M READY.
FIRST SET...
DEET DEET--DEET DEET--DEET DEET
SYSTEM RECALIBRATION?
NO...

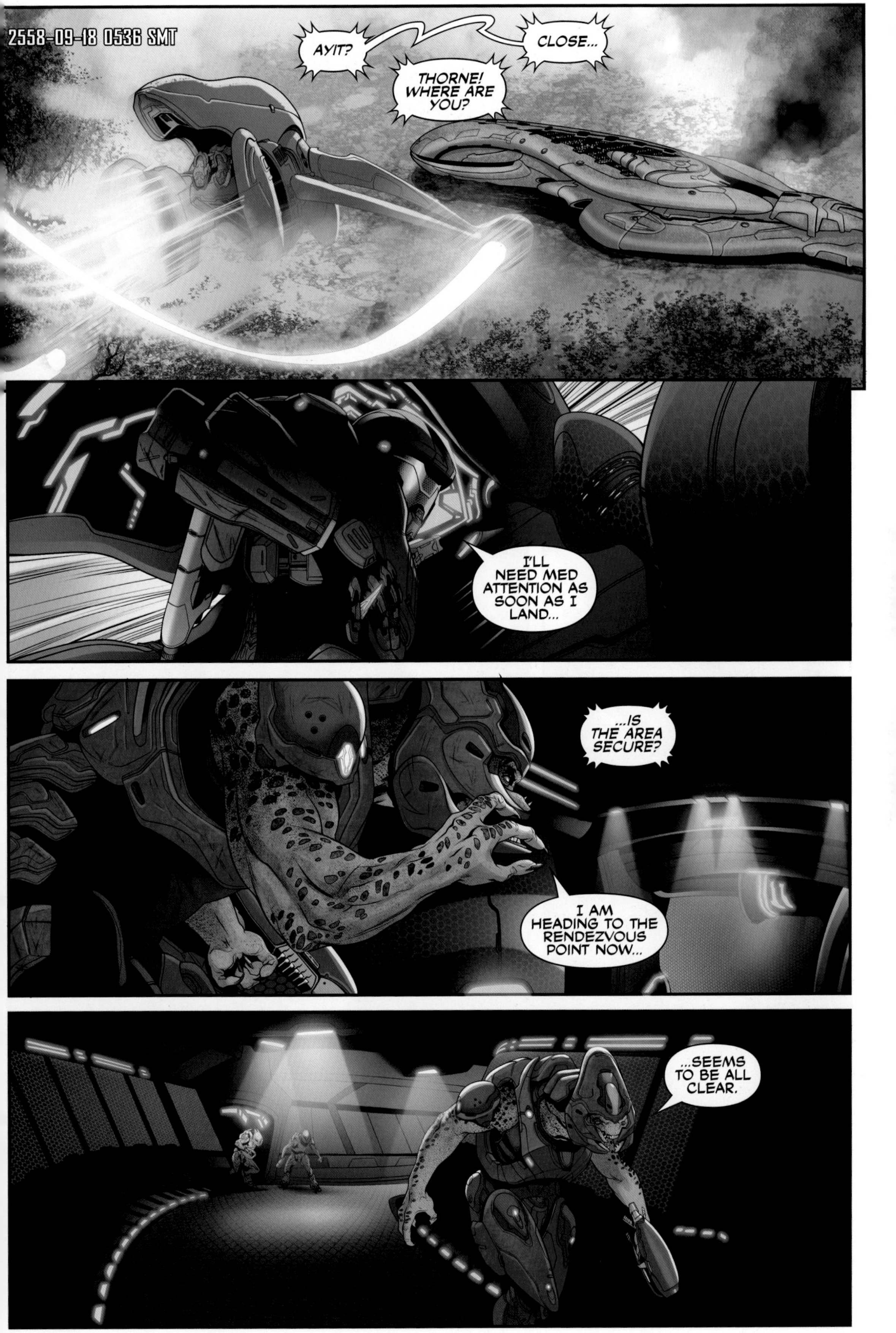
2558-09-18 0536 SMT
AYIT?
CLOSE...
THORNE! WHERE ARE YOU?
I'LL NEED MED ATTENTION AS SOON AS I LAND...
...IS THE AREA SECURE?
I AM HEADING TO THE RENDEZVOUS POINT NOW...
...SEEMS TO BE ALL CLEAR.

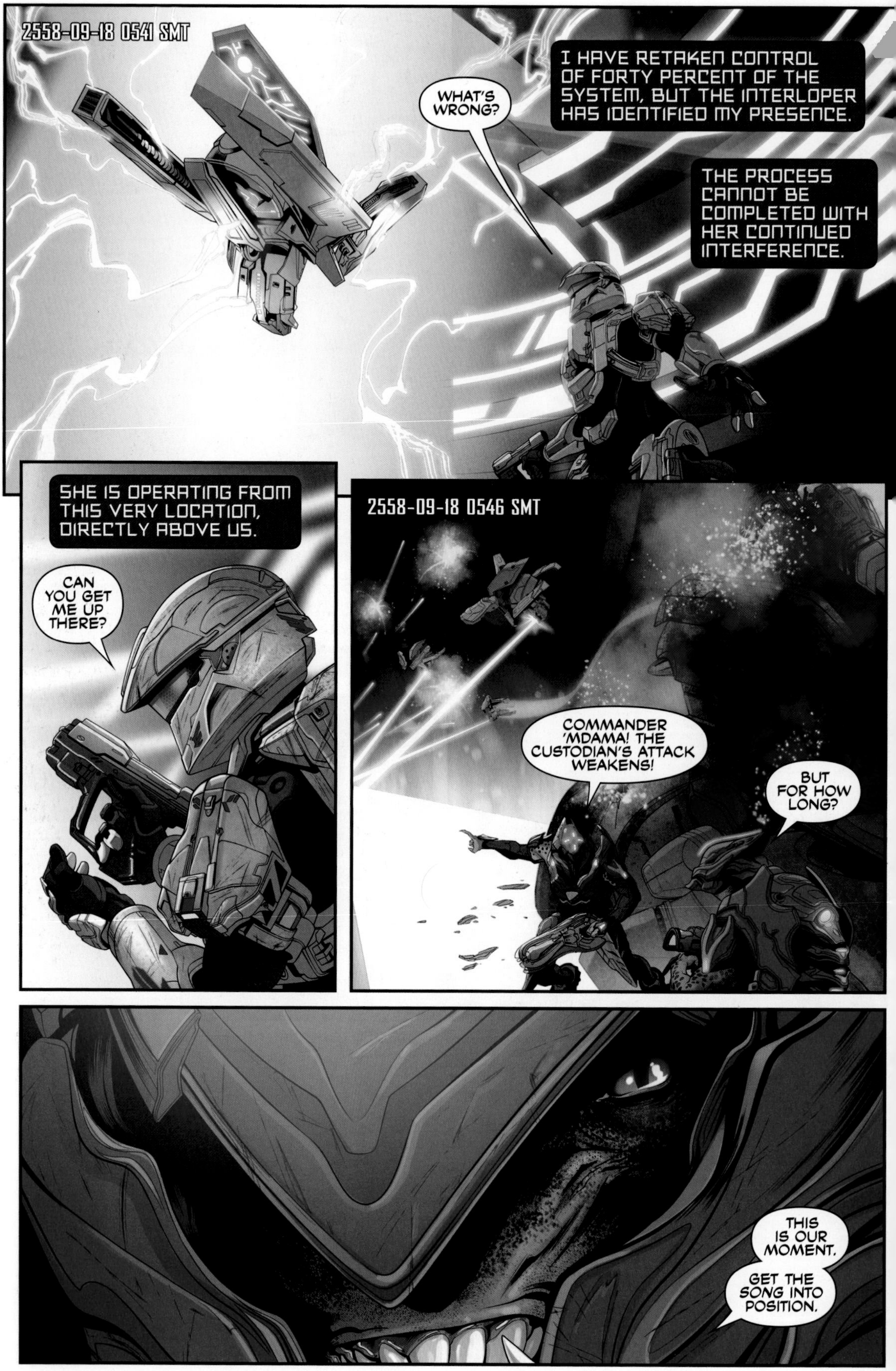
2558-09-18 0541 SMT
WHAT'S WRONG?
I HAVE RETAKEN CONTROL OF FORTY PERCENT OF THE SYSTEM, BUT THE INTERLOPER HAS IDENTIFIED MY PRESENCE.
THE PROCESS CANNOT BE COMPLETED WITH HER CONTINUED INTERFERENCE.
SHE IS OPERATING FROM THIS VERY LOCATION, DIRECTLY ABOVE US.
CAN YOU GET ME UP THERE?
2558-09-18 0546 SMT
COMMANDER 'MDAMA! THE CUSTODIAN'S ATTACK WEAKENS!
BUT FOR HOW LONG?
THIS IS OUR MOMENT.
GET THE SONG INTO POSITION.

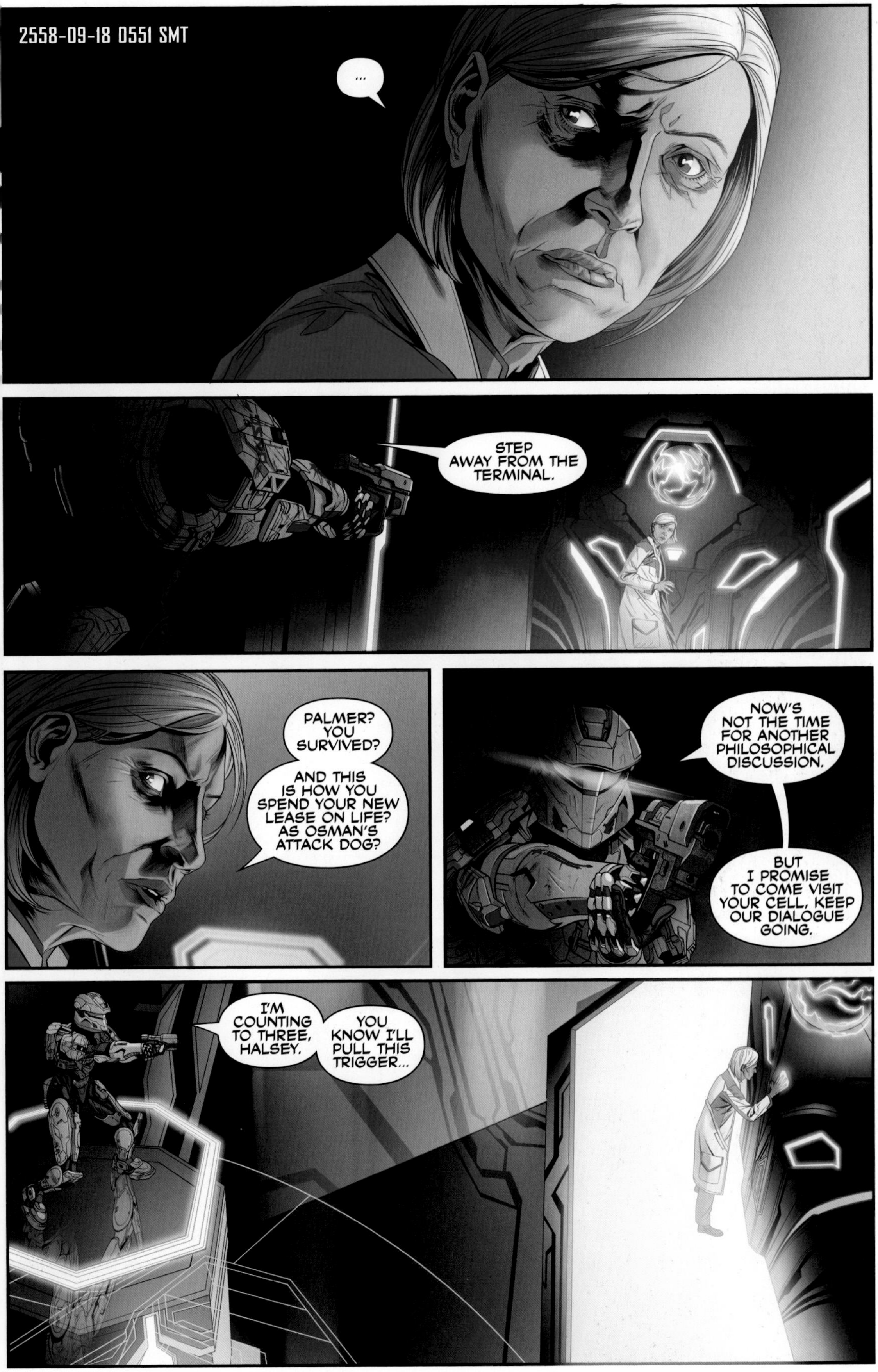
2558-09-18 0551 SMT
...
STEP AWAY FROM THE TERMINAL.
PALMER? YOU SURVIVED?
AND THIS IS HOW YOU SPEND YOUR NEW LEASE ON LIFE? AS OSMAN'S ATTACK DOG?
NOW'S NOT THE TIME FOR ANOTHER PHILOSOPHICAL DISCUSSION.
BUT I PROMISE TO COME VISIT YOUR CELL, KEEP OUR DIALOGUE GOING.
I'M COUNTING TO THREE, HALSEY.
YOU KNOW I'LL PULL THIS TRIGGER...

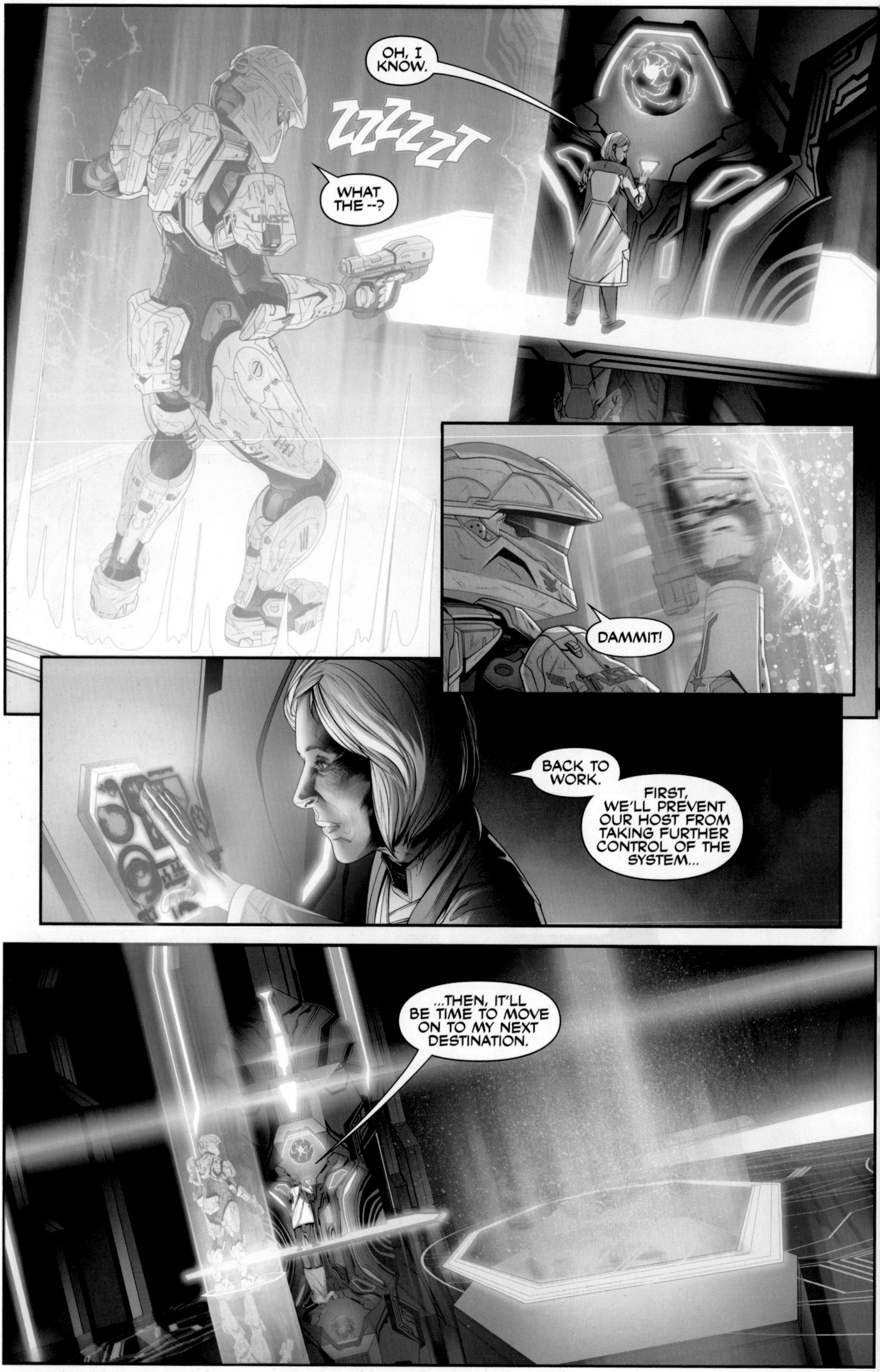
OH, I KNOW.
ZZZZZT
WHAT THE --?
UNSC
DAMMIT!
BACK TO WORK.
FIRST, WE'LL PREVENT OUR HOST FROM TAKING FURTHER CONTROL OF THE SYSTEM...
...THEN, IT'LL BE TIME TO MOVE ON TO MY NEXT DESTINATION.

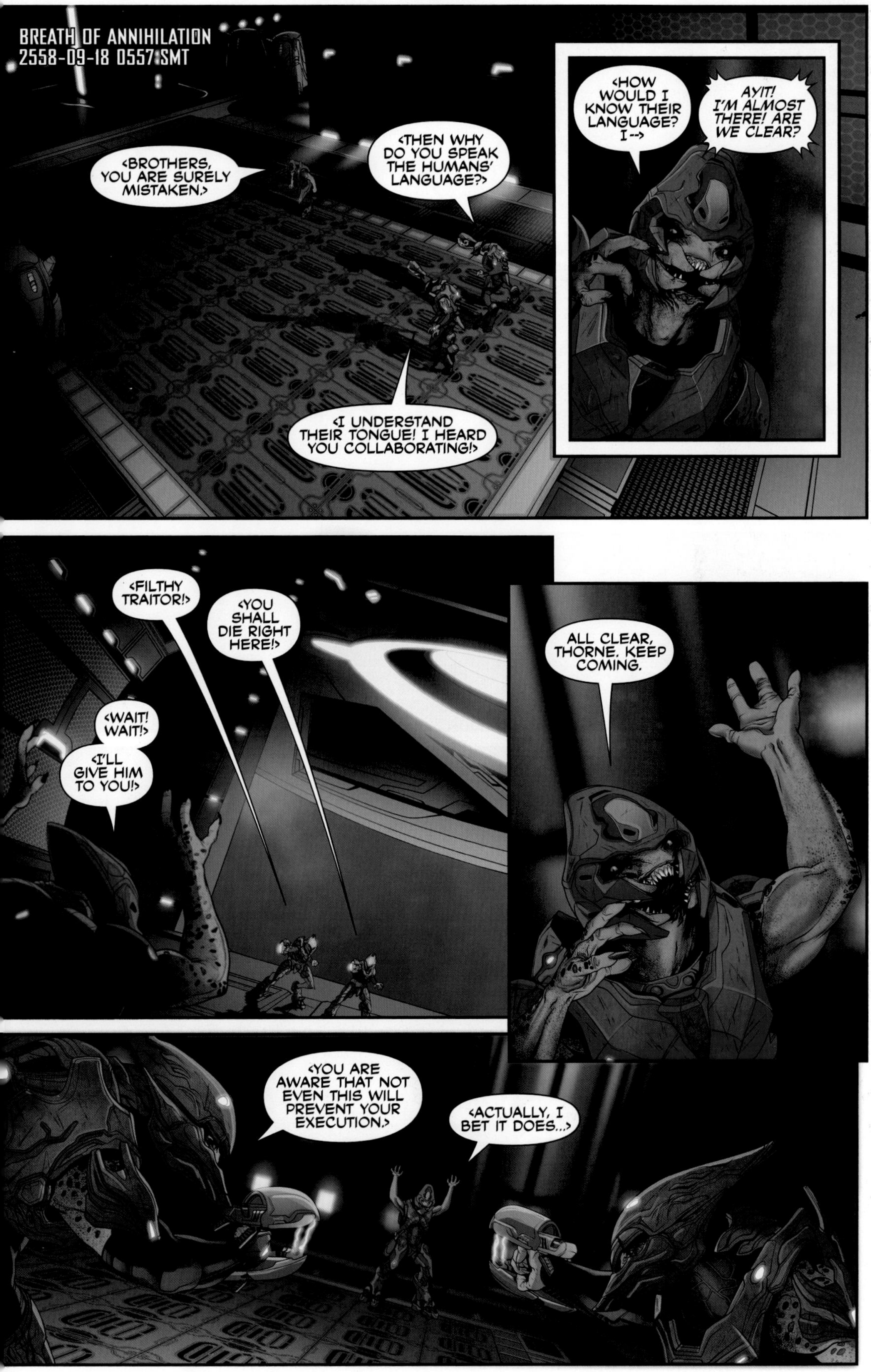
BREATH OF ANNIHILATION
2558-09-18 0557 SMT
<BROTHERS, YOU ARE SURELY MISTAKEN.>
<THEN WHY DO YOU SPEAK THE HUMANS' LANGUAGE?>
<I UNDERSTAND THEIR TONGUE! I HEARD YOU COLLABORATING!>
<HOW WOULD I KNOW THEIR LANGUAGE? I -->
AYIT! I'M ALMOST THERE! ARE WE CLEAR?
<FILTHY TRAITOR!>
<YOU SHALL DIE RIGHT HERE!>
<WAIT! WAIT!>
<I'LL GIVE HIM TO YOU!>
ALL CLEAR, THORNE. KEEP COMING.
<YOU ARE AWARE THAT NOT EVEN THIS WILL PREVENT YOUR EXECUTION.>
<ACTUALLY, I BET IT DOES...>

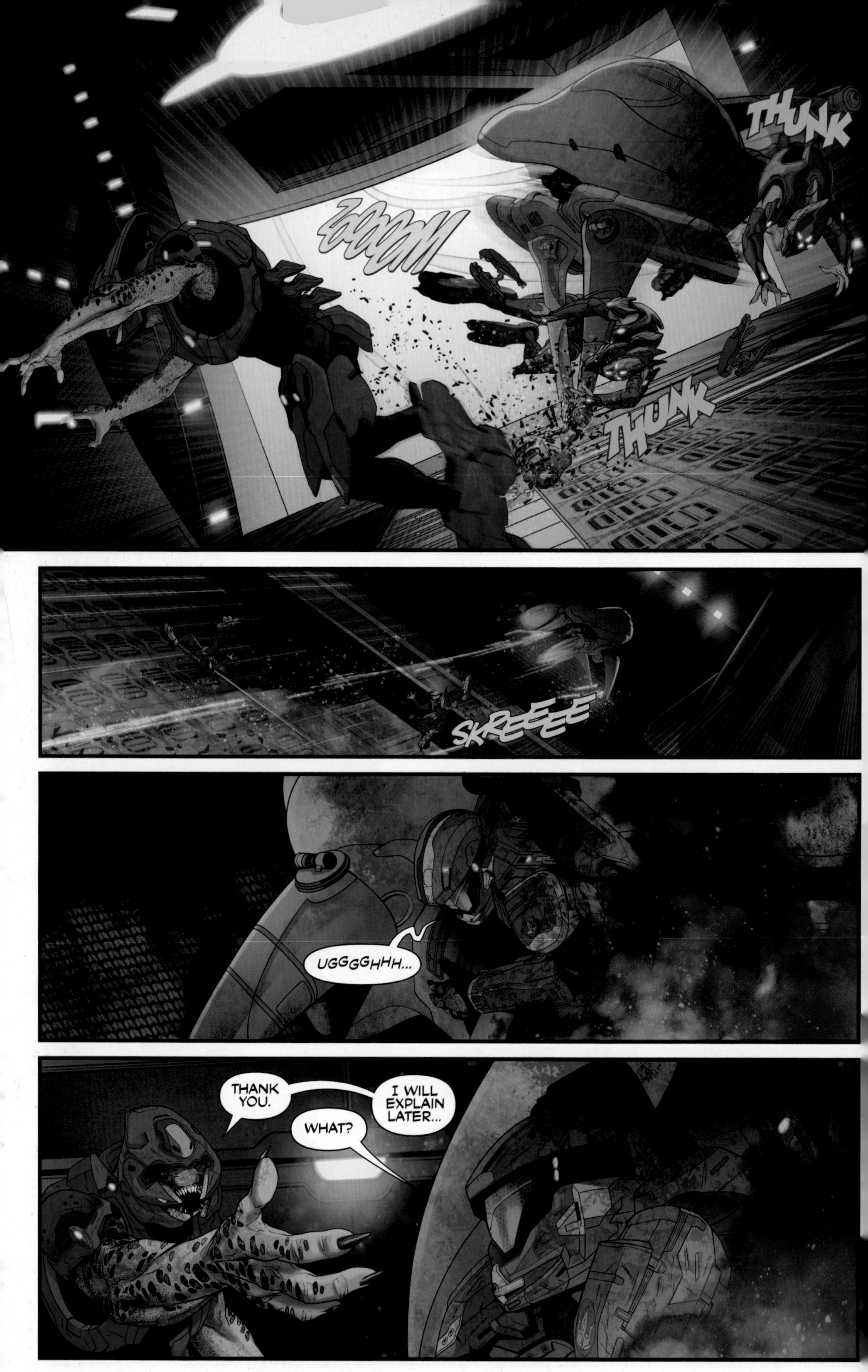

THUNK
ZOOOOM
THUNK
SKREEEEE
UGGGGHHH...
THANK YOU.
WHAT?
I WILL EXPLAIN LATER...

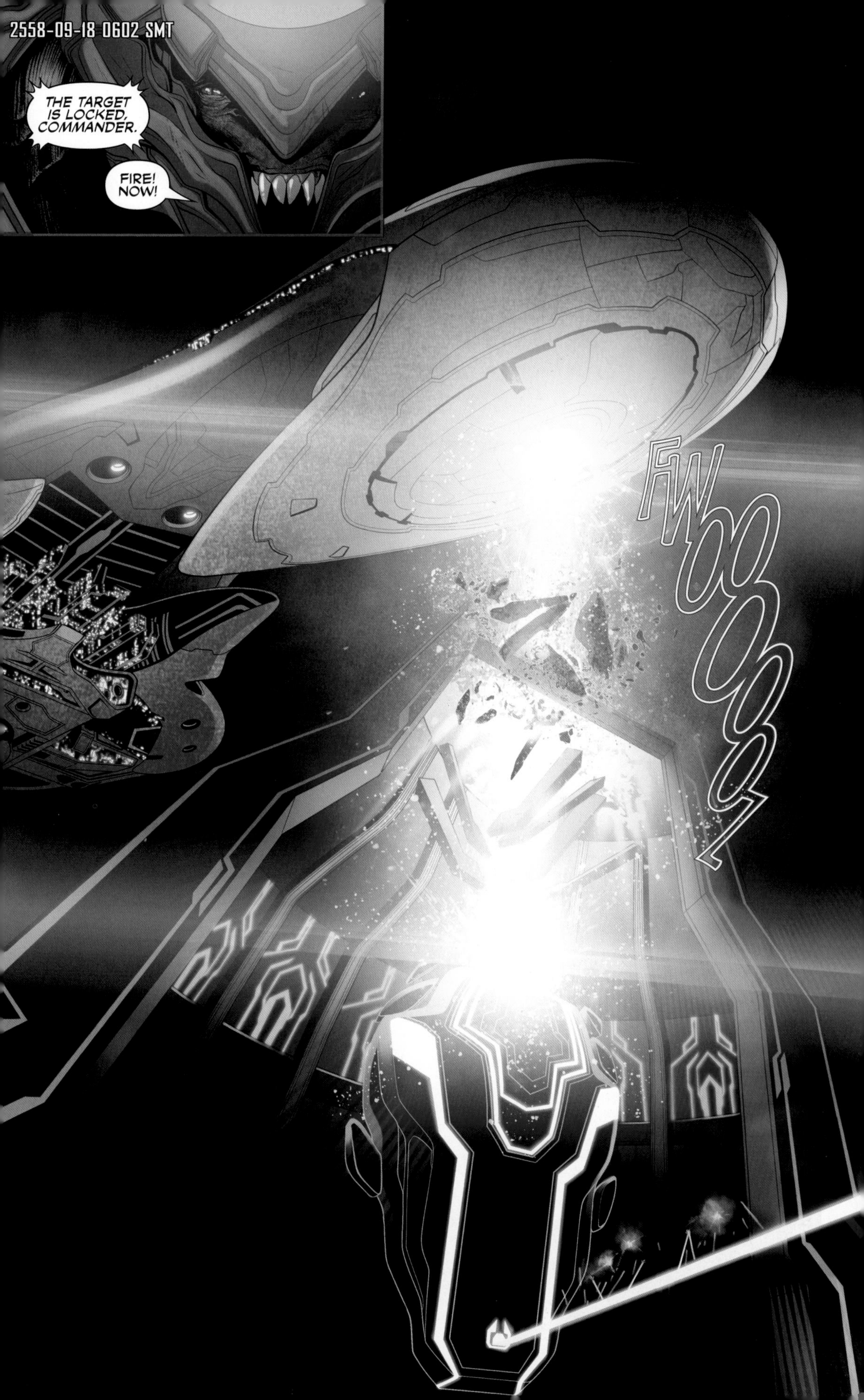
2558-09-18 0602 SMT
THE TARGET IS LOCKED, COMMANDER.
FIRE! NOW!
FWOOOOOOOZ

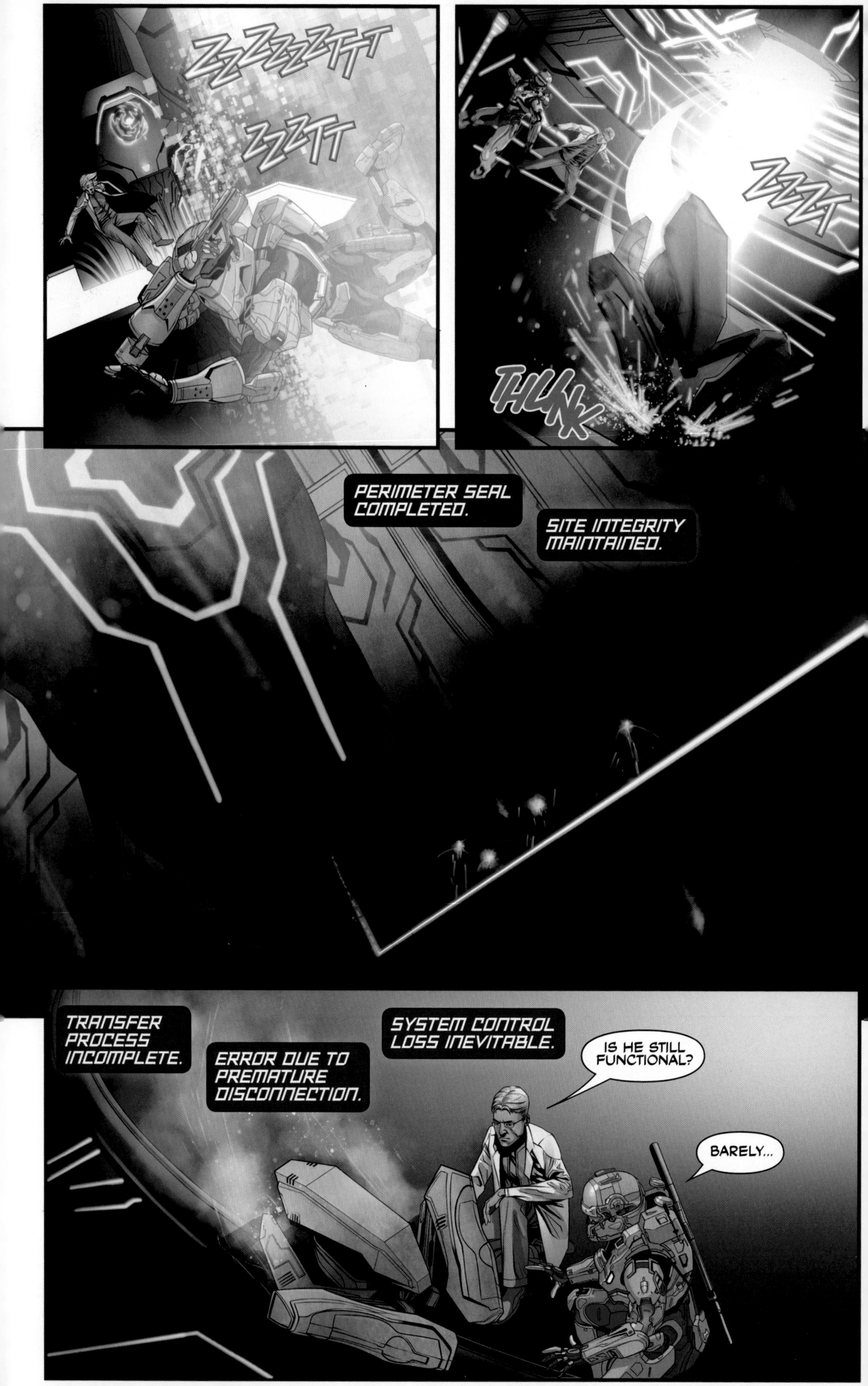

ZZZZZZTTT
ZZZTT
ZZZZT
THUNK
PERIMETER SEAL COMPLETED.
SITE INTEGRITY MAINTAINED.
TRANSFER PROCESS INCOMPLETE.
ERROR DUE TO PREMATURE DISCONNECTION.
SYSTEM CONTROL LOSS INEVITABLE.
IS HE STILL FUNCTIONAL?
BARELY...

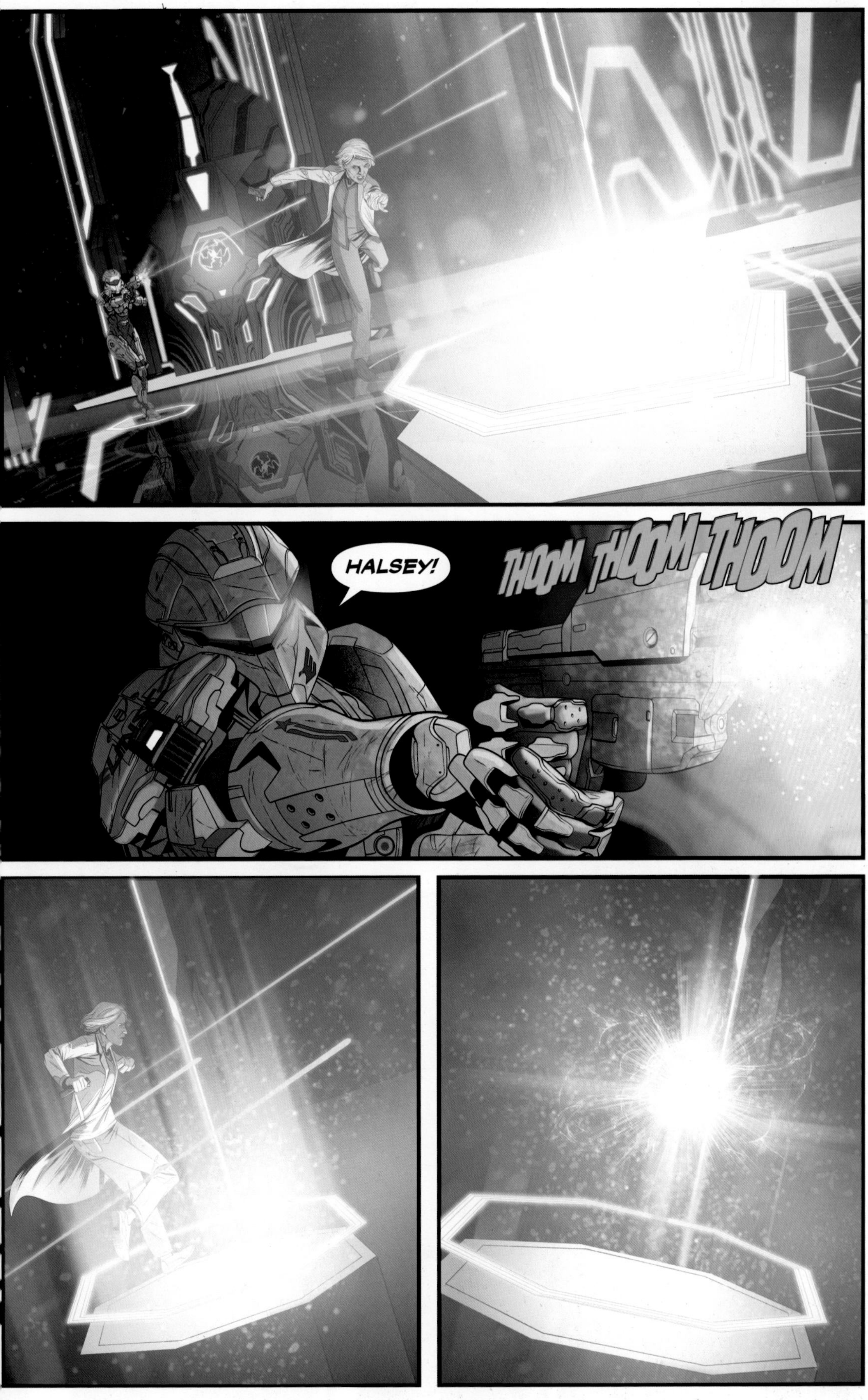
HALSEY!
THOOM THOOM THOOM

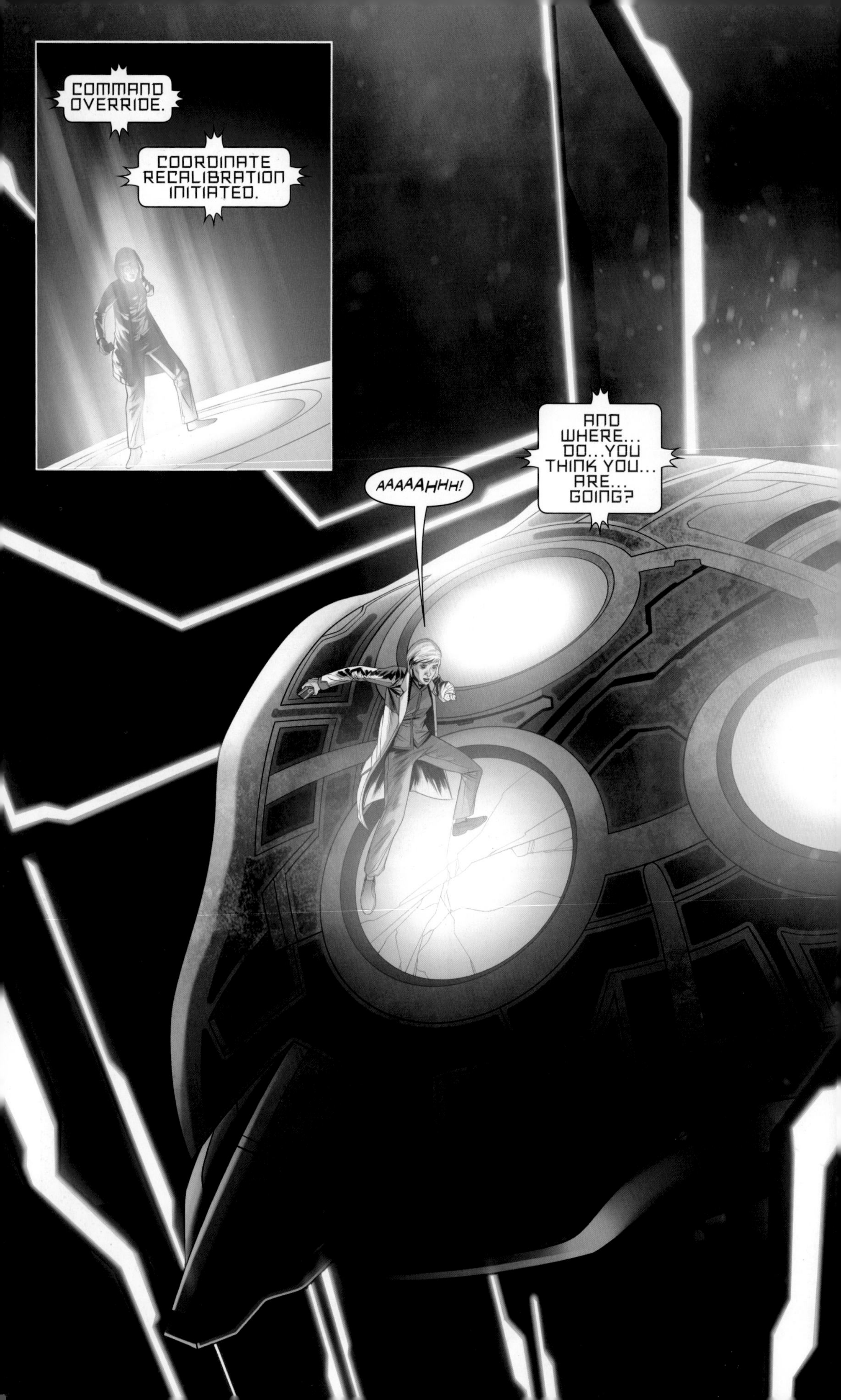
COMMAND OVERRIDE.
COORDINATE RECALIBRATION INITIATED.
AND WHERE... DO...YOU THINK YOU... ARE... GOING?
AAAAAHHH!

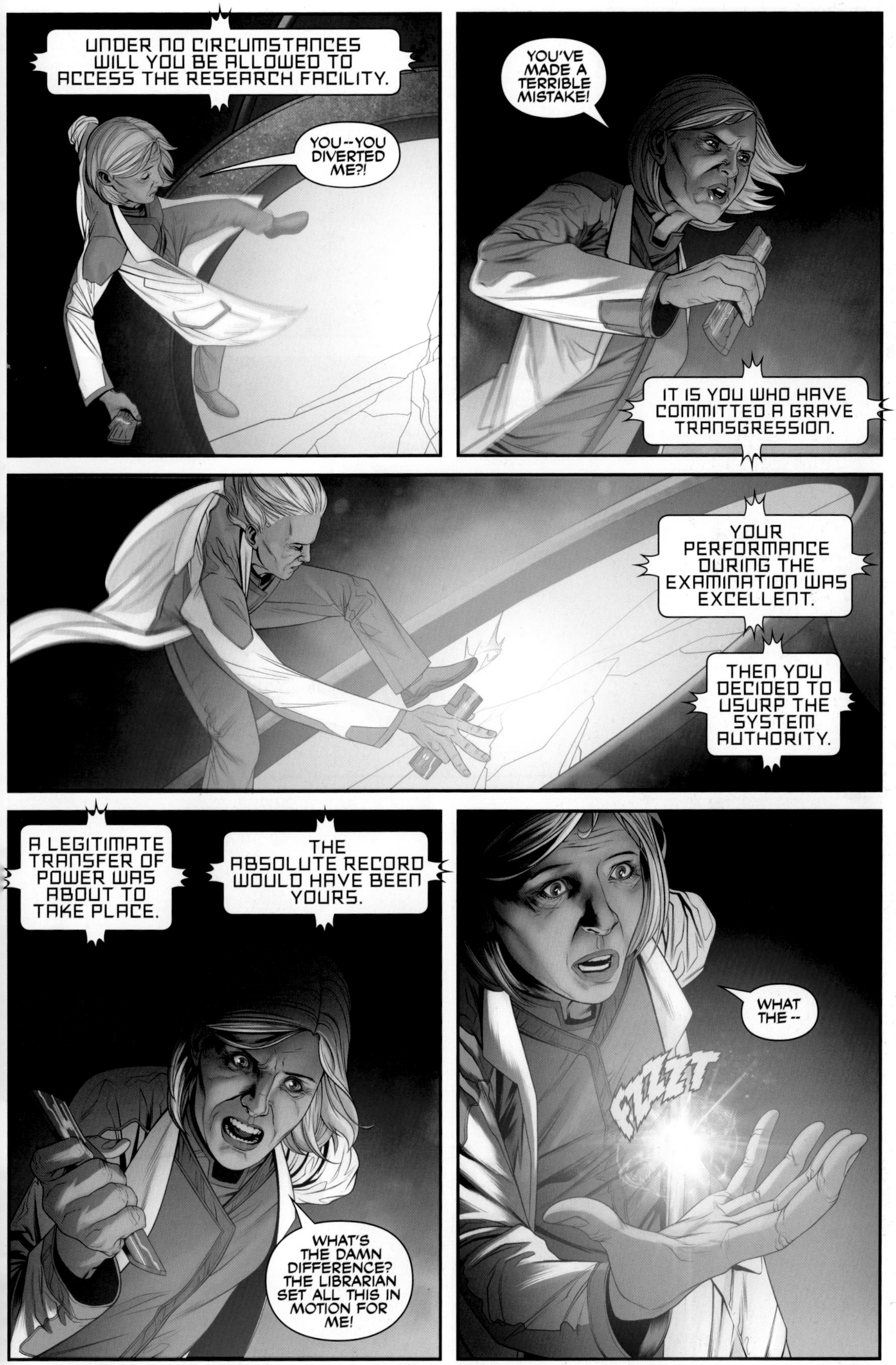
UNDER NO CIRCUMSTANCES WILL YOU BE ALLOWED TO ACCESS THE RESEARCH FACILITY.
YOU--YOU DIVERTED ME?!
YOU'VE MADE A TERRIBLE MISTAKE!
IT IS YOU WHO HAVE COMMITTED A GRAVE TRANSGRESSION.
YOUR PERFORMANCE DURING THE EXAMINATION WAS EXCELLENT.
THEN YOU DECIDED TO USURP THE SYSTEM AUTHORITY.
A LEGITIMATE TRANSFER OF POWER WAS ABOUT TO TAKE PLACE.
THE ABSOLUTE RECORD WOULD HAVE BEEN YOURS.
WHAT'S THE DAMN DIFFERENCE? THE LIBRARIAN SET ALL THIS IN MOTION FOR ME!
FZZZT
WHAT THE --

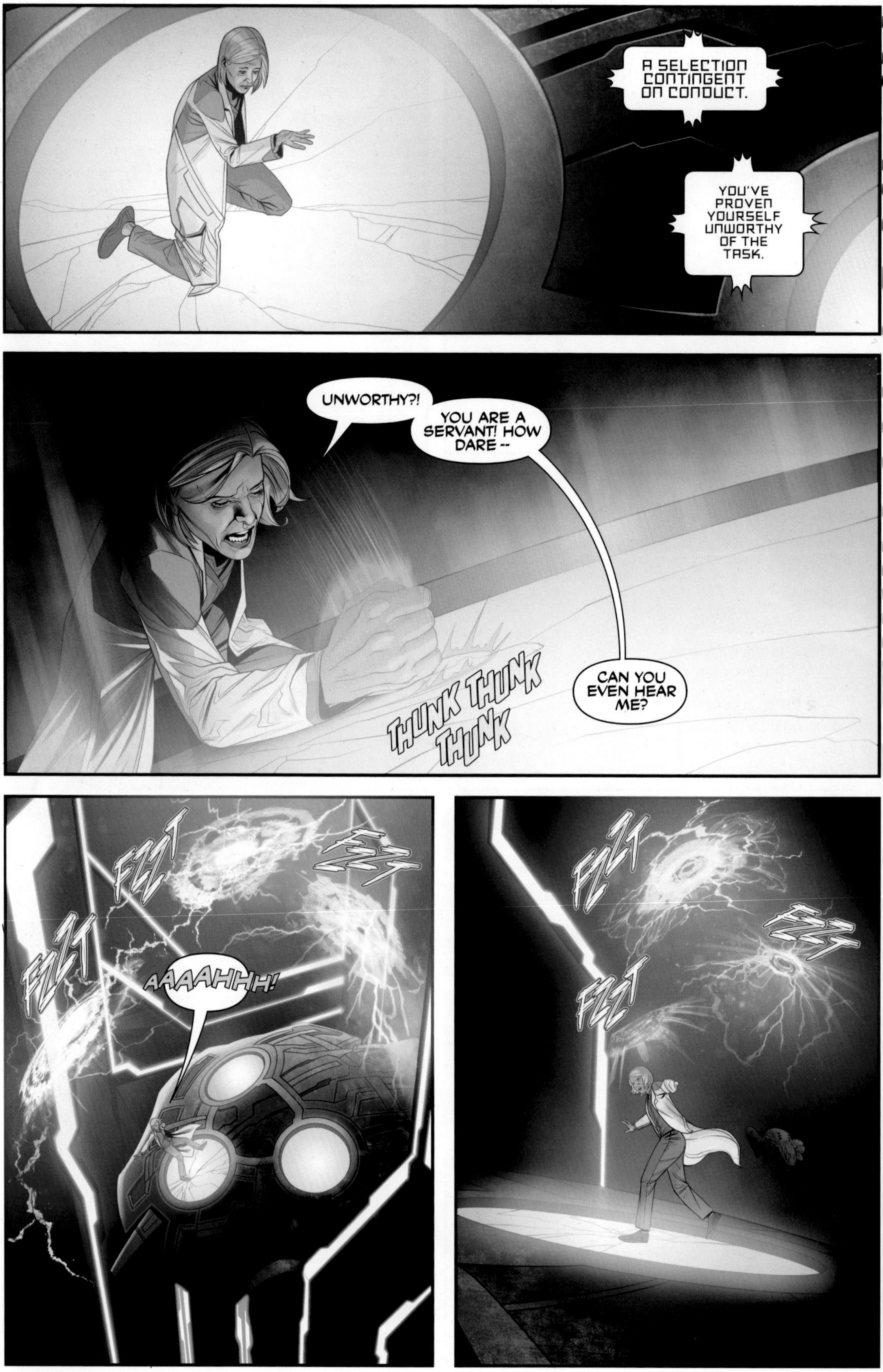
A SELECTION CONTINGENT ON CONDUCT.
YOU'VE PROVEN YOURSELF UNWORTHY OF THE TASK.
UNWORTHY?!
YOU ARE A SERVANT! HOW DARE --
CAN YOU EVEN HEAR ME?
THUNK THUNK THUNK
FZZT
FZZT
FZZT
AAAAHHH!
FZZT
FZZT
FZZT

OUR HOST IS FRIED.

THIS PLACE IS DISAPPEARING RIGHT OUT FROM UNDER US!

HEY! I THINK I FOUND OUR WAY OUT!

DURING THE EXAMINATION, THE CUSTODIAN DISPLAYED A MAP OF THE STAR SYSTEM IN WHICH THE ACCESS PORTAL IS LOCATED...

EXISTING FORERUNNER TECH IN THE AREA WAS LIT UP, ALL SCATTERED AROUND.

BUT I NOTICED AN ANOMALY WHERE MULTIPLE SIGNAL MARKERS WERE ALL CLUSTERED AROUND A SINGLE POINT. I'VE LOCATED THE COORDINATES HERE...

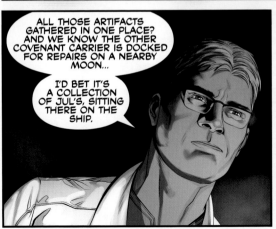

ALL THOSE ARTIFACTS GATHERED IN ONE PLACE? AND WE KNOW THE OTHER COVENANT CARRIER IS DOCKED FOR REPAIRS ON A NEARBY MOON...

I'D BET IT'S A COLLECTION OF JUL'S, SITTING THERE ON THE SHIP.

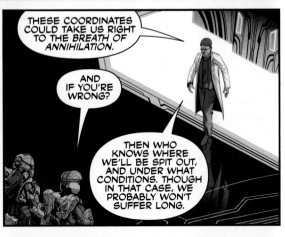

THESE COORDINATES COULD TAKE US RIGHT TO THE BREATH OF ANNIHILATION.

AND IF YOU'RE WRONG?

THEN WHO KNOWS WHERE WE'LL BE SPIT OUT, AND UNDER WHAT CONDITIONS. THOUGH IN THAT CASE, WE PROBABLY WON'T SUFFER LONG.

THE TRANSLOCATION PLATFORM IS READY WHEN WE ARE...

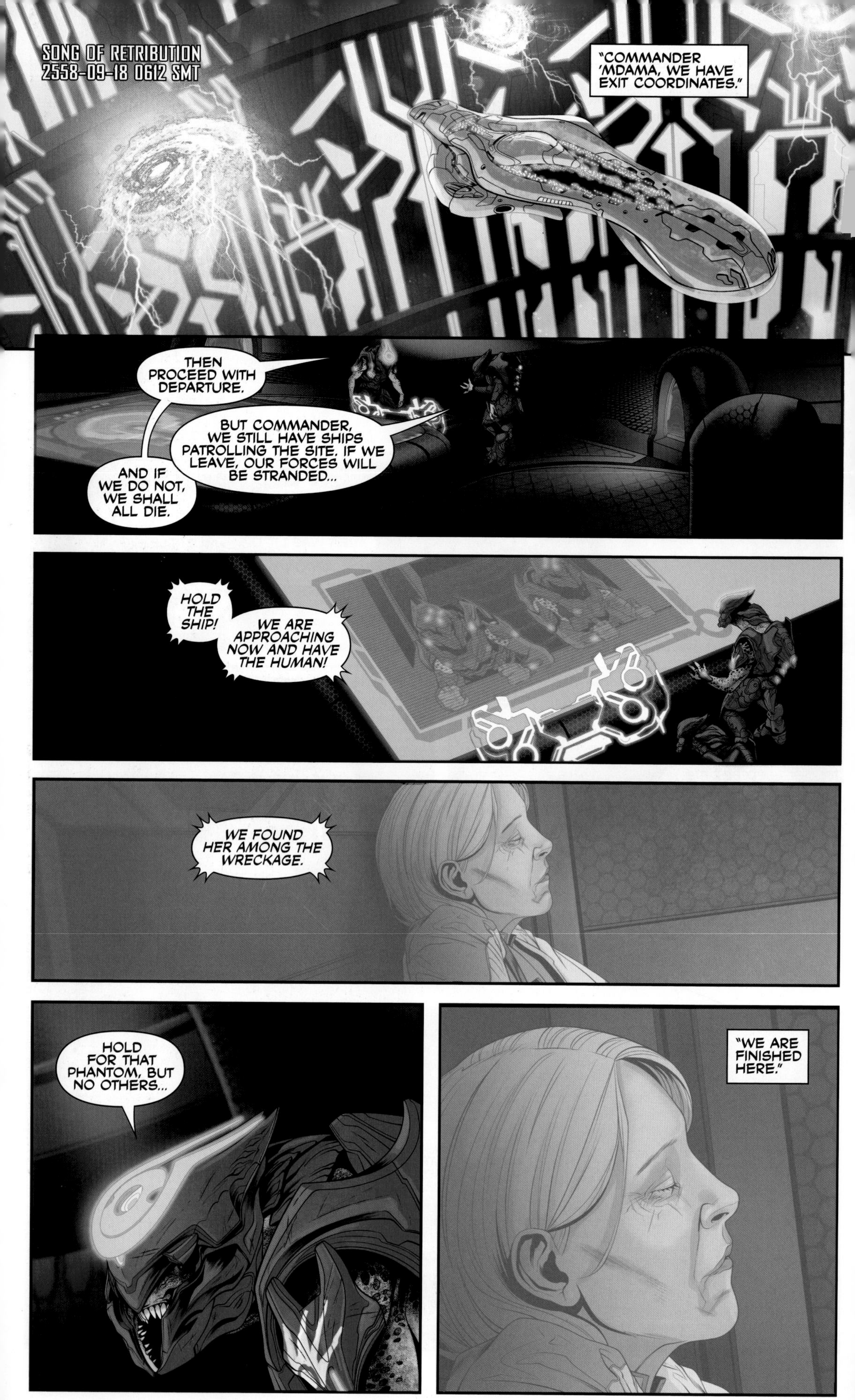
SONG OF RETRIBUTION
2558-09-18 0612 SMT
"COMMANDER 'MDAMA, WE HAVE EXIT COORDINATES."
THEN PROCEED WITH DEPARTURE.
BUT COMMANDER, WE STILL HAVE SHIPS PATROLLING THE SITE. IF WE LEAVE, OUR FORCES WILL BE STRANDED...
AND IF WE DO NOT, WE SHALL ALL DIE.
HOLD THE SHIP!
WE ARE APPROACHING NOW AND HAVE THE HUMAN!
WE FOUND HER AMONG THE WRECKAGE.
HOLD FOR THAT PHANTOM, BUT NO OTHERS...
"WE ARE FINISHED HERE."

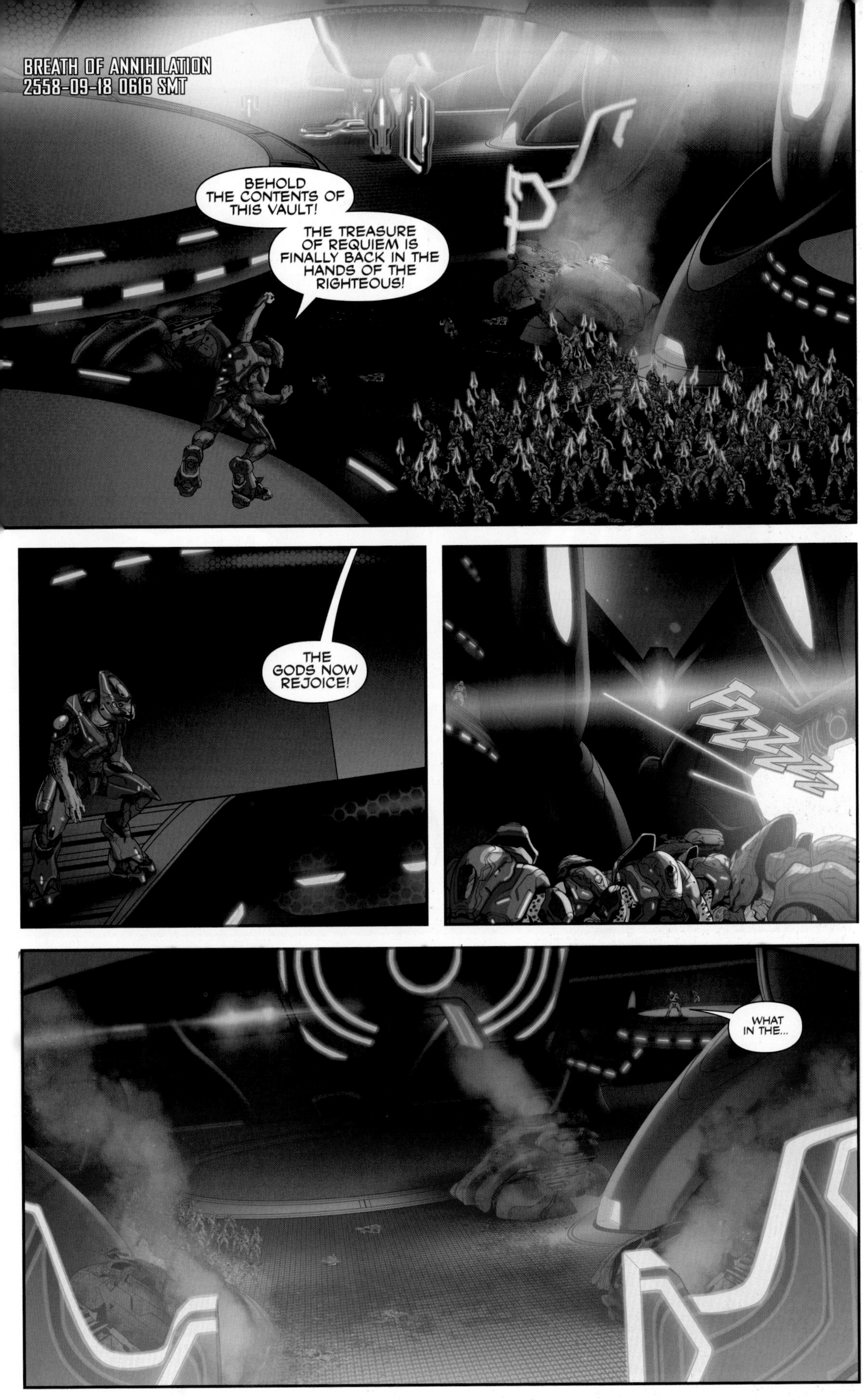
BREATH OF ANNIHILATION
2558-09-18 0616 SMT
BEHOLD THE CONTENTS OF THIS VAULT!
THE TREASURE OF REQUIEM IS FINALLY BACK IN THE HANDS OF THE RIGHTEOUS!
THE GODS NOW REJOICE!
FZZZZ
WHAT IN THE...

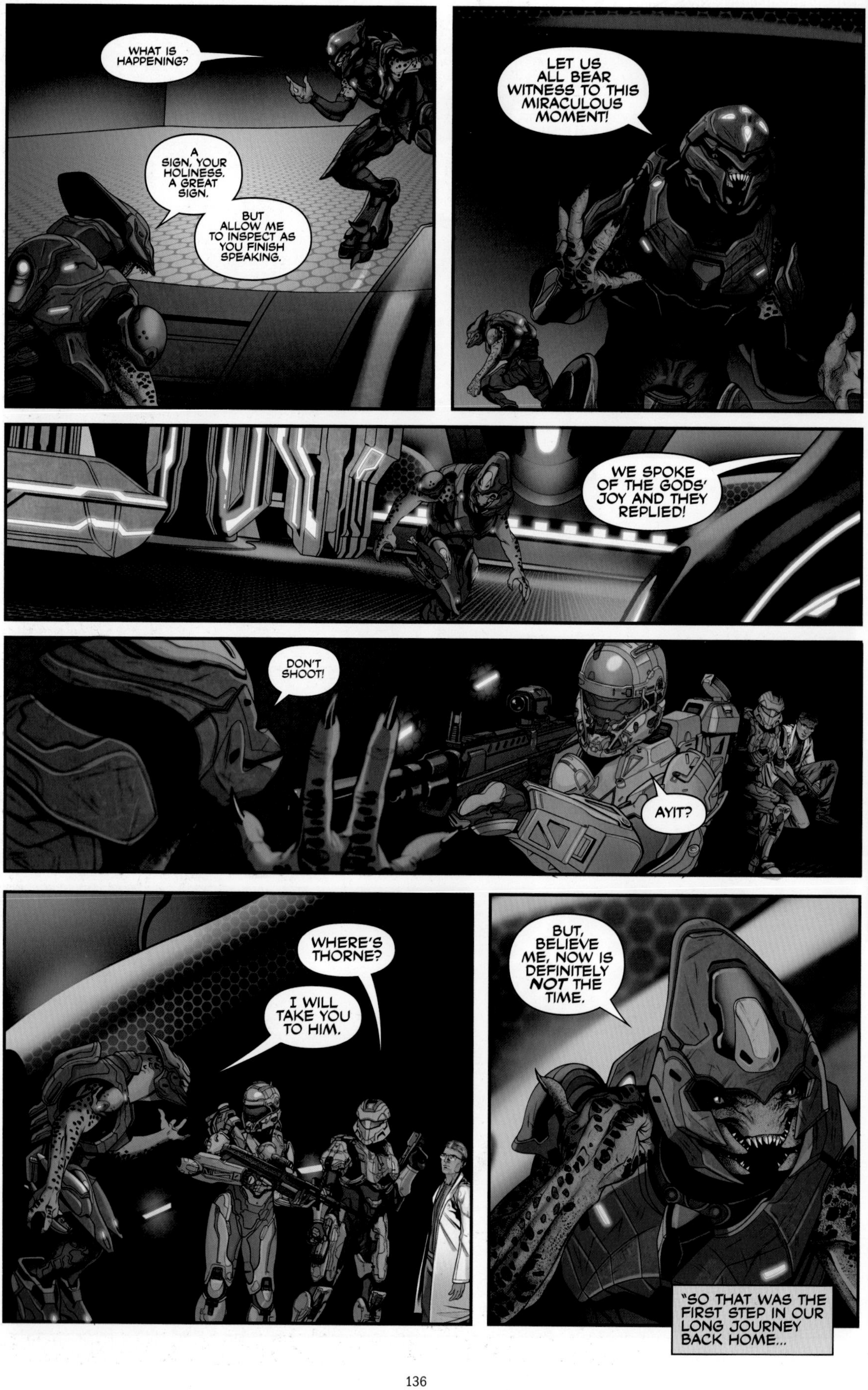
WHAT IS HAPPENING?
A SIGN, YOUR HOLINESS. A GREAT SIGN.
BUT ALLOW ME TO INSPECT AS YOU FINISH SPEAKING.
LET US ALL BEAR WITNESS TO THIS MIRACULOUS MOMENT!
WE SPOKE OF THE GODS' JOY AND THEY REPLIED!
DON'T SHOOT!
AYIT?
WHERE'S THORNE?
I WILL TAKE YOU TO HIM.
BUT, BELIEVE ME, NOW IS DEFINITELY *NOT* THE TIME.
"SO THAT WAS THE FIRST STEP IN OUR LONG JOURNEY BACK HOME...

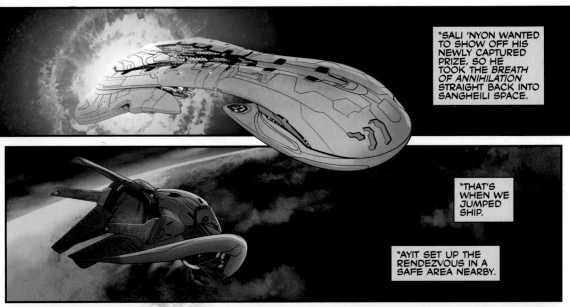

"SALI 'NYON WANTED TO SHOW OFF HIS NEWLY CAPTURED PRIZE, SO HE TOOK THE *BREATH OF ANNIHILATION* STRAIGHT BACK INTO SANGHEILI SPACE.

"THAT'S WHEN WE JUMPED SHIP.

"AYIT SET UP THE RENDEZVOUS IN A SAFE AREA NEARBY.

"ONI WAS WAITING, READY FOR OUR EXFIL.

"AND NOT A MOMENT TOO SOON...

"BECAUSE ALL HELL BROKE LOOSE.

"JUL SHOWED UP IN THE *SONG OF RETRIBUTION* AND THE TWO CARRIERS SLUGGED IT OUT.

"BUT JUL COULDN'T RETAKE THE SHIP.

"SO THE *BREATH* IS STILL OUT THERE. UNDER 'NYON'S CONTROL NOW."

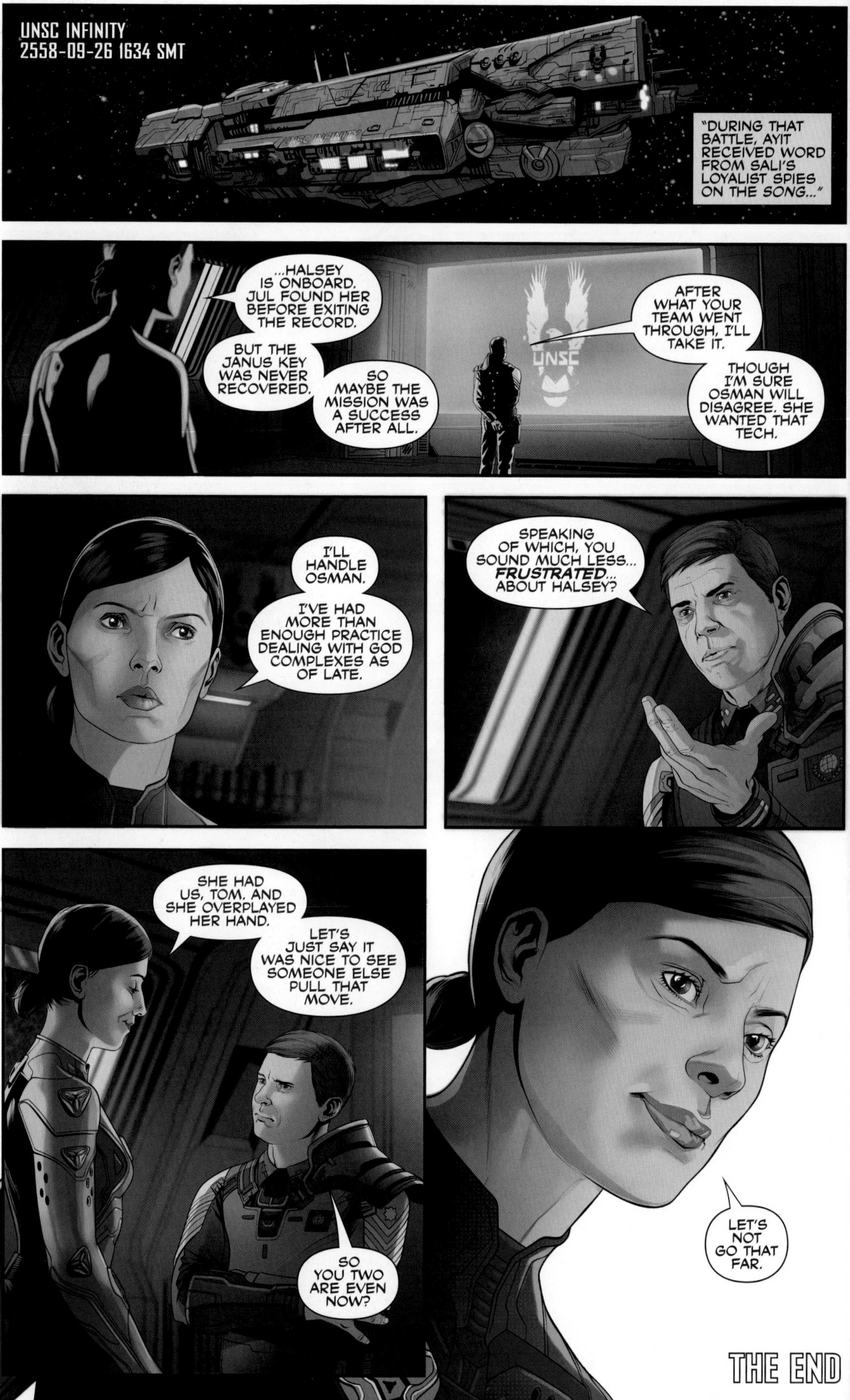
UNSC INFINITY
2558-09-26 1634 SMT
UNSC INFINITY
"DURING THAT BATTLE, AYIT RECEIVED WORD FROM SALI'S LOYALIST SPIES ON THE SONG..."
...HALSEY IS ONBOARD. JUL FOUND HER BEFORE EXITING THE RECORD.
BUT THE JANUS KEY WAS NEVER RECOVERED.
SO MAYBE THE MISSION WAS A SUCCESS AFTER ALL.
AFTER WHAT YOUR TEAM WENT THROUGH, I'LL TAKE IT.
THOUGH I'M SURE OSMAN WILL DISAGREE. SHE WANTED THAT TECH.
UNSC
I'LL HANDLE OSMAN.
I'VE HAD MORE THAN ENOUGH PRACTICE DEALING WITH GOD COMPLEXES AS OF LATE.
SPEAKING OF WHICH, YOU SOUND MUCH LESS... FRUSTRATED... ABOUT HALSEY?
SHE HAD US, TOM. AND SHE OVERPLAYED HER HAND.
LET'S JUST SAY IT WAS NICE TO SEE SOMEONE ELSE PULL THAT MOVE.
SO YOU TWO ARE EVEN NOW?
LET'S NOT GO THAT FAR.
THE END

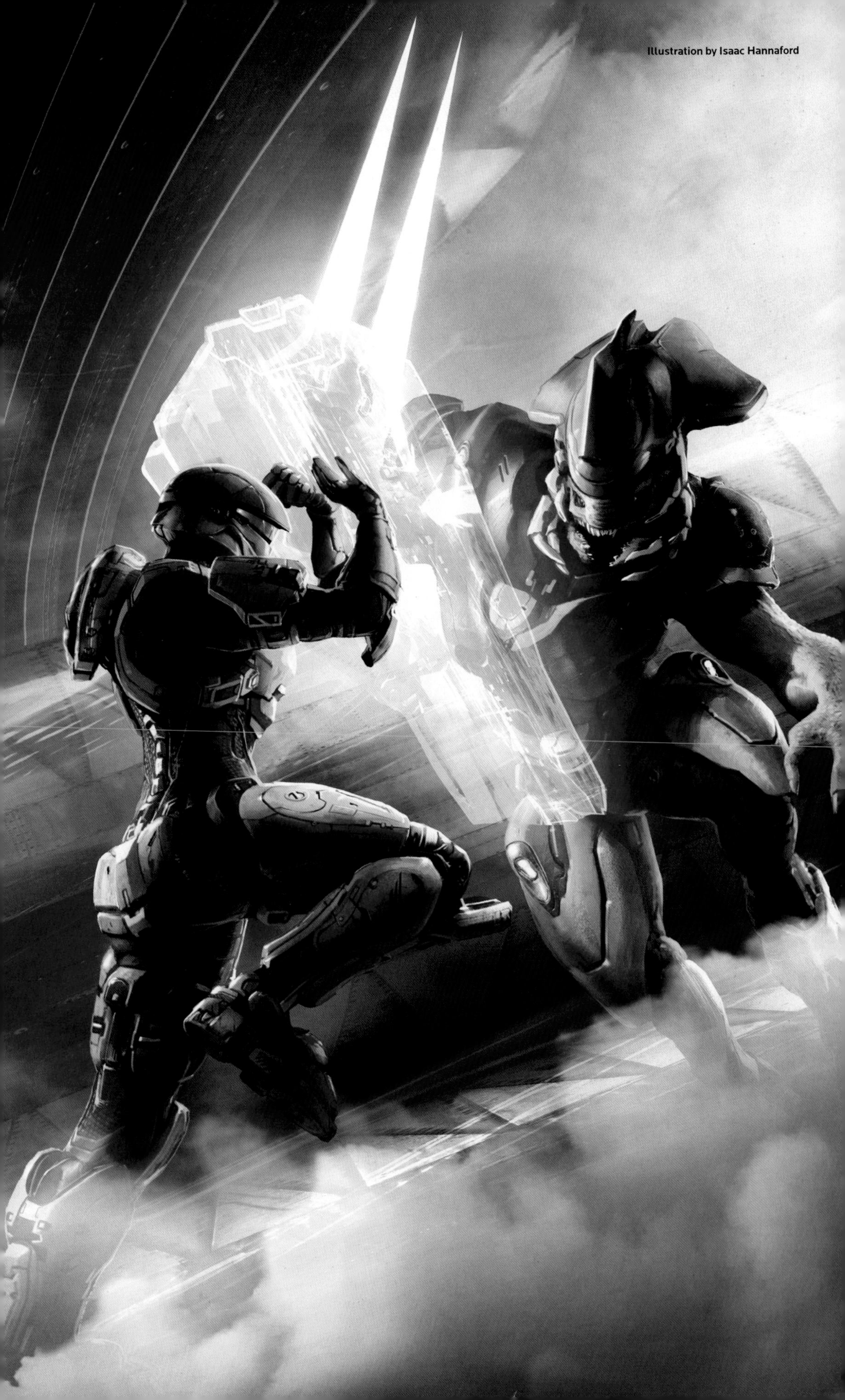

Illustration by Isaac Hannaford

Illustration by Jean-Sébastien Rossbach

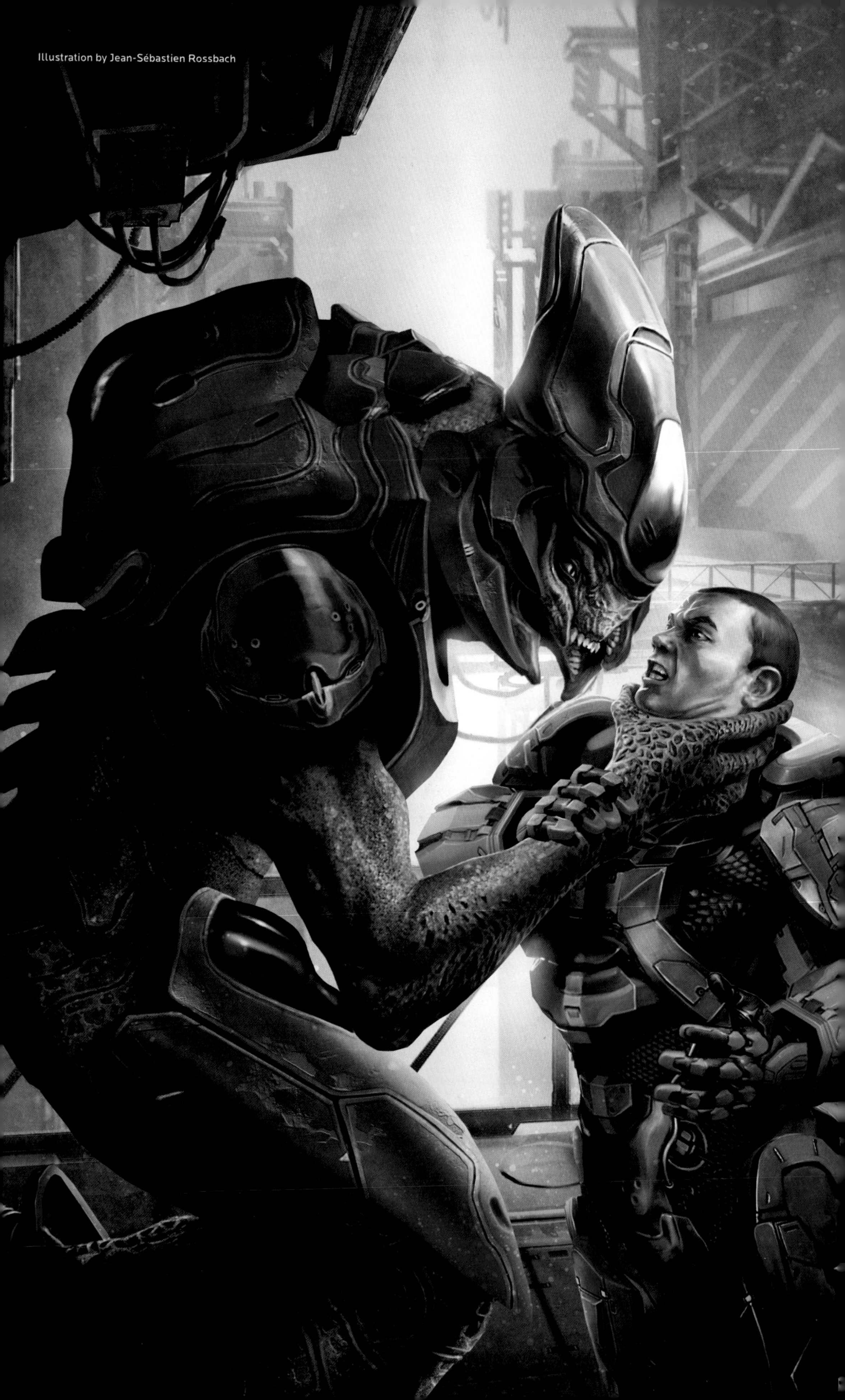

Illustration by Isaac Hannaford

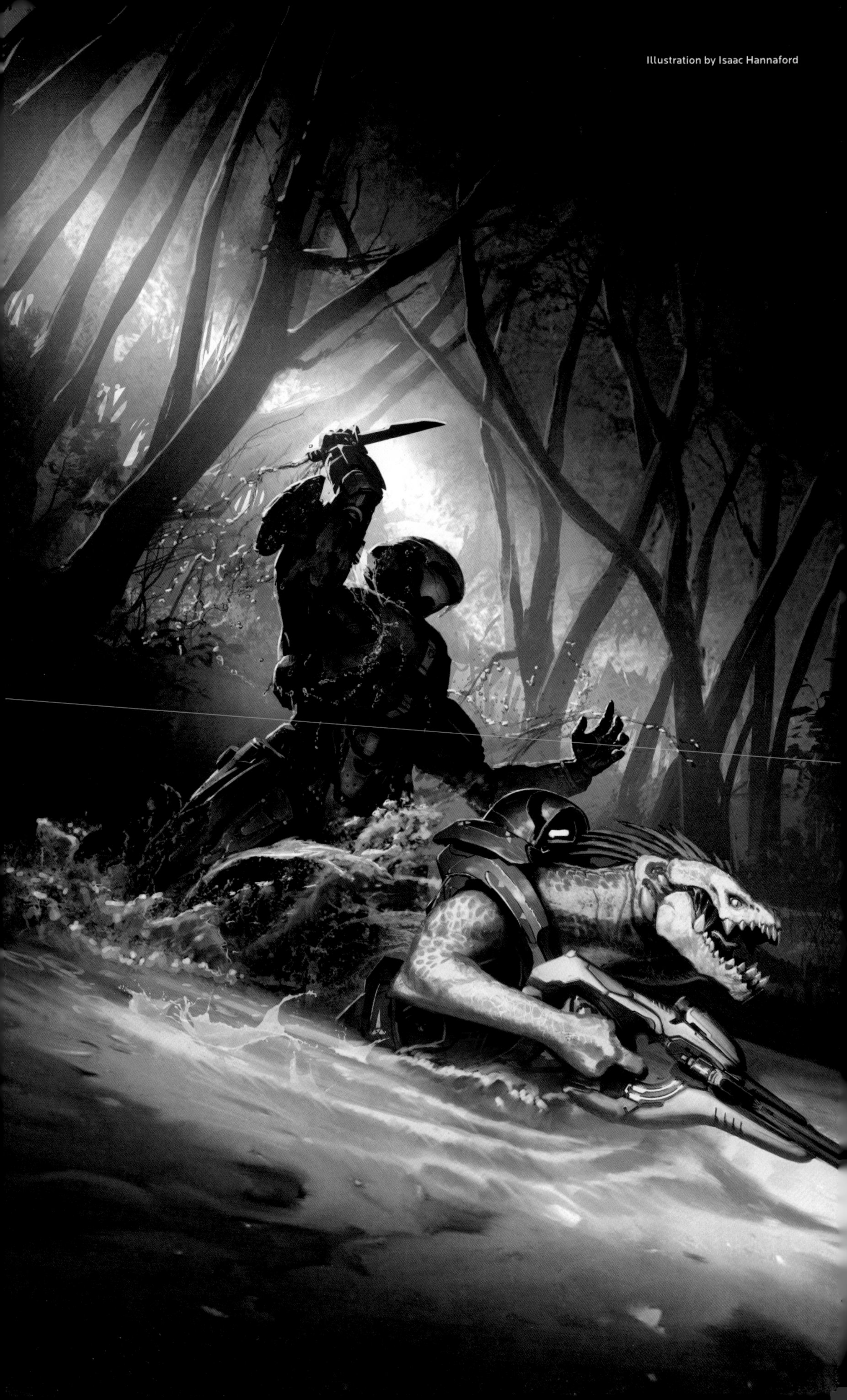

HALO

OFFICIALLY LICENSED FROM THE POPULAR VIDEO GAME FRANCHISE!

HALO UNSC INFINITY 9" REPLICA
Fully painted 9" miniature replica
$49.99

HALO UNSC PELICAN DROPSHIP 6" REPLICA
Fully painted 6" miniature replica
$39.99

HALO: INITIATION
978-1-61655-325-8
$14.99

HALO: ESCALATION VOLUME 1
978-1-61655-456-9
$19.99

HALO: ESCALATION VOLUME 2
978-1-61655-628-0
$19.99

DARKHORSE.COM | HALOWAYPOINT.COM

AVAILABLE AT YOUR LOCAL COMICS SHOP OR BOOKSTORE!

To find a comics shop in your area, call 1-888-266-4226. For more information or to order direct visit
DarkHorse.com or call 1-800-862-0052 Mon.–Fri. 9 am to 5 pm Pacific Time. Prices and availability
subject to change without notice.

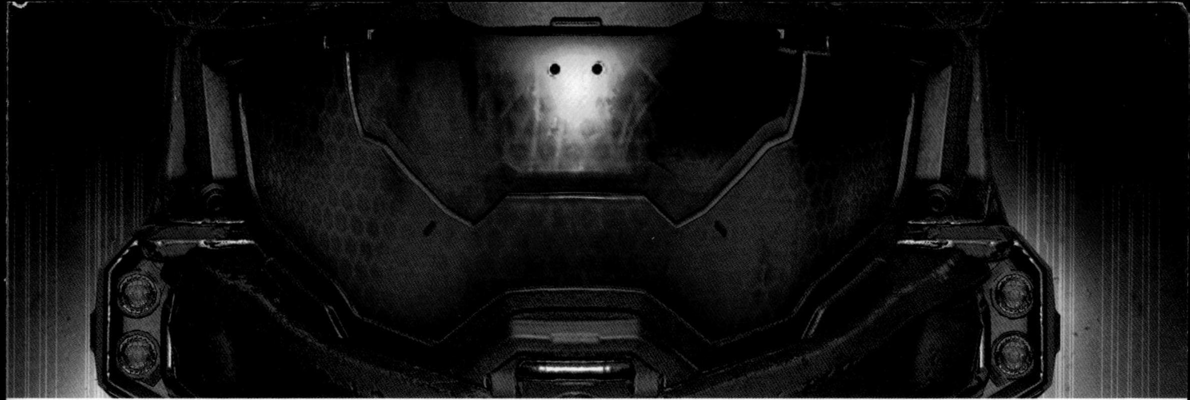

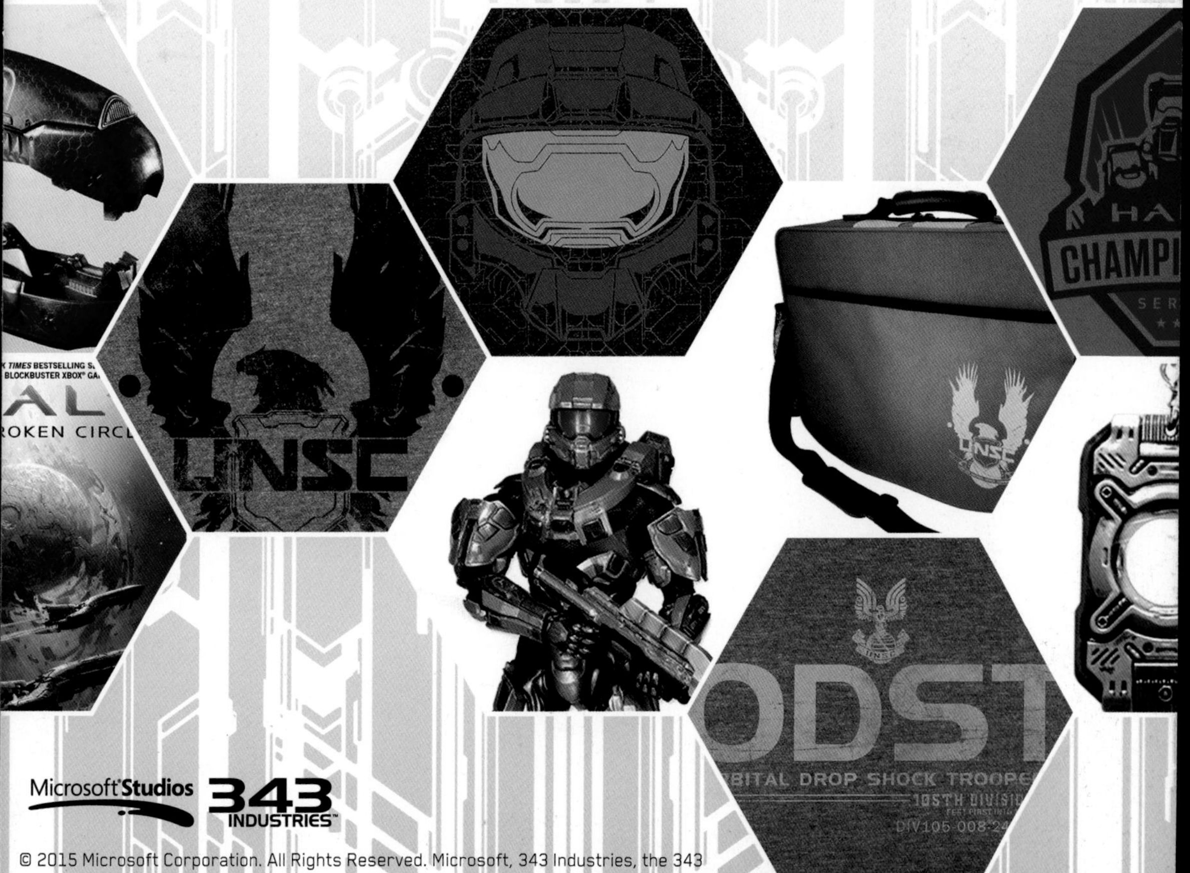
UNSC
ODST

PRESIDENT AND PUBLISHER
MIKE RICHARDSON

EXECUTIVE VICE PRESIDENT
NEIL HANKERSON

CHIEF FINANCIAL OFFICER
TOM WEDDLE

VICE PRESIDENT OF PUBLISHING
RANDY STRADLEY

VICE PRESIDENT OF BOOK TRADE SALES
MICHAEL MARTENS

VICE PRESIDENT OF MARKETING
MATT PARKINSON

VICE PRESIDENT OF PRODUCT DEVELOPMENT
DAVID SCROGGY

VICE PRESIDENT OF INFORMATION TECHNOLOGY
DALE LaFOUNTAIN

VICE PRESIDENT OF PRODUCTION AND SCHEDULING
CARA NIECE

GENERAL COUNSEL
KEN LIZZI

EDITORIAL DIRECTOR
DAVEY ESTRADA

EDITOR IN CHIEF
DAVE MARSHALL

EXECUTIVE SENIOR EDITOR
SCOTT ALLIE

SENIOR BOOKS EDITOR
CHRIS WARNER

DIRECTOR OF PRINT AND DEVELOPMENT
CARY GRAZZINI

ART DIRECTOR
LIA RIBACCHI

DIRECTOR OF DIGITAL PUBLISHING
MARK BERNARDI